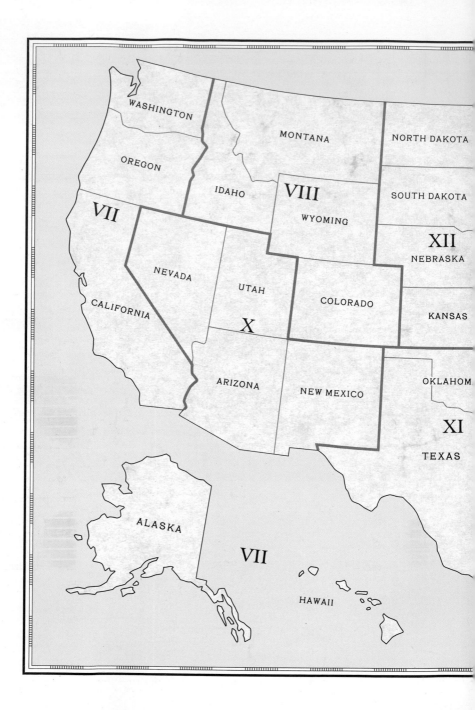

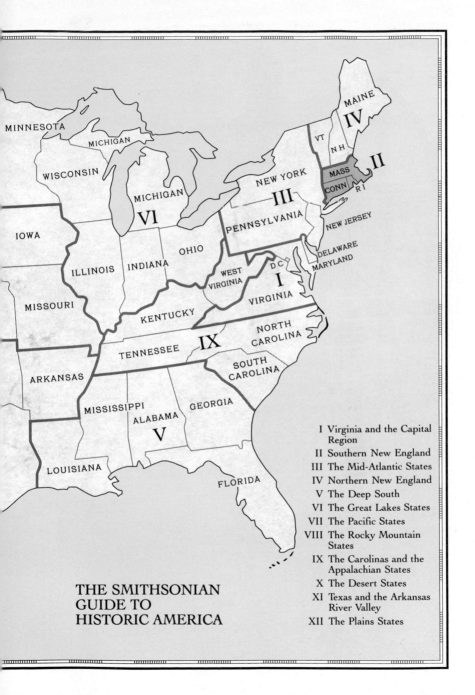

MAINE
IV
VT
N H
MASS II
CONN
R I

MINNESOTA
MICHIGAN
WISCONSIN
MICHIGAN
VI
NEW YORK
III
PENNSYLVANIA
NEW JERSEY
IOWA
OHIO
DELAWARE
ILLINOIS INDIANA
WEST D C MARYLAND
VIRGINIA I
MISSOURI
VIRGINIA
KENTUCKY
NORTH
CAROLINA
TENNESSEE IX
SOUTH
CAROLINA
ARKANSAS
MISSISSIPPI GEORGIA
ALABAMA
V
LOUISIANA
FLORIDA

I Virginia and the Capital Region
II Southern New England
III The Mid-Atlantic States
IV Northern New England
V The Deep South
VI The Great Lakes States
VII The Pacific States
VIII The Rocky Mountain States
IX The Carolinas and the Appalachian States
X The Desert States
XI Texas and the Arkansas River Valley
XII The Plains States

THE SMITHSONIAN GUIDE TO HISTORIC AMERICA

THE
SMITHSONIAN
GUIDE TO
HISTORIC AMERICA
SOUTHERN NEW ENGLAND

TEXT BY
HENRY WIENCEK

SPECIAL PHOTOGRAPHY BY
PAUL ROCHELEAU

EDITORIAL DIRECTOR
ROGER G. KENNEDY
DIRECTOR OF THE NATIONAL MUSEUM
OF AMERICAN HISTORY
OF THE SMITHSONIAN INSTITUTION

Stewart, Tabori & Chang
NEW YORK

Due to limitations of space, additional photo credits appear on
page 416 and constitute an extension of this page.

All information is accurate as of publication. We suggest
contacting the sites prior to a visit to confirm hours of operation.

Published in 1989 by Stewart, Tabori & Chang, Inc., 740 Broadway,
New York, NY 10003.

LIBRARY OF CONGRESS CATALOGING-IN-PUBLICATION DATA

Wiencek, Henry.
    Southern New England.

    (Smithsonian guide to historic America)
    Includes index.
    1. New England—Description and travel—1981-   —Guide-books.
    2. Connecticut—Description and travel—1981-   —Guide-books.
    3. Massachusetts—Description and travel—1981-   —Guide-books.
    4. Rhode Island—Description and travel—1981-   —Guide-books.
    I. Rocheleau, Paul.
    II. Title. III. Series.
    F2.3.W54 1989   917.4   88-15704
    ISBN 1-55670-051-2 (paper)   ISBN 1-55670-059-8 (hardcover)

Distributed by Workman Publishing, 708 Broadway, New York, NY 10003

Printed in Japan

10 9 8 7 6 5 4 3 2 1
First Edition

SERIES EDITOR: HENRY WIENCEK
EDITOR: MARY LUDERS
PHOTO EDITOR: MARY Z. JENKINS
ART DIRECTOR: DIANA M. JONES
ASSOCIATE EDITOR: BRIGID A. MAST
EDITORIAL ASSISTANT: BARBARA J. SEYDA
DESIGNERS: JOSEPH RUTT, PAUL P. ZAKRIS
CARTOGRAPHIC DESIGN AND PRODUCTION: GUENTER VOLLATH
CARTOGRAPHIC COMPILATION: GEORGE COLBERT
DATA ENTRY: SUSAN KIRBY

FRONT COVER: Block Island.
HALF-TITLE PAGE: Sign, Chatham, MA.
FRONTISPIECE: Dwight Barnard House, Deerfield, MA.
BACK COVER: Boston Public Library.

C O N T E N T S

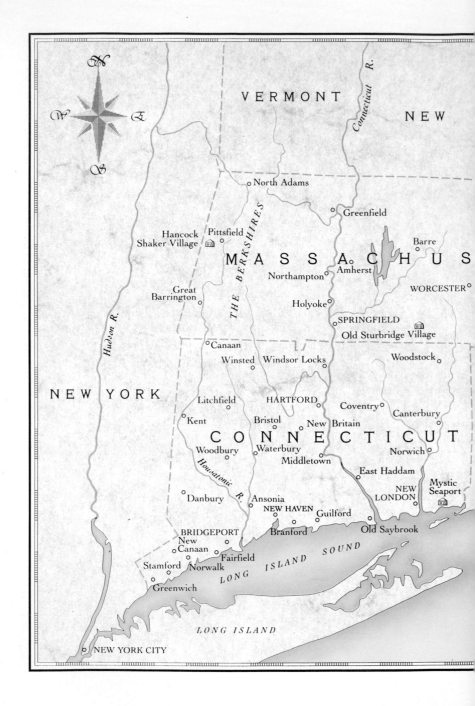

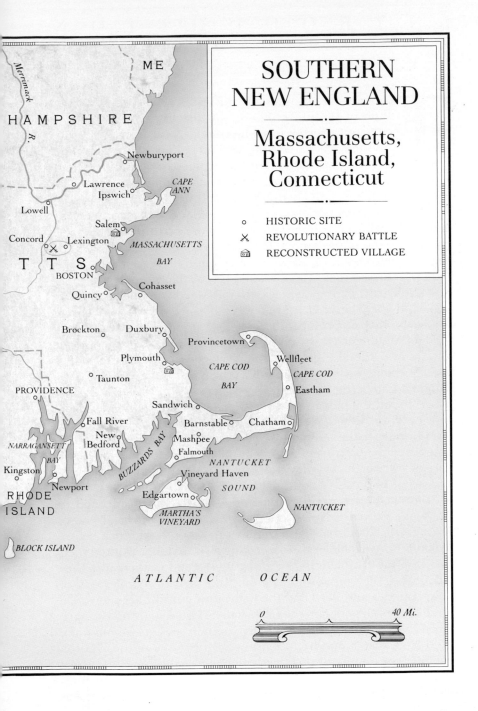

SOUTHERN NEW ENGLAND

Massachusetts,
Rhode Island,
Connecticut

- ○   HISTORIC SITE
- ✕   REVOLUTIONARY BATTLE
- 🏠   RECONSTRUCTED VILLAGE

ME

HAMPSHIRE

Merrimack

R.

Newburyport

Lawrence   CAPE
Ipswich   ANN

Lowell

Salem

Concord   Lexington   *MASSACHUSETTS*

T T S   *BAY*
BOSTON

Quincy   Cohasset

Brockton   Duxbury

   Provincetown

Plymouth   CAPE COD   Wellfleet

Taunton   *BAY*   CAPE COD

PROVIDENCE   Eastham

Sandwich

Fall River   Barnstable   Chatham

New   Mashpee
NARRAGANSETT Bedford

BAY   Falmouth

Kingston   *NANTUCKET*

Newport   Edgartown   *SOUND*

RHODE
ISLAND   Vineyard Haven

*MARTHA'S
VINEYARD*   *NANTUCKET*

BLOCK ISLAND

ATLANTIC   *OCEAN*

0   *40 Mi.*

INTRODUCTION

ROGER G. KENNEDY

Though some Bostonians still speak of their city as "the hub of the universe," it, and the three New England states of which it is the metropolis, owe their prosperity to their place upon the periphery. These are shoreline states. They are at the extremities of a continent and upon the edges of the watery world. Their people have been, by necessity, amphibian, living upon land and sea.

This was a very ancient intersection of land and water. For ten thousand years, a great glacier weighted the earth with billions of tons of ice, and in the process locked up enough water to raise the level of the oceans by perhaps five hundred feet. Earlier, the glaciers gathered rocks and sand and clay as they crept southward. Now the frozen booty was released and Martha's Vineyard, Cape Cod, and the Shinnecock Hills were born. Even Rhode Island acquired a modest protuberance, somewhat enthusiastically called "Badger Mountain," the summit of which remained seven hundred feet above sea level even after the glaciers melted and the waters rose. The long beaches and islands of the North Atlantic coast were inundated, to become the shoals and banks upon which later fishermen found the means to respond profitably to the protein deficiencies of the distant West Indies and of Europe.

Contrary to the "empty continent" myth the peopling of North America did not come first from the east. Not long after the glaciers retreated, America was discovered from the west, from Asia. Some of those we now call "Native Americans" (or by Columbus's mistaken description, "Indians"—no one seems inclined to the Norse word for North American natives, "Skraelings") were making fires upon the southernmost tip of South America before 10,000 B.C. Archeological evidence suggests that they worked their way from the Pacific to the Atlantic. By the end of their trek they had grown very numerous, creating the urban complexities of Meso-America and Peru and the enormous but simpler metropoli of the Hopewell period in the Ohio Valley, Louisiana, and Georgia. Our "New England" was at the fringe of their settlement, but there could have been a hundred thousand of them east of the Hudson in 1500. The density of their settlement amazed those Europeans; they had cleared much of the shore of Long Island Sound for a depth of six or seven miles. The penetration by Native Americans from the west and south took place over so protracted a period that we forget the magnitude of the achievement of these first pioneers.

At the eastern edge of the continent their hardiness was tested in their first encounters with the ferocious Scandinavians, about the year 1000. Those "Vikings," the terror of Europe, were themselves terrified by the "Skraelings" they found determined to defend their occupancy of the few meadows and shelters along that coast. Some footholds were secured by the Europeans, perhaps even as far along the coast as Rhode Island or Martha's Vineyard.

It is generally assumed that these early entrepots did not survive. But most historians are now prepared to admit that the absence of a document does not prove the absence of an experience, and it is entirely possible that there was sporadic European-American contact over the next four hundred years as Basque, Portuguese, French, and English West Country fishermen made their own essays in winter survival in a new world. The shallow offshore waters were crowded with fish, and, by 1525, were becoming crowded with fishermen. Some ragged settlements on shore may have lasted a year or so on Newfoundland or even farther south, but fishermen have never liked telling others where the "big ones" are to be found, so history has only the barest hints of what Bristol and Galway knew before Columbus.

By 1600, however, the Portuguese, French, and Spaniards had proven to the skeptical British that America was worth colonizing, and then, finally, there came to be some reason to apply the term "New England" to the southerly portion of the fishermen's shore. It was not the chief attraction of the Western World: its natural resources were scant; unlike Mexico, it had no silver and gold; unlike the West Indies it could not grow sugar; and Newfoundland offered far more cod, mackerel, and haddock. The shore between the lordly Hudson and the lazily looping Piscataqua seemed lean and irregular, bare and harsh.

What was the land like, then? Where can a curious traveller get a sense of what the terrain looked like before the advent of the Europeans? There are the beaches and the marshes, the off-shore islands with their colonies of gannets and gulls. There are inland swamps and barren, rocky hilltops. And, here and there, a pocket of old America, very much as it was. Off Pine Street, a little way up

Essex Road in Cornwall, Connecticut, the Nature Conservancy is tending the Cathedral Pines Preserve, and the Carlisle State Forest, near Carlisle, Massachusetts contains some very old growth pines and hemlocks in a remnant spared by logging and hurricanes.

In 1620, very late in the European investigations of the region, seventeen years after the French planted their gardens in Maine, the Pilgrims landed. Some of the Pilgrim Fathers and Mothers treated the Native Americans as respectfully as they themselves were at first treated. Their survival amply demonstrates that they knew how to draw forth reciprocal kindness, for they had little knowledge of the architectural and agricultural means by which to pass an American winter. From the Indians they learned about snow-shoes and moccasins, about corn and beans and squash, about building with saplings and with stockaded timbers.

The Pilgrims did not, of course, commence American history, even that part of our history dealing with European settlement. Our Thanksgiving feast can remind us of other harvests gathered, and other common meals: three quarters of a century before these reforming Protestants arrived, Spanish Catholics had been celebrating the Mass on the shores of Chesapeake Bay; Santa Fe is older than Plymouth. The region now contained within the United States was initially penetrated by Europeans from the south, not the northeast; and, even from that direction, the French under Jacques Cartier penetrated 1,000 miles into the interior in the 1530s, more than a century before the granite rock in Plymouth Bay felt John Winthrop's footfall. The French were in Wisconsin and Missouri before the English had passed beyond the Berkshires.

The English came so late because they had been distracted by their own civil and religious wars, and, perhaps, they required rehearsals in Ireland for their American experience. In Ireland they learned how to exterminate aborigines while forming "plantations"—the term has an Irish origin—and how to explain themselves to themselves. They wrote of the Irish, and, later, the Indians in ways which later became braided into the older histories of New England: the natives were "savages" and their religion "idolatrous;" they were "nomads" because they moved herds from summer to winter quarters.

In New England, the invaders ultimately triumphed after a century of uncertain skirmishes, massacres, and alliances among changing clusters of colonies and tribes. Contributing to that victory

—complete by 1760—were European diseases, and a combination of the adaptation by Europeans of the technology of gunpowder with that of snow-shoes and moccasins, and the abandonment of European mass-attacks in favor of dispersed "forest tactics."

Having learned their Irish lessons, the English were able to manipulate the rivalries of local chiefs and family groupings. Massacre, the killing of entire populations including non-combatants, seems to have been a European invention. Contrary to Indian experience, the English knew all about a strategy of starving their opponents into desperate errors or submission. They burnt off their food supplies, drove them from the small arable sections of the terrain, and left to them only the squalid life possible on barren headlands, rocky hills, sand dunes and marshes. What had worked well on one side of the Atlantic worked again on the other.

Along the Connecticut River, rough characters from the West Indies abraded further the worsening relations between the invading Europeans and the Native Americans. A freebooter named Stone provided the pretext for the First Puritan War of Conquest, or the Pequot War. Having been banished from Massachusetts, this pirate courted martyrdom by kidnapping Pequot Indians. After the Pequot violently terminated Stone's predations, the neighboring Narragansett, sensing that white settlers preferred to act as their own vigilantes, suggested a joint expedition to obliterate the Pequot, their traditional enemies. The Puritans made use of the Narragansett's knowledge of the terrain and of their disciplined troops, but the next generation of invaders turned upon their late allies. In the Second Puritan War of Conquest, they eliminated the Narragansett as a contending power and took possession of those lands in Rhode Island and Connecticut suitable for the simple sort of agriculture practiced by whites and Indians alike. (The Second Puritan War is more often called "King Philip's," not after the Spanish Hapsburg, but after the sachem of the Narragansett who led the last major Native American resistance in New England.)

Until the very end of the sixteenth century, the French were kept away from the Puritan colonies by the diplomacy of Charles II of England. After the subsidies he received from Louis XIV of France proved insufficient to his needs, and his subjects' lust for war, commercial and religious, could no longer be resisted, there ensued a hundred and fifty years of conflict between imperial Britain and imperial France. Southern New England sometimes profited and sometimes suffered from those endless struggles; the raids and counter-raids we call the "French and Indian Wars" were expressions of that world-wide contest; so was the profitability of privateering and smuggling; so also was one American co-belligerency with France that produced the victory at Yorktown. But by 1763, when France relinquished, to Britain, Canada and the eastern half of the Mississippi Valley, the direct impact of the Franco-British world wars was no longer felt in the area covered by this volume. Shifting alliances among European powers and Indian nations no longer produced much violence there. Native Americans had been ground between the great contenders, and, at the end, European victory was complete.

During this period, the fields and pastures won from the Indians produced increasing surpluses of food, which, along with fish, could be sold at great profits to the slave-driven plantations of the West Indies. Maine and New Hampshire survived on the sale of maritime supplies and fish to the islands; "South County," Rhode Island, like the Carolinas and New York's Shelter Island, was a Barbadian sub-colony, organized upon West Indian lines to send animals for power and protein to Caribbean sugar plantations. Bristol and Newport grew rich on the Caribbean slave-trade, and, later, upon the extension of that traffic to the descendants of the Barbadians in South Carolina.

By the beginning of the eighteenth century Boston was emerging as a center of commerce, with the West Indies and with the fishing towns and fishing fleets all the way to Newfoundland. Salem and Marblehead, mackerel and cod ports in Essex County, Massachusetts, were growing despite their meager hinterlands. New Englanders made the best of their position between fish and sugar, trading and trans-shipping in both directions. The sugar ports of Rhode Island increased in size and wealth as the riverside villages of Connecticut built and managed ships for the oceans of the world from yards that now appear hopelessly landlocked.

From far up the navigable rivers of New England, whalers set sail for the oceans of the world. Whaling had been practiced by the Indians and Cape Codders in the seventeenth century, but it was not until after 1720 that a desire for lighting and lubricating oil turned Nantucket, New Bedford, New London, Stonington, Edgartown and Provincetown into bases for expeditions ranging into the Arctic, Antarctic and Pacific. Oil from long-dead plants and animals was discovered in Titusville, Pennsylvania, in 1859; the Rockefellers and Harknesses and Pratts replaced the Rotches and Starbucks. Though, in the 1870s, whale-bone stays for corsets and umbrellas brought some old whalers back into action, it was no longer necessary to kill for light.

The industrial development of New England began at the fall-line. The rough and dangerous water that earlier frustrated those who wished to bring ocean-going shipping into the interior now produced power. The Connecticut and Merrimack were spared industry at their mouths, but where they broke into rapids they nurtured mills. At Pawtucket a waterfall, entrepreneurial genius, and English technology gave rise to the Slater Mill.

Capital was released from fishing and smuggling, from the West Indies and China trades, to textiles, as it would later be into railroad and real estate, and, after them, into electronics and financial services. Boston's ruling elite is phenomenally adaptable, perhaps because it has been content with a realistic self-definition: it is no small thing to be a part of a commercial class, led by intellectuals, continuous in some families over three centuries. Boston and Hartford, unlike Saybrook or Portsmouth, harbored no cast-off aristocrats to complicate the clarity of commercial vision. New England was spared the Cavalier pretensions that disabled the merchant-planters of tidewater South Carolina and Virginia. The "Brahmins" never relinquished the counting house, as did the risen merchants of Charleston, who could not adapt themselves to the imperatives of the nineteenth century.

This is not to suggest that all those imperatives were noble, or that their consequences were pretty. Historians have been learning in the last thirty years or so how to cut below the picturesque surfaces of many villages to discover how artificial is the present aspect of places that purport to show what "colonial" or "Federal" New England was like. It is remarkable just how skillfully that reality was altered after 1880, to accommodate the daintier preferences of those who had inherited that landscape. The industrialization of New England began in the eighteenth century, and, with it, the exploitation of women and children. This story does not require retelling here, but travellers may want to know what they are seeing when visiting "mill towns" like Harrisville, New Hampshire, or Slatersville, Rhode Island. The former is largely the creation of Austin Levy, who owned a woolen mill there, and, after 1918, built twenty-two "colonial revival" workers houses, a town hall, a library, and court house. Under his philanthropic direction, the Universalist Church was remodelled from the Victorian to the "colonial," and the Roman Catholic congregation was persuaded to build compatibly. The result is handsome, but no picture of what Harrisville would have been in 1800.

Slatersville was a real textile village, with a fascinating past; but while Mr. Levy was reconstructing Harrisville, Slatersville's multiple-family cottages were given side-porches, porticoes, and a coat of white paint, and gentrified into single-family occupancy.

More important was the reconstruction of the entire shape of colonial towns by giving them the park-like "greens" which the nineteenth and twentieth centuries thought appropriate to the seventeenth and eighteenth.

Few villages were sufficiently affluent to follow the lead of Litchfield, Connecticut, which engaged Frederick Law Olmsted to redesign the center of town, and went on to remodel Victorian buildings into "the Federal," painting over in white the varicolored residences that had persisted until 1890. They turned commercial structures into residences, and reconstructed the Town Hall and the Tapping Reeve Law School. But the pattern of settlement in colonial times was obscured, and colonial history made considerably duller, by reconstruction and bowdlerizing.

Town names like Longmeadow, Springfield, Enfield, Topsfield, Hatfield, Bloomfield, and Greenfield remind us that European settlers found waiting for them "fields" and "meadows" cleared and planted by previous occupants. Upon those sites they spread themselves out, very widely, for land was cheap: only rarely did they congregate around a central church until the industrial phase of New England began. The "nuclear village" of England was transplanted to New England in very few instances; Concord, Massachusetts, was the only inland town of any size that developed a commercial core before 1740 or 1750. "Highway villages" like Wethersfield and Northfield spread out along a single spine, on the terraces the Indians had made habitable and arable. After they felt safe in leaving their initial stockades (faithfully reproduced at Plymouth), or the defensive gatherings of the first generation, the colonials betook themselves to dispersed homesteads.

What of the white "colonial" village church, with its Gibbsian spire, and that well-mowed Green before it? The spire was a nineteenth-century addition, except for a few prototypical examples in major shipping cities like Boston and Newport. The "Green," as a park or "common" is a product of the nostalgia of the industrializing phase of the nineteenth century, or even of the "colonial revival" of the turn of this century. "Until then," we have learned from Thomas Lewis, "most commons were barren, unsightly places covered with stumps, stones, stagnant puddles and dead trees." This is how they appear in nineteenth-century photographs, taken after the first meeting house, for which the commons was created, had collapsed, or the local clergyman, for whom it may have been a "glebe," had relinquished it.

We have our own interior images of the New England past, more powerful than any photographs. We insist upon how our ancestors must have lived, though we may deprive them of the credit they deserve for surviving the harshness of their actual existence. If all was sweet and untroubled in colonial times, the triumph of democracy and tolerance would not be so remarkable. If serenity and openness and love predominated in the Peaceable Kingdoms of our imagination, Anne Hutchinson and William Lloyd Garrison would have had tranquil lives, and those calls to conscience for which New England has been famous would have been unnecessary.

The history of New England did not stop when the nineteenth century began, when industrialism grew, when immigrants from other nations were added to those from East Anglia, when determined men and women strove to live considered and responsible lives despite unprecedented bafflements and complexities. This essay must break off here, ruefully acknowledging that in an effort to give enough information to counteract some of the pernicious simplicities that have obstructed our vision of the accomplishments of southern New England, it has run out of space. That is how history is: it can only be an invitation to inquire, never a complete story. Though a little skeptical about some traditional tales about "colonial" life, we close in grateful acknowledgement of the past— including the recent past that created, or re-created, among the folded hills and in the Atlantic mists, some villages as beautiful as the land itself, the delight of Native Americans, the Vikings, and the Pilgrim Fathers, when first they laid eyes upon this wonderful edge of the continent.

BOSTON
AND
ENVIRONS

OPPOSITE: Boston's waterfront, where new hotels and offices dwarf Custom House tower, once New England's tallest structure.

"In whatever part of the world you may meet with him you can tell a Bostonian a mile off," Samuel Adams Drake wrote in 1900; "The Bostonian knows that his own is preeminently the historic city of America, and he feels that no small part of its worldwide renown has descended to him as his peculiar inheritance." Not even in Charleston, South Carolina can one find such self-assurance, and it is unlikely that anyone in Santa Fe would make such a statement about that considerably older city. The tangible portion of the Bostonian's peculiar historical inheritance includes the Common, Faneuil Hall and the Bunker Hill battlefield, Harvard and Beacon Hill, Paul Revere's house and Harrison Gray Otis's mansions, the architecture of Charles Bulfinch and Henry Hobson Richardson. The city's intellectual and literary heritage is prodigious.

From the start, Boston's fortunes depended on the sea. The settlers who arrived in 1630 under the leadership of John Winthrop found the land poor for farming but the waters rich in cod. By the 1640s, Boston ships were carrying dried cod to feed the African slaves who worked the British-owned sugar plantations in the West Indies. Boston also found a market for dried cod in the Roman Catholic Mediterranean. The Puritans reviled the Pope, but grew rich from his prohibition of meat on Friday. In exchange for their fish, flour, dried beef, and barrel staves, Bostonians got wine, sugar, molasses, and gold. By the 1670s, Boston had the lion's share of the West Indian shipping business; and by 1700, the city was the third busiest port in the British realm, after London and Bristol. Until 1755, when Philadelphia took the lead, Boston was the largest town in British America.

In large measure the city had the "Sacred Cod" to thank for its prosperity, and Boston did not forget it. In 1784 one of Boston's representatives proposed "that leave might be given to hang up the representation of a Codfish in the room where the House sit, as a memorial of the importance of the Cod-fishery to the welfare of this Commonwealth." The motion was approved, and the Sacred Cod still graces the representatives' chamber in the State House.

From the days of the earliest settlements Bostonians displayed an independence of spirit that rankled the Crown's officers. In the 1600s Bostonians twice prepared to take up arms to defend themselves when Britain threatened to revoke the charter that granted certain powers of self-government. Massachusetts Puritans did not take happily to the "restoration" of King Charles II in place of the

Paul Revere's engraving of the Boston Massacre. On sale three weeks after the shooting, this further inflamed anti-British sentiment in Boston.

Puritan commonwealth of Oliver Cromwell. In the 1760s, Boston was the epicenter of resistance to England's attempts to curtail the individual rights of the colonists, to tax them without representation in Parliament, and to control their trade.

Riots here forced the British to send troops to occupy the city in 1768. Tension between the town and the troops culminated in the deaths of five men in what became known as the Boston Massacre of 1770. Three years later, two hundred men descended on the waterfront and tossed three shiploads of tea into the harbor

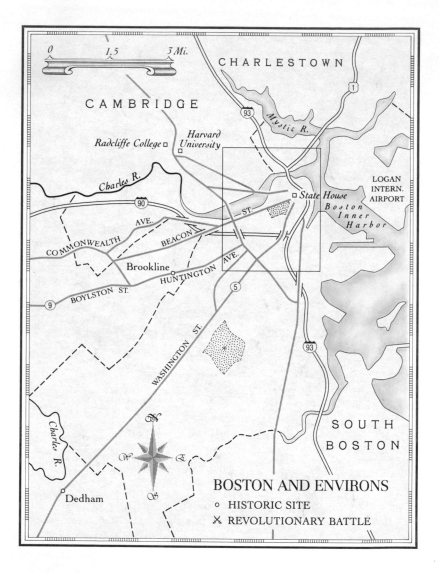

BOSTON AND ENVIRONS

○ HISTORIC SITE

✕ REVOLUTIONARY BATTLE

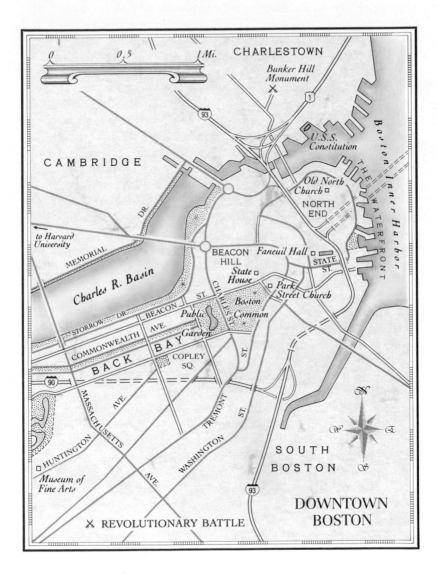

0   0.5   1 Mi.   CHARLESTOWN

Bunker Hill
Monument

93

1

CAMBRIDGE

U.S.S.
Constitution

Old North
Church

NORTH
END

to Harvard
University

MEMORIAL
DR.

Charles R. Basin

BEACON
HILL

Faneuil Hall

STATE
ST.

State
House

Park
Street Church

STORROW DR.

BEACON

CHARLES ST.

ST.

Boston
Common

Public
Garden

COMMONWEALTH

AVE.

BACK BAY

COPLEY
SQ.

CHARLES ST.

90

MASSACHUSETTS

AVE.

TREMONT

ST.

WASHINGTON

SOUTH
BOSTON

HUNTINGTON

AVE.

93

Museum of
Fine Arts

✕ REVOLUTIONARY BATTLE

DOWNTOWN
BOSTON

Boston Inner Harbor

THE WATERFRONT

to protest the tea tax. In response, King George closed the port and sent more troops to Boston, which the British then turned into their stronghold. All over New England militia units drilled and piled up supplies: A military confrontation was inevitable.

The Revolution began in and around Boston. The first shots were fired at Lexington and Concord, and from April 1775 to March 1776, Boston was the focus of the war. The British were penned into the city by a siege ring of militia units, over which George Washington took command in July 1775. The Americans briefly took possession of the high ground at Breed's Hill in Charlestown, but were driven off the same day. The British victory was costly: It made their officers wary of tangling with the rebels, and put them in a mood for retreat. When Washington fortified Dorchester Heights in a single night, the British realized their position was militarily untenable. They evacuated the city on March 17, 1776. Thereafter the fighting never again touched Boston.

After the Revolution, Boston's economy sank into a depression caused by the loss of British markets, and the city set out to find new markets and new goods for trade. In 1790 a Boston vessel, the *Columbia,* returned after a three-year voyage around the world, the first circumnavigation by an American ship. *Columbia*'s owners were not interested in setting records, but rather in establishing trade in the furs of the Northwest. The Far East was the next logical place, and Boston's ships were soon bringing the silks, spices, and porcelain of Asia to American buyers. Trade came to a halt with President Jefferson's embargo in 1807, and again during the War of 1812, but Boston recovered and thrived for the next several decades. The 1850s saw the brief and beautiful reign of the clipper ships—trim, speedy vessels handcrafted with the utmost care. The premier clipper builder was Boston's Donald McKay, who constructed such world-famed vessels as the *Flying Cloud.* The era of the clipper was cut short by the development of metal, steam-powered ships—which Bostonians did not trust and would not build. The city's merchants shifted their capital to manufacturing, and the harbor went into a long decline.

In the middle of the nineteenth century the social and historical character of Boston was defined by Beacon Hill, the elite residential district of elegant but sturdy brick houses erected on foundations of granite, at whose peak is the State House—which Oliver Wendell Holmes declared was "the hub of the solar system." Beacon Hill was the abode of the "Boston Brahmins" (another Holmes coinage), "with their houses by Bulfinch, their monopoly of Beacon Street, the ancestral portraits and Chinese porcelain, humanitarianism, Unitarian faith in the march of mind, Yankee shrewdness and New England exclusiveness." Behind the graceful facades of Beacon Hill's townhouses lived some of the sharpest commercial

The Tea Party, *painted by Henry Sargent about 1824, is believed to show a gathering of Bostonians at the artist's house, which was designed by Charles Bulfinch.* OVERLEAF: A Bird's Eye View of Boston (1858), *by J. Bachman.*

minds in America, the founders and managers of empires in shipping, trading, finance, and manufacturing. The mill cities of Lowell and Lawrence bear the names of Beacon Hill entrepreneurs who had the energy, vision, and, of course, the capital to embark on grand industrial enterprises. Beacon Hill's Frederick Tudor is another example of Yankee commercial shrewdness. In 1805 an acquaintance at a wintertime party remarked it was a shame that New England's ice could not be transported to the West Indies, where it would surely make a fortune. Tudor seized upon the idle joke, spent nearly thirty years developing methods of storing and shipping ice in tropical climes, and reaped the fortune that earned him the name, "The Ice King."

As Boston's wealth grew, so did the city itself. At the outset it was situated on a knob of land, covering about 740 acres, connected to the mainland at Roxbury by a narrow neck. Lapping up against the edge of Boston Common were the shallow waters of Back Bay. In 1821 a mile-and-a-half-long dam was built from the corner of Charles and Beacon streets to Brookline. In succeeding decades, railroad lines were built across the bay and it became a fetid dumping ground for the city's trash and sewage. But in 1857 the city began to fill in the bay, creating a flat tract of new land upon which was built the handsome residential district that retains the old name of Back Bay.

This powerful commercial city, one that had produced some of eighteenth-century America's most influential political figures, declined in economic importance relative to the rising West. Nevertheless, in the nineteenth century it was home to some of the country's most prominent intellectuals. "All I claim for Boston," wrote Holmes, "is that it is the thinking center of the continent, and therefore of the planet." On the roll of Boston's eminent thinkers were the historians Francis Parkman, William H. Prescott, and John Lothrop Motley, the psychologist William James, the poets Henry Wadsworth Longfellow and James Russell Lowell, the philosopher George Santayana, the social theorists and activists Margaret Fuller, Bronson Alcott, Julia Ward Howe, Horace Mann, William Ellery Channing, and William Lloyd Garrison.

Edgar Allan Poe was born here in 1809 to indigent actors; Hawthorne clerked in the Custom House; William Dean Howells, an Ohioan who came to Boston to edit the *Atlantic Monthly,* promoted literary realism when it was new and controversial; and beneath the elms of Boston Common, Ralph Waldo Emerson strolled with a young New York poet, Walt Whitman, urging him to delete the indelicate passages from *Leaves of Grass.* But the city's literary history had begun long before, with its very first settler. The Reverend William Blaxton lived at a remove from other Europeans, his only companions being the Indians, who were illiterate, but his library had some two hundred volumes. In his literary history *The Flowering of New England* Van Wyck Brooks remarked that there were books in Boston when wolves still howled on the hills.

The character of this archetypal Yankee city was forever changed by the great influx of Irish immigrants that began in the 1840s, spurred by the potato famine and a depression in British manufacturing. For decades the target of discrimination by old-line Bostonians, the Irish grew numerous enough to take political control of the city. In 1885 the first Irish mayor was elected, starting a Hibernian political tradition that continues today.

Beginning in the 1960s, Boston underwent an urban renewal in which some old, low-rise residential and commercial sections were razed to make way for highways, Government Center in downtown Boston, and the Prudential Center in Back Bay. The 1970s and 1980s saw massive development in the financial district and along the deteriorated waterfront, where some of the granite warehouses were converted to apartments and offices. Despite these changes, Boston preserves much of its past. Sixteen historical landmarks are located along the Freedom Trail, a self-guided walking tour that begins at the Common, winds its way through the downtown area, and finishes in Charlestown. Beacon Hill looks much the same as it did in the first half of the nineteenth century. The downtown area retains the crooked street pattern pounded out by the feet, carts, and cattle of the first settlers, and is a marked contrast to the neat grid of Back Bay.

This chapter is divided into several parts. The first begins at the Common, proceeds through downtown Boston to the financial district, the waterfront, and thence to the North End. The next begins on Beacon Hill, proceeds through Back Bay and the Copley Square area to the museums on and near Huntington Avenue, while a third part covers South Boston and Charlestown. Finally, separate sections are devoted to Cambridge and suburban sites.

BOSTON COMMON

The oldest public park in the eastern part of the country, the Common is the symbolic and historical heart of Boston. It was the site of the first settlement: Before the Puritans arrived, the Reverend William Blaxton had built a house here. John Winthrop and his band of Puritans originally settled in Charlestown, but the water supply there was poor, so Blaxton invited them to his domain. It is said he repented the invitation, unhappy in the midst of so many Englishmen, and he rode off to Rhode Island on the back of a bull. He came back briefly, twenty-five years later, to find a wife.

In 1634 the Bostonians set aside Blaxton's acres as common ground, specifically as a cattle pasture and drilling field for the militia. (Cattle roamed the Common until 1830, when they were finally banned.) The Common was also the site of executions. The Puritans hanged criminals here, as well as people who had violated religious laws—adulterers, witches, and Quakers.

In the eighteenth century Back Bay still lapped at the edge of the Common, along present-day Charles Street. When the British military occupation of Boston began in 1768, the Common was the Redcoats' main encampment. The troops who marched on Lexington and Concord began their ill-fated campaign on boats launched from the Common, at Charles and Boylston streets. The movement was supposed to be a carefully guarded secret, but Patriot spies uncovered the plans. After watching the embarkation, British commander Lord Percy was walking across the Common when he heard a man say, "The British troops have marched, but they will miss their aim." Percy, startled, asked the man, "What aim?" "The cannon at Concord," came the answer.

On the Boylston Street side of the Common is the **Central Burying Ground,** started in 1756. Gilbert Stuart, the painter whose portrait of George Washington is one of the most famous images in American art, died penniless in 1828 and was buried here in an unmarked vault. Here also many Revolutionary Patriots and British soldiers, who fell at Bunker Hill, lie side by side in unmarked graves.

The city's **Visitor Information Booth** is on the Common at Tremont Street, a few steps from the 1868 **Brewer Fountain,** bought in Paris by Gardner Brewer for his Beacon Hill home, and later donated to the city. The streetcar subway line that runs below the Common along Tremont and Boylston streets was the country's

The Public Garden (foreground), Boston Common, and Beacon Hill (upper left).

first subway, opened in 1897. **St. Paul's Cathedral** at 138 Tremont Street, completed in 1820, was designed by Alexander Parris in the Greek temple form. The walls were constructed of Quincy granite. The cathedral has a distinctly unfinished look because a relief planned for the pediment was never installed.

Park Street Church

Built in 1809, Park Street Church is both an historical and architectural landmark. The British architect Peter Banner's majestic, 217-foot steeple and spire echo the style of Christopher Wren's London churches. Henry James called it "perfectly felicitous . . . the most interesting mass of brick and mortar in America." Its location is known as Brimstone Corner because powder was stored in the church basement during the War of 1812. Abolitionist William Lloyd Garrison made his first antislavery speech in this church in 1829, and in 1831 the song "America" was sung here for the first time. The church replaced what was then the biggest building in the city, a granary so large that it was used as a sail loft in which the sails for the USS *Constitution* were made.

LOCATION: Corner of Park and Tremont streets. HOURS: July and August: 9–3:30 Daily. FEE: None. TELEPHONE: 617–532–3383.

Old Granary Burying Ground

One of the greatest posthumous gatherings of Founding Fathers, including three signers of the Declaration of Independence, this cemetery was named for the granary that stood on the site of the Park Street Church. Started in 1660, it has some 1,600 graves, including those of Paul Revere, John Hancock, Samuel Adams, Peter Faneuil, the five men killed by British soldiers in the 1770 Boston Massacre, and many other notable Bostonians. A twenty-foot granite obelisk marks the graves of Benjamin Franklin's parents. The original, a modest stone put up by Benjamin, was re-

Tombstones in the Old Granary Burying Ground.

placed by this imposing marker in 1827. The cemetery's gateway was built in 1830. The actual grave sites may not correspond with the markers, as tombstones were moved around by grounds-keepers in the 1800s to improve the graveyard's appearance.

LOCATION: Tremont Street, next to Park Street Church. HOURS: 8–5 Daily. FEE: None.

King's Chapel

Originally an Anglican church, King's Chapel became the first church of the Unitarian denomination after the Revolution. Its Anglican worshippers had been Loyalists for the most part, and half left when the British Army evacuated Boston in 1776. Construction of the present church began in 1750, with plans provided at no charge by Peter Harrison, the Newport architect. The church, of Quincy granite, was built around an old wooden structure which was then broken up and removed in pieces through the windows. Funds were short, so the portico was not added until the late 1780s and a planned spire was never completed. The interior is beautiful, with Corinthian columns, the old wooden church's altar table presented to the congregation by William and Mary in 1696, and a carved monument to Frances Shirley, the wife of a royal governor. George Washington attended services here as well as a musical entertainment intended to raise money for construction.

The **King's Chapel Burying Ground** is the oldest in the city. In 1630 Isaac Johnson was buried here, at his own request, near property he owned. Others decided they wanted to be laid to rest near him, and the cemetery thus began. The burying ground contains the graves of the first colonists, including John Winthrop, the colony's first governor. The writer Nathaniel Hawthorne often visited the graveyard, where he may have noticed the 1704 grave of Elizabeth Pain, reputedly imprisoned for adultery and branded with the letter "A." It was, in fact, the practice of the Puritans to brand criminals with the initial letter of their offence, and Pain may have been the inspiration for Hester Prynne in Hawthorne's novel *The Scarlet Letter*.

LOCATION: Corner of Tremont and School streets. HOURS: 10–4 Tuesday–Saturday. FEE: None. TELEPHONE: 617–523–1749.

Old City Hall, 45 School Street, was built between 1862 and 1865 to a design by Gridley J. F. Bryant and Arthur Gilman in the

French Second Empire style. The committee that approved the design assessed it as "graceful and harmonious in proportion and detail...light and cheerful in its prevailing character." Statues of Benjamin Franklin and Josiah Quincy, mayor of Boston from 1829 to 1845, flank the entrance. The city hall until 1968, it now houses private offices.

Old Corner Bookstore

Recently restored as the Globe Corner Bookstore, this was one of Boston's literary gathering places in the mid-nineteenth century— "the Exchange of Wit, the Rialto of current good things, the hub of the Hub." From 1845 to 1865 the store housed the office of Ticknor & Fields, which published works by Hawthorne, Whittier, Longfellow, Thoreau, and Stowe. Many Boston authors gathered here for conversation, and both Charles Dickens and William Makepeace Thackeray called here during their visits. The building may be the oldest brick structure in the city, built after the fire of 1711 on the site of Anne Hutchinson's house. Hutchinson was banished from the colony, by the ecclesiastical court, for heretical teachings.

> LOCATION: Corner of School and Washington streets. HOURS: 9–6 Monday–Friday, 9:30–6 Saturday, 12–5 Sunday. TELEPHONE: 617–523–6658; 800–358–6013.

Old South Meeting House

The Old South may be the most revered shrine of the Revolution in Boston. Its commodious hall, almost seventy feet wide, made it a useful forum for mass meetings before the Revolution, when Patriots such as Samuel Adams and James Otis roused citizens with rebellious fervor. On the morning of December 16, 1773, some five thousand patriots gathered inside and outside the meeting house to discuss the tea tax. Many in the audience knew a more vigorous protest had been secretly planned for that night; and those who did not may have wondered at Samuel Adams's shouted query: "Who knows how tea will mingle with salt water?" After a day-long discussion during which the Patriots sought some compromise with the royal governor, Samuel Adams proclaimed, "This meeting can do nothing more to save the country!" Shortly thereafter the Boston

Tea Party took place, when Patriots disguised as Indians dumped four hundred crates of tea into Boston Harbor.

Puritan and Presbyterian churches were thought to be revolutionary cells by the British. During the British occupation of Boston in the winter of 1775–1776, General John "Gentleman Johnny" Burgoyne, in a calculated insult to the people of the city, had the pews torn out and the floor spread with sand so he could drill his horsemen indoors. The British also looted the minister's library, which included the priceless manuscript of William Bradford's *History of Plimoth Colony.*

At the close of the Revolution, Old South was once again used as a house of worship, and remained so until 1872 when the congregation moved to its present site in Copley Square. The meetinghouse, aging and up for sale, was saved from destruction in 1876 by a determined group of preservationists. Their stated goal of ". . . acquiring and holding Old South Meeting House for public, historical, memorial, educational, charitable, and religious uses," is in evidence today.

Now restored to its eighteenth-century appearance, Old South also houses a multimedia exhibition combining audio re-creations of the fiery Tea Party meeting and other historic events with an array of visual and literary displays, a scale model of Colonial Boston, life-size figures out of Old South's past, and more. It is also still frequently used for public programs and meetings.

LOCATION: 310 Washington Street, at Downtown Crossing. HOURS: April through October: 9:30–5 Daily; November through March: 10–4 Monday–Friday, 10–5 Saturday and Sunday. FEE: Yes. TELEPHONE: 617–482–6439.

Old State House

Built in 1713 to replace a townhouse that burned in 1711, the Old State House is Boston's oldest public building. It was the seat of British government up to the Revolution, and home of the early provincial Massachusetts legislature, or General Court.

The Old State House was the setting for many patriotic speeches against the British Crown. In 1761 it saw James Otis's eloquent and impassioned plea against the legality of the Writs of

OVERLEAF: Interior of the Old South Meeting House.

Assistance, which allowed homes to be searched upon the mere suspicion that smuggled goods might be hidden therein. John Adams, who was present at the speech, said, "then and there the child independence was born." The royal governor, for his part, called Otis, "a passionate, violent, and desperate man. . . . The troubles of this country take their rise from [him]." It was Otis, a lawyer who had resigned his position with the royal government to champion the patriotic cause, who focused American protest upon the "tyranny of taxation without representation." Such oratory no doubt led to the 1766 installation of a visitor's gallery, for the first time allowing citizens to see their representatives debating the popular issues of the day.

The Declaration of Independence was read from the balcony over State Street on July 18, 1776—one of its first public readings. Afterwards the statues of a lion and unicorn on the roof—symbols of the British Crown—were tossed into the street and burned. The statues seen today are reproductions. After the British left Boston in 1776, Washington came here to receive the thanks of the legislature. When the Commonwealth of Massachusetts was established, the building became the first state capitol, and John Hancock became the first elected governor in 1780.

When the new State House on Beacon Hill was opened in 1798, all state offices moved and this building was rented out to merchants and tradesmen. From 1830 to 1841 it was the city hall. In 1835 the abolitionist William Lloyd Garrison sought protection here from a lynch mob. The mayor had Garrison arrested for rioting in order to get him into a safe jail and out of the mob's hands. The building returned to commercial use, suffering many alterations and a general decline, until it was restored in 1881 through the efforts of the Bostonian Society.

Since 1882 it has been maintained as an excellent museum devoted to the history of Boston as well as to Revolutionary and maritime history. The collection contains paintings, prints, ship models, furniture, and other objects, including tea from the Boston Tea Party, objects made and used by Paul Revere, and a drum that sounded at Bunker Hill. Two video documentaries, "Boston and Paul Revere" and "The Growth of Boston," are also shown.

LOCATION: 206 Washington Street. HOURS: November through March: 10–5 Monday–Friday, 9:30–5 Saturday, 11–5 Sunday; April through October: 9:30–5 Daily. FEE: Yes. TELEPHONE: 617–242–5655.

OPPOSITE: Old State House cupola and unicorn reproduction.

A circle of cobblestones marks the spot of one of the most famous incidents of American history, the **site of the Boston Massacre**. On the night of March 5, 1770, a mob of angry Bostonians surrounded a detachment of British soldiers on the street in front of the State House. Hurling snowballs packed with rocks and ice, the crowd surged around the frightened soldiers, who fired into their tormentors, killing five men. Boston exploded in fury, and the royal governor feared that "the town would be all in blood." Patriot anger was tempered by the rumor that the massacre had been deliberately incited by Sam Adams, who wished to create a bloody incident to stir up the city.

Patrick Carr, who died of his wounds several days after the shooting, stated on his deathbed that the soldiers had fired in self-defense. Eight soldiers and an officer were tried for murder; two were found guilty of manslaughter, and the rest were acquitted. Their defense was handled by two attorneys with impeccable patriotic credentials, John Adams and Josiah Quincy, Jr.

Faneuil Hall

Known as the "Cradle of Liberty," Faneuil Hall resounded with the patriotic rhetoric of James Otis, Samuel Adams, and others in the tense years leading up to the Revolution. The building seen today is the third Faneuil Hall, a renovation of 1806 by Charles Bulfinch. The original was built in 1742 with funds donated by the prosperous slave trader, Peter Faneuil, who thought it practical that the city have a central market—an idea that many merchants opposed, partly because they didn't want to make it convenient for inspectors and tax collectors to regulate their businesses. The first floor held market stalls and the upper floor a public meeting room. Faneuil died, at the age of forty-two, a few months before the hall's opening; the first public meeting held here was his memorial service.

A fire destroyed the first hall; the second, identical in design, was completed in 1763. In the 1760s and 1770s this was the favorite forum for Boston's revolutionaries. During the Revolution, the British stored confiscated weapons here and used the hall as a theater (in defiance of a 1750 city law prohibiting plays). The British officer corps was at the hall enjoying a farce written by Burgoyne, *The Blockade of Boston,* when a voice cried out, "The rebels! The rebels! They're attacking the Neck!" The audience roared until they realized it wasn't a joke, and rushed out to discover the Americans were indeed marching on Charlestown Neck. In the nineteenth century, Fanueil Hall was the site of abolitionist meetings. In December 1837 a meeting was planned to denounce the murder, in Illinois, of Elijah P. Lovejoy, an abolitionist killed defending his printing press from a mob. When the mayor refused permission to use the hall, Wendell Phillips thundered, "When Liberty is in danger, Faneuil Hall has the right, it is her duty, to strike the key-note for the United States." A meeting held here in 1850 formed a Vigilance Committee to render assistance to runaway slaves.

The old market stalls have been removed from the sides of the building but a familiar Boston landmark remains—the four-foot-long grasshopper weathervane of gilded copper. The ground floor contains a modern shopping mall; the second floor holds the historic meeting hall, and the third is the armory of the Ancient and Honorable Artillery Company, the nation's oldest military group, founded in 1638. The third floor also contains a museum that includes a cannon captured from the British at Yorktown.

LOCATION: Below Government Center. HOURS: 10–9 Daily. FEE: None. TELEPHONE: 617–523–3886.

East of Faneuil Hall are three commercial buildings, **Quincy Market** and its flanking warehouses called **North and South Market,** designed by Alexander Parris. They were built in 1825 and 1826 at the behest of Mayor Josiah Quincy to expand the facilities of Faneuil Hall. Quincy Market has impressive granite porticoes at each end. In the 1970s the historic trio was renovated; they now contain shops and restaurants.

FINANCIAL DISTRICT

Boston's modern financial district has long been the city's commercial center. From Boston's earliest days, this area was the domain of the wharves, warehouses, and counting houses that provided the wealth to create Beacon Hill. The shoreline has been much changed since colonial times, as Bostonians were in the habit of filling in the Harbor whenever pressed for space. At the corner of

OVERLEAF: *The assembly room in Faneuil Hall, with George P. A. Healy's painting of the January 1830 debate between Senators Daniel Webster and Robert Y. Hayne.*

Batterymarch and Franklin streets is the site of Fort Hill, one of Boston's three original hills, carted away for landfill between 1866 and 1872. Faneuil Hall and the Custom House, landmarks originally right on the water, are inland today. It is said that the bowsprits of docked ships could brush the windows of the Custom House (which was erected on pilings). Some of the old wharves have been preserved, their warehouses converted into offices or apartments.

State Street

The financial district's main thoroughfare has always been State Street, originally named King Street (the name was changed after the Revolution). One of the first streets in the city, it became one of the busiest after the construction of Long Wharf at its foot in 1710. Sailors, merchants, customs inspectors, and travelers shared the street with wagons carrying the exotic goods of the Far East from the ships to warehouses. In the 1700s, business was transacted in the street and at taverns, but in the nineteenth century the city's business barons erected office buildings that were badges of their prosperity. In 1872, Samuel Adams Drake wrote, "It is the busy mart and exchange of the city, sacred to the worship of Mammon. Bills, stocks, and bonds are its literature, and in its vaults are fifty millions of dollars." The National Park Service maintains a visitor center at 15 State Street (617–242–5642).

The **Brazer Building** (1897) at number 27 State was designed by Cass Gilbert, who also did the Woolworth Building in New York. The adjacent **Worthington Building,** at number 33, dates to 1894. Only the facade of the 1891 **Boston Stock Exchange** remains; the interior has been rebuilt for modern offices. Three plaques on the building note that Governor John Winthrop's house was on this site from 1630 to 1643; that this was the site of the Bunch of Grapes Tavern, a meeting place for revolutionaries; and that a Masonic Lodge was established here in 1733.

The **Richards Building,** 114 State Street, has a cast-iron facade and was built in the 1850s for a clipper ship company. Anchors and dolphins adorn the entrance of the adjacent **Cunard Building,** built in 1902 and designed by Peabody and Stearns for the steamship line. The block opposite is taken up by the 1901 **Board of Trade Building,** its facade also enlivened by nautical motifs.

Custom House

A decade in construction (1837–1847), the Custom House is one of the largest American buildings in the Greek Revival style outside the nation's capital. Walt Whitman called it, "one of the noblest pieces of commercial architecture in the world." Designed by Ammi B. Young, and built of Quincy granite, the massive Grecian temple—topped by a Roman dome with a skylight that illuminated the interior—cost one million dollars.

When it was built, it stood at the water's edge between Long Wharf and Central Wharf. Young drove three thousand pilings into the floor of the Harbor to provide a foundation. Each column is a single piece weighing forty-six tons. Originally the building consisted only of the ground floor: The 29-story, 495-foot tower was added in 1915, making the Custom House the tallest structure in New England at the time. A museum is planned for the original rotunda inside, to be open to the public along with the observation deck on the twenty-fifth floor after the building's redevelopment.

LOCATION: Corner of State and India streets. TELEPHONE: 617–722–4300.

The **State Street Block,** across McKinley Square from the Custom House, was built in 1858 by Gridley J. F. Bryant. What remains is only a fifth of what was there originally—sixteen warehouses—and has been converted into offices.

On Milk Street, reachable via India Street, are brick warehouses of the old **Central Wharf,** built in 1816 and perhaps designed by Bulfinch. The **Flour and Grain Exchange Building,** erected in 1892, is a flamboyant castle of commerce. The bulky tower over the entrance, with its conical roof surrounded by dormer windows, resembles a crown.

WATERFRONT

By 1700 Boston was the third-busiest seaport in the British Empire, after London and Bristol. The first round-the-world voyage by an American ship was undertaken by a Boston vessel, the *Columbia,* which returned in 1790 after three years at sea. In the early 1850s, Boston was preeminent in the building of clipper ships, thanks to Donald McKay, but the era of the clipper was a short one. By the

The Destruction of Tea at Boston Harbor, a lithograph by Currier.

1860s, steam was replacing sail, New York City was steadily drain-
ing Boston's shipping away, and the city's business community
turned to manufacturing.

A dozen old wharves line the waterfront from Congress Street
to the North End, along Atlantic Avenue and Commercial Street.
These have been extensively redeveloped, and some historic buildings have been adapted to modern use. The **New England Aquar-
ium** (617–973–5200) stands on Central Wharf, built in 1817. On
Long Wharf, the **Gardiner Building,** erected in 1830, now houses
a restaurant, and the **Custom House Block,** warehouses built in
1837, are now offices.

The original Long Wharf extended two thousand feet into the
Harbor. British troops landed on it in 1768 at the beginning of
the military occupation of Boston. It was the embarkation point
for the Battle of Bunker Hill and for the British evacuation in 1776.
The waterfront was also the site of another of Boston's famed
Revolutionary exploits: the Tea Party.

Boston Tea Party Ship and Museum

On the evening of December 16, 1773, some two hundred Patriots
in Indian disguises (they had darkened their skin to a copper color,

muffled themselves in blankets, and masked their faces) descended
on Griffin's Wharf, where three ships were moored with chests of
tea. To protest the nominal tax on tea, they opened the chests and
heaved the tea into the harbor. Despite the festive name, "Boston
Tea Party," the act was carried out in virtual silence because all
concerned were aware of the seriousness of the business, which
amounted to the criminal destruction of property. John Adams
wrote in his diary, "This destruction of the tea is so bold, so daring,
so firm, intrepid and inflexible, and it must have important consequences." Indeed, the consequences were grave: An enraged British government closed the port of Boston, placed the city under
martial law, and imposed a new set of laws that quickly became
known as the Intolerable Acts. In May 1774, General Gage arrived
with fresh troops, which were quartered in private homes.

The *Beaver II*, a Danish brig launched in 1908, has been fitted
out as a replica of one of the Tea Party ships. The museum has
displays of eighteenth- and nineteenth-century shipbuilding,
hands-on exhibits (including tossing tea chests overboard), and
guides dressed in Colonial costumes.

LOCATION: Congress Street Bridge. HOURS: 9–dusk Daily. FEE: Yes.
TELEPHONE: 617–338–1773.

The buildings on **Commercial Wharf,** dating to the early 1830s,
have been renovated as offices, apartments, and shops. Across the
street from the wharf are warehouses built in the 1830s and the
Mercantile Wharf Building, constructed in 1857 to designs by
Gridley J. F. Bryant.

Lewis Wharf and its 400-foot-long granite warehouse dating
to the 1830s, served the clipper ships. The 1863 **Pilot House** was
originally a depot of the Union Railroad. **Union Wharf's** row of
granite warehouses from the 1840s are now apartments.

Harbor Islands State Park

Of the thirty islands of various size which dot Boston Harbor, eight
are included in the state park. When Captain John Smith explored
the Harbor in 1614, he found evidence of Indian habitation on the
islands, noting that many were "planted with corn, groves, mulber-
ries, savage gardens." Georges Island is the site of **Fort Warren**
(617–727–5250), an impressive bastion begun in 1833. A visitor in

1845 called the fort "probably the most magnificent piece of masonry in this or any other country," and marveled at the size of the twelve-foot-thick foundation walls. During the Civil War, a thousand Confederate prisoners were confined here. The fort is said to be haunted by the ghost of a southern woman, the "Lady in Black," who slipped into the fort disguised as a man to help her husband escape. She was caught and hanged.

NORTH END

The North End of Boston preserves the city's oldest house, its second-oldest cemetery, and its only surviving church designed by Charles Bulfinch. The area is rich in Revolutionary history: Paul Revere and Benjamin Franklin were North Enders, and the British directed the Battle of Bunker Hill from its high points. The district has always had a sense of separateness from the rest of the city. It was originally linked to the city only by a narrow neck of land. In colonial times North Enders and "South Enders" (those from Boston proper) staged a mock battle every year on Guy Fawkes Day. The battle, which often ended in wild fistfighting, symbolized the fierce neighborhood loyalties. With difficulty, Patriot leaders persuaded North Enders to put aside their local feelings and join the rest of Boston in common cause against the British. The North End remains cut off from downtown Boston by an elevated highway, the Central Artery. The city's Italian neighborhood, it has an ethnic identity of its own. Hanover Street, cut in two by the Central Artery, is the main thoroughfare, leading to the waterfront.

Paul Revere House

There are few names in American history more famous than that of Paul Revere—silversmith, engraver, businessman, industrialist, public official, and one of the men who alerted the countryside to the approach of a British expedition on the night of April 18, 1775. The house, built shortly after the Great Fire of 1676, was first owned by a wealthy merchant. In 1770, when the house was ninety years old, Paul Revere purchased it and lived there until 1800. In the nineteenth century, the building was used as a tenement and to house shops. Although recognized very early as being historically

OPPOSITE: The seventeenth-century Paul Revere House.

significant, the house was not saved until 1907 when threat of demolition led a group of preservationists to buy and restore it. A museum since 1908, the house is Boston's only seventeenth-century structure—making it Boston's oldest surviving building.

While the exterior is architecturally typical of the seventeenth century, with an overhanging second story and small, diamond-shaped window panes, the interior has been restored to reflect both that century and the time of Revere. On exhibit are some original Revere family items, including furniture and personal possessions such as his saddlebags. Works of silver and other artifacts are also on display. On the grounds is a courtyard and colonial garden with an 1804 Revere-made church bell. Adjacent is the **Pierce-Hichborn House** (29 North Square), a Georgian style, brick dwelling built about 1711 and owned by Revere's cousin Nathaniel Hichborn after 1781. The house is still under restoration but has limited tours on a regular basis.

LOCATION: 19 North Square. HOURS: April 15 through October: 9:30–5:15 Daily; November through April 14: 9:30–4:15 Daily. Closed Mondays, January through March. FEE: Yes. TELEPHONE: 617–523–2338.

Hanover Street is dominated by the red-brick tower of **St. Stephens Church** (Hanover and Clark streets). Built in 1804, it is the only one of the Boston churches designed by Charles Bulfinch that still stands. Originally a Congregational church, it was acquired in the 1860s by the Catholic diocese to serve the neighborhood's growing immigrant population. In the 1960s, the church was restored to its original appearance inside and out. The dome atop the spire is gilded, but originally it was covered with copper plates provided by Paul Revere. (Revere also cast the original bells, which are visible from Hanover Street.) Bulfinch based his design for the tower on Italian Renaissance models. Inside the barrel-vaulted church, a gallery is supported by Doric and Corinthian columns; the Tracker organ dates to the 1830s.

Across Hanover Street is **Paul Revere Mall,** a public park with benches and trees, and the often-photographed **statue of Paul Revere** astride a horse. Designed in 1885 by Cyrus Dallin, the work was not cast and put up until 1940. Beyond the statue is the entrance to the Old North Church.

Old North Church

Old North is the popular name for Christ Church, Boston's second Anglican church, built in 1723. On the night of April 18, 1775, sexton Robert Newman, on instructions from Paul Revere, hung two lanterns from the 190-foot steeple to alert Patriots in Charlestown that the British were starting out on their Concord raid by boat from Boston Common, rather than by land across Boston Neck. On June 17, 1775, British commander General Thomas Gage went up into the belfry to observe the assault on Bunker Hill, and saw his officers and men relentlessly cut down by American fire. Major John Pitcairn, a British officer who died of wounds received at Bunker Hill, was buried in the crypt below the church, and his remains may still be there. In 1860 Henry Wadsworth Longfellow climbed the steeple and was inspired a few days later to begin writing "Paul Revere's Ride." The steeple seen today is a

Interior of Old North Church. Brass plates on the pews identify original owners.

modern (1955) reproduction. The original was knocked down in a hurricane in 1804, and the replacement itself toppled in a 1954 hurricane. In its design, the building is similar to churches in London designed by Christopher Wren. The church's chandeliers, organ, and clock all date to the eighteenth century. As a teenager, Paul Revere was among a group of boys who rang the church's bells. The eight bells in the belfry, installed in 1745, have sounded for every significant event in the nation's history.

LOCATION: 193 State Street. HOURS: 9–5 Daily. FEE: None. TELE-PHONE: 617–523–6676.

Copp's Hill Burying Ground

Dating to 1659, the cemetery, at Hull and Snow Hill streets, is the second oldest in the city, predated only by the one at King's Chapel. It was named after William Copp, a farmer who worked part of the hill in the middle of the seventeenth century. In April 1775, just after the battles of Lexington and Concord, the British placed several naval guns here. During the Battle of Bunker Hill in June, the guns pounded the Americans entrenched on Breed's Hill, with little effect, and hurled incendiary shells at Charlestown, with devastating effect. General John Burgoyne, who observed the battle from the cemetery, wrote "we threw a parcel of shells, and the whole [town] was instantly in flames." Musketballs and cannonballs were unearthed here during restorations in 1838 and 1878.

The British apparently used the gravestones for target practice, since those of Daniel Malcolm and Grace Berry show the marks of musketball hits. Grace Berry's stone is the source of some controversy because its date, 1625, would make it the oldest in the burying ground and would place her death five years before the city was settled. Some say that the date on the stone was altered from 1695 as a prank, while others maintain that Mrs. Berry died in Plymouth and was reburied here when her husband moved to Boston. The oldest uncontested grave is that of David Copp, who died in 1661. Three of Boston's most famous eighteenth-century ministers, Increase, Cotton, and Samuel Mather, are buried in the Mather tomb.

OPPOSITE: Stairway to the belfry of Old North Church, which sexton Robert Newman climbed to hang the signal lanterns on the night of April 18, 1775.

B   E   A   C   O   N   H   I   L   L

One of America's great architectural and historic treasures, Beacon
Hill is a superbly preserved nineteenth-century district. From the
time of its origins as a real estate development in the early 1800s,
the southern part of Beacon Hill was the geographical and social
apex of the city. Occupying the highest ground in Boston, Beacon
Hill was the home of the elite—merchants, bankers, doctors, lawyers, writers, and intellectuals. Referring to Beacon Street, Oliver
Wendell Holmes called it, "the sunny street that holds the sifted
few."

The northern slope of Beacon Hill, from Pinckney Street to
Cambridge Street, was built up first. In the eighteenth century,
when it was the site of ropewalks (long sheds where rope was
woven), houses of ill repute, and other sailor's haunts, the area was
known as "Mount Whoredom." In the nineteenth century this part
of the hill was also home to a thriving black community. Several
sites important in the history of black Bostonians are on Beacon
Hill, notably the Smith Court Residences and the Abiel Smith
School. At the end of the eighteenth century, the land south of
Pinckney was still largely rural. Atop Beacon Hill stood the signal
lamp that gave the hill its name. (The beacon was put up to give
warning of invasion, but it was never used.) The construction of the
State House on the peak of Beacon Hill made it an attractive area
for development. In 1795 a group of entrepreneurs called the
Mount Vernon Proprietors, which included architect Charles Bulfinch and prominent lawyer Harrison Gray Otis, purchased eighteen and a half acres on the hill's southern slope, from painter John
Singleton Copley, for about $1,000 an acre. The Proprietors
planned to build mansions with ample grounds, but the plan
proved too costly in the economic downturn caused by the 1807
embargo and the War of 1812. The lots were subdivided and put
up for sale. The result, architecturally, was a happy one—Mount
Vernon and Chestnut streets are among the most beautiful in the
country, presenting elegant blocks of red-brick townhouses that
blend together harmoniously. Decoration is minimal: tasteful
wrought-iron railings and fences; slender columns flanking doorways; delicate fanlights.

OPPOSITE: Mount Vernon Street on Beacon Hill.

Whereas a later generation of wealthy Bostonians would proclaim their prosperity by building chateaux and castles along Commonwealth Avenue, on Beacon Hill the unspoken but unbreached rule was restraint. Testing the edge of what that might mean, Harrison Gray Otis built three houses here, all designed for him by Bulfinch. Otis was beloved for his lavish entertaining, and his houses were obviously expensive, but the fronts of all three present a properly austere face to the public.

Beacon Hill residents later took pride in purple panes of glass. An 1818 shipment of glass from Hamburg contained traces of manganese oxide that, after years of exposure to sunlight, darkened to a rich purple. This consignment of glass was used up by 1825; thus possession of a purple pane is a badge of age, cherished alike by descendants of the venerable "sifted few" and by the new tycoons of finance and high technology who have purchased property on Beacon Hill in the boom years of the 1980s.

Boston Athenaeum

Behind a dark, sandstone facade is one of the finest private libraries in the country, established in 1807 as "a retreat for those who enjoy the humanity of books," and as an art museum. Ralph Waldo Emerson was one of the ten founding members. The building was completed in 1849, and enlarged in 1914. The Athenaeum's collection includes the libraries of George Washington and Henry Knox, who was a bookseller in Boston before winning fame in the Revolution as the man who transported Fort Ticonderoga's cannon across Massachusetts, and the King's Chapel library of theological books donated to the church by King William III. The Athenaeum's original art collection grew so large that it had to be housed separately, and formed the nucleus of the Museum of Fine Arts when it was established in 1876. Today the Athenaeum displays a notable collection of portraits, including works by Gilbert Stuart, Thomas Sully, and John Singer Sargent. The barrel-vaulted reading room on the fifth floor is the epitome of the book-lover's retreat.

LOCATION: 10 1/2 Beacon Street. HOURS: Tours at 3, Tuesday and Thursday, by appointment. FEE: None. TELEPHONE: 617-227-0270.

OPPOSITE: Reading room of the Boston Athenaeum. Once described by Henry James as "this honoured haunt of all the most civilized — library, gallery, temple of culture," the Athenaeum has provided a haven for such luminaries as Emerson, Longfellow, and Hawthorne.

STATE HOUSE

The State House is Charles Bulfinch's great contribution to the city and to American architecture. Bulfinch submitted his plans for the new state house only a few years after independence had been won. His majestic portico and resplendent dome embodied the values everyone hoped would guide government thenceforth: dignity, restraint, and loftiness of purpose. The cornerstone was laid in 1795 by two stalwart revolutionaries, Samuel Adams and Paul Revere. Revere also supplied a copper sheath for the dome, a covering replaced in 1874 by gold leaf. The building seen today is flanked by wings (added during World War I) that significantly detract from the visual impact of the Bulfinch design.

On the ground floor is the Doric Hall, an imposing columned hall with a statue of Washington. Also on the ground floor is the Hall of Flags in which the colors of state military units are displayed. A double staircase ascends to the chamber of the House of Representatives. Built in 1895, this domed, oval-shaped room is adorned with murals depicting episodes from Massachusetts history. The chamber also contains the Sacred Codfish, a gilded, carved-wood depiction of the fish that was a staple of the first settlers' diet and a valuable commodity in the Bay State's international trade. The Senate Chamber is part of the original building as well. This domed and columned room displays the first weapon captured from a British soldier in the Revolution.

In the **archives and museum** in the basement, the state charter granted by King Charles I and carried across the Atlantic by the Puritan settlers in 1630 is on display, as are the manuscript of Bradford's history of Plymouth (looted by the British during the Revolution and later recovered in London), and Bradford's copy of the Mayflower Compact.

Behind the State House, in the legislators' parking lot, is a nineteenth-century reproduction of a granite obelisk Bulfinch raised on the site of the original beacon.

LOCATION: Corner of Park and Beacon streets. HOURS: 10–4 Monday–Friday. FEE: None. TELEPHONE: 617–727–3676.

OPPOSITE ABOVE: The State House and its twentieth-century wings. BELOW: Statue of General William Francis Bartlett by Daniel Chester French and, on the left, Bela Pratt's memorial to Civil War nurses, in the State House Annex.

BEACON STREET

The apartment building at **34½ Beacon Street** was named after Frederic Tudor, the "Ice King," who shipped blocks of New England ice to the Caribbean and the Far East. His house stood on this site before the present building went up in 1896. The pair of houses at **39–40 Beacon** were both erected in 1819, and designed by Alexander Parris. **Number 39** (private) was the home of Nathan Appleton, one of the developers of the textile mills in Lowell, Massachusetts. In this house, Appleton's daughter Fanny married the poet Henry Wadsworth Longfellow in 1843. **Number 40** was the home of Daniel Pinckney Parker, a China-trade merchant; it is now occupied by the Women's City Club of Boston and may be toured by appointment (617–227–3550). Appleton and Parker, briefly business partners, were life-long friends, and this friendship is aptly expressed in the design of their houses, which are mirror images, inside and out. The handsome interior of number 40 features curved mahogany doors that slide into curved walls. Both houses boast a few panes of the rare purple glass.

Number **45 Beacon** is Harrison Gray Otis's third house on Beacon Hill. Now hemmed in on both sides, the house originally stood free. The private **Somerset Club** occupies **42 Beacon,** one half of which was designed by Alexander Parris as a residence on the site of John Singleton Copley's house. The Club, founded in 1852, moved here twenty years later. In the 1880s, one Bostonian described it as "that reservoir of Boston blue blood." A plaque at **50 Beacon** marks one corner of the landholdings of William Blaxton, Boston's original settler. The **Founder's Monument,** across the street, depicts Blaxton's first encounter with John Winthrop.

On Beacon Street, across from the State House, is the **Shaw Monument,** a sculpture in relief by Augustus Saint-Gaudens in a setting designed by McKim, Mead & White. Dedicated in 1897, the monument recalls the Fifty-Fourth Massachusetts Regiment, a Civil War unit made up entirely of black soldiers and commanded by white officers under Colonel Robert Gould Shaw, who was killed in battle at Charleston, South Carolina in 1863. A member of this unit, Sergeant William Carney, was the first black to win the Congressional Medal of Honor. The relief depicts the regiment's farewell march down Beacon Street, past the residence of Colonel

OPPOSITE: Entrance of the Appleton House on Beacon Street. One of Beacon Hill's rare purple panes of glass is in the window on the right.

Shaw's family, at number 44. Shaw's sister watched her twenty-six-year-old brother's departure, and later wrote, "his face was as the face of an angel and I felt perfectly sure he would never come back."

Prescott House

Number 55 Beacon Street, probably designed by Asher Benjamin, was the home of the distinguished historian William Hickling Prescott from 1845 to 1859. He was the grandson of Colonel William Prescott, who commanded the American forces at Bunker Hill. Blinded in one eye during a food fight at Harvard, and almost blind in the other, Prescott was unable to read longer than ten minutes at a time. Friends sometimes read to him, and he developed prodigious powers of memory. Unable to write things down efficiently, he composed in his head, memorizing as many as seventy-two pages of prose, which he mentally "rewrote" until it was ready to be put to paper. In this difficult fashion he wrote monumental histories of Spain, Mexico, and Peru. In 1837 Prescott made his reputation with the publication of *The Reign of Ferdinand and Isabella,* which brought him international acclaim and surprised his

The Shaw Monument, which took Augustus Saint-Gaudens thirteen years to complete.

Beacon Hill neighbors, who thought he was passing his time in idleness. Now the headquarters of the Colonial Dames of America, the house has been restored. There is an elegant second-floor drawing room with a view of the Common. Prescott's private study, on the third floor, includes a device called a noctograph, which he used as an aid to writing his manuscripts.

LOCATION: 55 Beacon Street. HOURS: 10–4 Wednesdays, and by appointment. FEE: Yes. TELEPHONE: 617–742–3190.

CHESTNUT STREET

Charles Bulfinch designed the three townhouses at **13–17 Chestnut** for three sisters, and they were built between 1806 and 1808. From 1863 to 1865, **number 13** was the home of Julia Ward Howe, lyricist of "The Battle Hymn of the Republic." Richard Henry Dana lived at **number 43.** Poor eyesight caused by measles forced him to give up his studies at Harvard and he went to sea. Later he vividly described his experiences in *Two Years before the Mast.*

    The historian Francis Parkman lived at **50 Chestnut Street** from 1863 to 1895. In those decades he authored some of the most

Acorn Street, on Beacon Hill.

influential histories written during the nineteenth century, including *The Discovery of the Great West*. To research the book, he traveled the routes of explorers and pioneers along the Oregon Trail.

MOUNT VERNON STREET

Nichols House Museum

This 1804 brick house, attributed to Bulfinch, was the home of Rose Standish Nichols (1872–1960), a noted landscape architect, author, and advocate of international cooperation. She was a founder of what later became the Foreign Policy Association. The interior of the house has been preserved as it was at Nichols's death in 1960, displaying her collection of art, needlework, and furniture, including a chair once owned by Governor John Winthrop, and bronzes by Augustus Saint-Gaudens, her uncle.

> LOCATION: 55 Mount Vernon Street. HOURS: March through May and September through November: 1–5 Monday, Wednesday, Saturday; June through August: 1–5 Tuesday–Saturday; December through February: 1–5 Saturday. FEE: Yes. TELEPHONE: 617–227–6993.

Daniel Webster lived at **57 Mount Vernon** from 1817 to 1819 when he was a Boston lawyer. From 1885 to 1907 **number 59** was the residence of Thomas Bailey Aldrich, editor of the *Atlantic Monthly*. **Number 85** was Harrison Gray Otis's second mansion on Beacon Hill, built in 1800. In the 1870s, Henry James lived for a brief time in **number 131,** where he finished the novel *Daisy Miller*.

LOUISBURG SQUARE

This rectangle of handsome brick residences, built between 1834 and 1847, faces a private park that was laid out in 1826. The square was named in tribute to the Massachusetts troops who, in 1745, helped capture Fort Louisburg, Nova Scotia, from the French. The statues of Columbus and Aristides the Just in the park were donated in 1850 by the Turkish Consul, who lived at **3 Louisburg Square.** The influential writer and editor William Dean Howells lived at **number 4** from 1883 to 1884. Novelist Louisa May Alcott lived at **number 10** from 1885 to 1887. At that time she was severely ill from mercury poisoning developed from a cure for a fever contracted while a nurse in the Civil War. She died in 1888. Samuel Gray Ward of **number 20** handled the financing for the $7.5 million purchase of Alaska from Russia. The famed opera singer Jenny Lind, the "Swedish Nightingale," was married in this house.

PINCKNEY STREET

Pinckney Street, the border between proper Boston and the less-elegant precincts on the north slope of the hill, was the address of numerous literary figures and two prominent black men in the nineteenth century. **Number 86 Pinckney** was the home of John J. Smith, the second black to serve on the Boston Common Council. Born in Virginia, he was first a barber and owned a number of barber shops. After serving in the Civil War, he was elected to the Massachusetts state legislature for three terms. Louisa May Alcott lived at both **43** and **81 Pinckney Street.** John P. Marquand moved to **number 57** in 1914, after graduating from Harvard. Nathaniel Hawthorne lived at **54 Pinckney Street** from 1839 to 1842, when he was a customs inspector. Bronson Alcott and his family lived at **20 Pinckney Street** from 1852 to 1855. **Number 15** had one of the first kindergartens in the country, started by Elizabeth Peabody, and **14 Pinckney Street** was the home of William D. Ticknor of Ticknor and Fields. What today constitute **numbers 5 and 7** were originally one building which was the home of George Middleton, a noted black veteran of the Revolutionary War. He held the rank of colonel, leading a company of black soldiers called "The Bucks of America."

Smith Court, on the north slope of Beacon Hill above Cambridge Street, is the location for the **African Meeting House** (617–742–1854), which has been restored. Opened in 1806, it is the oldest surviving black church in the country. An important center of the abolitionist movement, the church earned the nickname, the Black Fanueil Hall, because of its frequent and fiery antislavery meetings. The **Smith Court Residences,** a group of brick and clapboard houses facing a narrow court, represent typical homes of the city's black community in the nineteenth century.

The building at 46 Joy Street and Smith Court houses the **Museum of Afro American History** (617–742–1854). The museum shows a film on the history of blacks in Boston and has a permanent exhibit on the history of the civil rights movement. Tours of historic sites on the **Black Heritage Trail** depart from the museum. The building was formerly the **Abiel Smith School,** founded in 1835 for the private education of black children. Although many members of the black community had been dissatisfied with the quality of the education at the two grammar schools the city set aside for blacks, they also had ambivalent feelings about the Abiel Smith School, believing it might actually encourage segregation. A few years after the school opened, black parents led by a resident of Smith Court, the historian William C. Nell, formed the Equal School Association, calling for an end to segregated education and a boycott of the Smith School. The controversy dragged on for a decade, as a parent sued to force the city to admit his daughter to a public school near her home. The state's highest court ruled in 1850 that the Smith School provided an education that was equal to that of the public schools, so blacks did not have to be admitted to the public system. But in 1855 the state legislature outlawed school segregation, and the Smith School closed.

The **Lewis and Harriet Hayden House** (66 Phillips Street, private) was a station on the Underground Railroad. In 1853, Harriet Beecher Stowe, the author of *Uncle Tom's Cabin,* visited the house and met with a group of thirteen escaped slaves. The **Charles Street Meeting House** (Mount Vernon and Charles streets) was an important forum for abolitionists. Wendell Phillips, William Lloyd Garrison, and Frederick Douglass all spoke here. The building, erected in 1807, has been converted to offices.

HARRISON GRAY OTIS HOUSE

A severe facade masks an interior of great beauty and elegance. Certainly among the most beautiful homes of its day, it is a triumph of post-Revolutionary taste. The rooms are adorned with bright, patterned wallpapers, vivid carpets, and furniture that belonged to the Otis family and to John Osborn, who purchased the house in 1801. Perhaps the most impressive room in the house is the draw-

OPPOSITE: The second-floor drawing room in the Harrison Gray Otis House. Bulfinch's plain, almost austere, facade merely hints at the gracious interiors of Otis's first grand home on Beacon Hill.

Detail of mantel relief ornament in the Otis House drawing room.

ing room on the second floor, with its elaborate woodwork and mirrored doors.

Harrison Gray Otis, lawyer, politician, and real estate entrepreneur, was one of the five Proprietors who developed Beacon Hill. The house was designed for Otis by Charles Bulfinch, and built in 1795 and 1796. It is now the headquarters of the Society for the Preservation of New England Antiquities. The basement of the house contains an architectural museum.

LOCATION: 141 Cambridge Street. HOURS: Tours at 10, 11, 1, 2, and 3, Monday–Friday. FEE: Yes. TELEPHONE: 617–227–3956.

A few steps away from the Otis House is **Old West Church,** built in 1806 by Asher Benjamin. Four blocks west at the end of Cambridge Street is the dour **Charles Street Jail,** erected in 1851. The jail was designed with the help of a prison reformer who suggested that every cell have some sunlight. One block north of the jail, Fruit Street leads to the Massachusetts General Hospital. The **Bulfinch Pavilion** of the hospital, designed by Charles Bulfinch and built between 1818 and 1821, was the site of the first medical use of an anaesthetic. The historic operation took place in 1846, in an operating theater under the building's dome, now known as the Ether Dome. A dentist, William T. G. Morton, administered ether to a patient before the removal of a tumor under his jaw. The medical community was amazed when the patient said he had experienced no pain during the operation.

B   A   C   K   B   A   Y

The filling in of the Back Bay in the late 1800s provided an opportunity for large-scale city planning. The result was a remarkably graceful, architecturally distinguished area. In the early nineteenth century a dam was built across Back Bay from the foot of Beacon Street, at the corner of Charles, to present-day Kenmore Square, thereby harnessing the tides to provide power for mills. Later, railroad lines were built across the Bay, impeding the flow of water. The semistagnant Bay became a dumping ground and sewage outlet. Resolved to do something about this health hazard, the city began filling in the Bay in 1857, a project completed in stages by the end of the century.

Upon this new land arose a residential district. The spine of the new neighborhood was and is Commonwealth Avenue, a beautiful, 240-foot-wide boulevard, with a mall running down its center. Four streets run parallel: Marlborough and Beacon to the north, and Newbury and Boylston to the south. The cross streets were named in alphabetical order, beginning at the Public Garden: Arlington, Berkeley, Clarendon, Dartmouth, Exeter, Fairfield, Gloucester, and Hereford. The Back Bay ends at the next cross street, Massachusetts Avenue.

Statue of abolitionist William Lloyd Garrison, by Olin Levi Warner, on Commonwealth Avenue.

PUBLIC GARDEN

The first botanical garden in the country, the Public Garden was unofficially established in 1837 by a group of horticultural minded Bostonians after years of struggle against real estate developers. In 1859 the city enacted a law forbidding any building, except a city hall, between Arlington and Charles streets. In the following year the Boston landscape architect George F. Meacham laid out the serpentine walks and flower beds that are seen today. Among the monuments in the Garden are a 1924 bronze statue of a maiden, by Daniel Chester French, memorializing the philanthropist George Robert White; an 1867 monument to the first use of ether as an anaesthetic during an operation; and a bronze tribute to George Washington, dedicated in 1869. A tradition in the Garden's pond since 1877 are "swan boat" rides, powered by a helmsman who pedals the boat from behind a large swan.

COMMONWEALTH AVENUE

The **First Baptist Church,** at the corner of Clarendon, was designed by Henry Hobson Richardson and was built in the early 1870s. Its square tower looms over the avenue, with a frieze at the top designed by Frédéric Auguste Bartholdi, the sculptor of New York's Statue of Liberty. On the next corner, at Dartmouth Street, is the **Ames-Webster Mansion,** built in 1872 and now converted to offices. Farther along the avenue are the area's two most imposing mansions. The **Albert E. Burrage Mansion** (private), at Hereford Street, was built in 1899 for a lawyer and financier who made a fortune in copper and gas. The architect derived the detailing for the mansion from a French chateau, then added a profusion of gargoyles and cherubs. The **Oliver Ames Mansion** (355 Commonwealth Avenue, private), is in the same style.

Gibson House Museum (137 Beacon Street, 617–267–6338) was built in 1860. The house provides a glimpse of the way of life enjoyed by the Boston rich in the latter half of the nineteenth century. The house is furnished with items of the period, including many original furnishings.

The **Arlington Street Church,** at the corner of Boylston, is a Georgian-style building erected a half century after the style was no

OPPOSITE: The pond in the Public Garden and a Japanese lantern at the water's edge.

longer fashionable. It features a sturdy stone tower in the design of Christopher Wren.

The **Church of the Covenant** (Newbury and Berkeley streets) had the city's tallest tower—236 feet—when built in 1866. Inside are superb stained-glass windows from the shop of Louis Comfort Tiffany, depicting the birth and resurrection of Christ.

COPLEY SQUARE

Copley Square is the site of masterworks by two of America's greatest architects: Trinity Church, designed by Henry Hobson Richardson, and the Boston Public Library, largely by Charles Follen McKim of McKim, Mead & White.

Trinity Church

Trinity Church took four years to build, from 1873 to 1877, using Massachusetts materials: granite from Dedham and red sandstone from Longmeadow. The church represents the culmination of Richardson's life-long fascination with the beauties and mysteries of medieval architecture. In an essay he wrote describing the church, Richardson said its design was a "free rendering of the French Romanesque," in which he found grandeur, repose, and enlightenment. The enormous tower that dominates both church and square echoes, he said, the domes of Venice and Constantinople. In Richardson's brilliant plan, the massive stone structure appears vibrant, almost in motion, with its patterns of slender archways and columns. The interior is richly ornamented, notably by frescoes painted by John LaFarge and by stained glass prepared under his direction. The ceiling of the tower, more than one hundred feet above the floor, is decorated with biblical scenes.

LOCATION: Copley Square. HOURS: 8–6 Daily. FEE: None. TELE-PHONE: 617–536–9044.

Boston Public Library

Completed in 1895, the Boston Public Library was designed by Charles Follen McKim to be a sumptuous public palace devoted to learning. The building was inspired by Italian Renaissance palazzi

OPPOSITE: *Panelled ceiling below the tower of Trinity Church, with arabesques and Biblical frescoes by John LaFarge.* OVERLEAF: *Main entrance hall of the Boston Public Library. The lions were sculpted in Siena marble by Louis Saint-Gaudens; the murals of the muses were done by Puvis de Chavannes.*

WINCHESTER · 1862 · CEDAR MOUNTAIN
ANTIETAM · CHANCELLORSVILLE
GETTYSBURG · RESACA · ATLANTA
THE MARCH TO THE SEA · SAVANNAH
SHERMAN'S CAROLINA CAMPAIGN

and has a broad granite facade dominated by tall, arched windows; its massive bronze doors are decorated with reliefs by Daniel Chester French. The grand entrance hall boasts a handsome marble staircase, the first landing of which overlooks a central courtyard. In addition to French, two other noted artists of the period created works for the library. The second-floor room that contains the circulation desk is surrounded by a mural painted by Edwin Austin Abbey depicting *The Quest and Achievement of the Holy Grail*. The room's design was based on the library of the Doge's Palace in Venice. On the third floor, a long corridor is lined by a series of murals by John Singer Sargent, who worked on these paintings off and on for thirty years. They are entitled *Judaism and Christianity*.

LOCATION: Copley Square. HOURS: 9–9 Monday–Thursday, 9–5 Friday–Saturday, 2–6 Sunday (closed Sundays in summer). FEE: None. TELEPHONE: 617–536–5400.

The **New Old South Church** (Boylston and Dartmouth streets) was built in 1875 in Anglo-Ruskinian Gothic style. The church has noteworthy stained-glass windows.

Christian Science Center

A complex of modern buildings surrounds the original Mother Church, built in 1894, and the extension added to it in 1906. The extension is a huge, domed building of Indiana limestone, with Byzantine and Italian Renaissance architectural elements. The *Christian Science Monitor* building contains the impressive Mapparium, a thirty-foot-wide, stained-glass globe, through which visitors can walk on a footbridge. Mary Baker Eddy, born in New Hampshire in 1821, founded the Christian Science church in the 1870s after she was healed of the effects of a serious injury. Coming to believe that all sickness can be cured through faith, she attracted 100,000 followers before she died in 1910.

LOCATION: One Norway Street. HOURS: 8–4 Monday–Friday, 10–3:45 Saturday, 11:15–3:45 Sunday. FEE: None. TELEPHONE: 617–450–2000.

MUSEUM OF FINE ARTS

Founded in 1870, the museum has grown to encompass one of the finest and most wide-ranging art collections in the world. Its collection of Asian art is without peer in the Western Hemisphere. The museum has sponsored archaeological digs in Egypt since the 1880s; from 1905 until 1945, in partnership with Harvard, it conducted extensive explorations along the Nile at sites ranging from the pyramids outside Cairo to areas in the Sudan. As a result, the MFA possesses a superb collection of Egyptian antiquities.

The museum has also energetically acquired American paintings, sculpture, furniture, and decorative arts. The broad collection of American art includes paintings by every prominent American artist of the eighteenth and nineteenth centuries, such as John Singleton Copley, Benjamin West, John Trumbull, Samuel F. B. Morse, Thomas Sully, Thomas Cole, Albert Bierstadt, George Inness, Winslow Homer, Thomas Eakins, and John Singer Sargent. Perhaps the historical prizes of the American art collection are the portraits of George and Martha Washington painted by Gilbert Stuart in 1796, shown here and at the National Portrait Gallery in Washington, DC in alternating three-year periods.

The **Department of American Decorative Arts and Sculpture** displays an outstanding collection of furniture, silver, pewter, glass, ceramics, and folk art. With an emphasis on works created in New

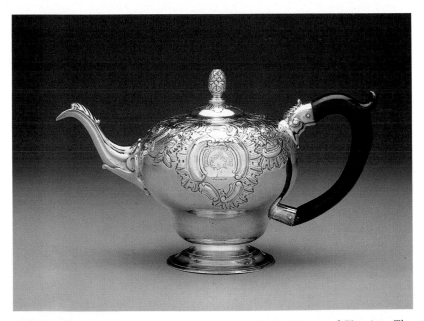

A silver teapot, made by Paul Revere in the 1760s, in the Museum of Fine Arts. The Revolutionary War hero was also one of the finest silversmiths in the country.

Meditation by the Sea, painted by an unknown artist in the 1850s, in the collection of the Museum of Fine Arts.

England before the Civil War, it includes among its notable works the silver "Liberty Bowl" made by Paul Revere, in 1768, and engraved with the names of fifteen members of the Sons of Liberty.

The **American Period Rooms** display furnishings of the eighteenth and nineteenth centuries in authentically arranged settings—some reconstructed from actual historic houses. The rooms make use of architectural elements, such as panelling, windows, and fireplaces, purchased or salvaged from houses facing demolition.

LOCATION: 465 Huntington Avenue. HOURS: 10–5 Tuesday, Saturday, Sunday; 10–10 Wednesday–Friday. FEE: Yes. TELEPHONE: 617–267–9377.

ISABELLA STEWART GARDNER MUSEUM

One of the nation's cultural treasures, this museum was built and filled with works of art by Mrs. Gardner in the late nineteenth and early twentieth centuries. Having begun collecting art on a trip she took to Europe in an effort to recover from the death of her only child, she developed a keen eye for quality, and was later assisted in her art acquisitions by Bernard Berenson, a respected connoisseur of Renaissance painting. To house the collection—and to provide a home for herself—Mrs. Gardner built a Venetian-style palace with a grand courtyard that rises the full four-story height of the building. Mrs. Gardner opened the museum to the public in 1903, and lived here until her death in 1924. It is a treasure house of works ranging in period from ancient Egypt to the late nineteenth century. Mrs. Gardner still presides over the house in the form of her controversial portrait painted by John Singer Sargent in 1888. It caused a Boston scandal because Mrs. Gardner appeared in what was then considered to be a revealing, low-cut gown.

LOCATION: 280 The Fenway (next to the Museum of Fine Arts). HOURS: 12–5 Wednesday–Friday, 10–5 Saturday–Sunday, 12–8 Tuesday (July–August, 12–5). FEE: Donation suggested. TELEPHONE: 617–734–1359.

SOUTH BOSTON

A 215-foot-high marble tower stands at **Dorchester Heights National Historic Site** where, overnight, American engineers built the fortifications that forced the British army and fleet out of Boston in 1776. Militia units had penned the British into the city since the preceding spring, but neither side had the strength to defeat the other. Then Henry Knox arrived with the fifty-nine cannon that Ethan Allen had captured at Fort Ticonderoga in upstate New York, and Knox had dragged by oxen across the intervening three hundred miles. On the night of March 4, 1776, some two thousand troops slipped into Dorchester Heights, followed by a wagon train of equipment, ammunition, and cannon. At dawn the next day, the British were utterly astounded to see a formidable complex of fortifications that seemed to have come by magic—out of "Aladdin's lamp," as one British officer wrote. The works withstood British bombardment from Castle Island, then known as Castle William, and an attempt to attack the Heights was broken up by a sudden storm. The British command had great respect for the skill of American artillerymen, and realized that their position in Boston was untenable. They evacuated Boston on March 17, never to return.

OVERLEAF: Courtyard of the Isabella Stewart Gardner Museum.

Castle Island

Strategically located near the harbor's main shipping channel, Castle Island has been continuously fortified by a series of eight fortifications since 1634. The island's present fortification, the massive, star-shaped **Fort Independence,** was completed in 1851.

In March 1776, Castle William, the British stronghold on the site, was forced to return the fire from the American rebel position on Dorchester Heights, the only time the island's guns were fired in war. The rebels' advantageous position forced the British to evacuate Castle Island and Boston. Castle Island was linked to the South Boston mainland by a wooden drawbridge in 1891, and then by a causeway in the 1920s. Fort Independence is partially restored and is open to the public on a seasonal basis.

LOCATION: William J. Day Boulevard. HOURS: May through October: weekends, hours vary. FEE: None. TELEPHONE: 617–268–5744.

John F. Kennedy Library

Housed in a striking building designed by I. M. Pei and overlooking the Harbor, the Kennedy Library contains the president's pa-

Fort Independence in South Boston. During his brief army career, Edgar Allan Poe was stationed on the island for a few months in 1827, when he was eighteen years old.

pers and a museum that is open to the public. Displays of documents and historical photographs trace the rise of the Kennedy and Fitzgerald families to wealth and political prominence. Personal items on exhibit include the president's desk and the coconut shell on which he carved a plea for help after his PT boat was sunk during World War II.

LOCATION: Columbia Point. HOURS: 9–5 Daily. FEE: Yes. TELEPHONE: 617–929–4523.

CHARLESTOWN

Charlestown was settled before Boston by a group of pioneers from Salem who arrived in the dead of winter, in January 1629. Many died from cold and starvation. John Winthrop and his Puritan followers arrived in Charlestown in 1630, but soon moved across the river to Boston.

Charlestown was virtually destroyed by the British bombardment during the Battle of Bunker Hill. Some eighteenth-century houses survive, nonetheless, but the important historic sites are the Navy Yard and the Bunker Hill Monument. The Charlestown Bridge ends at City Square. A few blocks east, on Water Street, is the **Bunker Hill Pavilion,** the city's tourist information center, where a slide show about the Bunker Hill battle is presented. The Pavilion is close to the entrance of the Navy Yard.

USS Constitution and Charlestown Navy Yard

Launched in 1797 at a Boston shipyard, the frigate *Constitution* won two famous victories against British ships during the War of 1812, thereby buoying American spirits amid disastrous defeats on land. On August 19, 1812, under Captain Isaac Hull, the *Constitution* destroyed the *Guerrière* in a fierce thirty-minute exchange of broadsides. It was in this battle that the ship won the nickname "Old Ironsides," when British cannonballs bounced off her oak hull. On December 29, the skilled gunners of the *Constitution* reduced the *Java* to a wreck in two hours. Her final battle was fought in February 1815, during which she captured two British ships off Madeira by superior ship-handling.

OVERLEAF: USS Constitution. Once each year—Independence Day—throngs gather to witness the "turning" of "Old Ironsides" as the ship sails through the harbor before returning to her berth.

In 1830 the navy planned to scrap the *Constitution*, but Oliver Wendell Holmes, then a law student at Harvard, wrote an impassioned poetic plea ("Nail to the mast her holy flag / Set every threadbare sail / And give her to the god of storms / The lightning and the gale!") which was published in newspapers throughout the country. The ensuing public outcry saved the ship, now the oldest commissioned vessel in the navy. The ship has been completely refurbished (less than 10 percent of her timbers are original) and is open for tours. Docked next to the *Constitution* is the World War II destroyer *Cassin Young*, which saw action at Iwo Jima and Okinawa. Nearby is the **Constitution Museum,** displaying some of the famous hull, nautical equipment, and prizes won by her captains.

A path leads from the *Constitution* to the Navy Yard, which was established in 1800 and was active until 1974. An information center, housed in an 1816 building, provides tour information and a slide show. Several of the yard's facilities are open, including the quarter-mile-long **ropewalk** (which produced all the navy's rope until 1955) and the **Commandant's House,** built in 1805.

LOCATION: Historic Waterfront. HOURS: USS *Constitution:* 9:30–3:50 Daily; *Navy Yard:* 9–5 Daily. FEE: Yes. TELEPHONE: 617–426–1812.

Bunker Hill Monument

A 220-foot-high granite obelisk marks the site of one of the most heroic engagements of the Revolution. The battle, which took place on the afternoon of June 17, 1775, actually occurred on Breed's Hill, where the monument stands. Bunker's Hill, northwest of Breed's, was the site of the American fall-back entrenchment. The American commander, Colonel William Prescott, had been ordered to occupy Bunker's Hill in order to forestall a British plan to occupy Dorchester Heights. When he arrived on the scene the night of June 16, 1775, either Prescott or his officers decided that Breed's Hill would suit their purposes better. Working in the dark, Prescott's militia units managed to build a sturdy rectangular redoubt with a breastwork in front of it. Colonel John Stark's New Hampshire militia, who arrived the next afternoon, improvised a wall of stones and rails that ran north to the Mystic River.

When sentries aboard a British ship in the Charles River noticed the American earthworks at 4 AM, the ship began a bombardment which was also taken up by the battery on Copp's Hill in the North End. The British organized an amphibious assault across the

John Trumbull's dramatic painting of the final British assault on Breed's Hill.

Charles River from Boston. Two courageous advances, planned and led by Major General William Howe, were beaten back and resulted in heavy casualties. Aware that it was strategically essential to dislodge the rebels from their redoubt, Howe ordered a final, desperate attack supported by accurate artillery fire. Prescott's men, almost out of powder, held their fire until the British were within twenty yards.

Once again the British line was shattered, but they surged into the redoubt amid hand-to-hand fighting. One British officer wrote, "Nothing could be more shocking than the carnage that followed." Major John Pitcairn, who had commanded the British troops on Lexington Green, was mortally wounded; the patriot leader Joseph Warren was killed instantly by a musketball through his head. Thirty other defenders were bayonetted. The Americans fled to Bunker's Hill, and then to their camps in Cambridge. Although the Americans had been defeated, the British suffered terrible losses, particularly among the officers, whom rebel sharpshooters had singled out. In his report to London, General Gage wrote bitterly, "I wish this cursed place was burned."

LOCATION: 43 Monument Square. HOURS: 10:30–4 Daily. FEE: None. TELEPHONE: 617–242–8220.

C A M B R I D G E

Founded in 1630, the same year as Boston, Cambridge was originally named New Towne and was the colony's first capital. Harvard College, the first college in the nation, was founded here in 1636. Two years later the name of the town was changed to Cambridge, after the English university town.

The focus of modern Cambridge and of the city's historic district is Harvard Square, a busy commercial center where the main entrance to Harvard Yard is located. On the night of April 18, 1775, William Dawes rode through Harvard Square on his way to Lexington and Concord. North of the Square is **Cambridge Common** where, on July 3, 1775, George Washington is said to have stood under a tree (thereafter known as "the Washington Elm") and taken command of the Continental Army which marched before him in review. (Historians now believe that the story is little more than a charming local legend. The nascent Continental Army was better at guerrilla warfare than at marching in a straight line.) On the night he arrived in Cambridge, Washington attended a party at which General John Glover's Marblehead officers had quite a lot to drink and entertained their new commander in rousing song. Washington's residence in Cambridge was a house on Brattle Street which would later be owned by Henry Wadsworth Longfellow. Brattle Street is the location of Cambridge's finest eighteenth- and nineteenth-century houses, nearly all of them private, known in Revolutionary times as Tory Row. Many of their owners moved to Boston at the outbreak of hostilities.

HARVARD UNIVERSITY

The first college in the country, Harvard was founded to provide training for ministers in 1636, just six years after the establishment of the colony of Massachusetts Bay. It was named Harvard in 1638 after a minister, John Harvard, who had bequeathed money and books to the school. They had no legal power to grant degrees, but did so anyway. The foundation of the college signaled that the colonists intended to be as independent as possible in educational, theological, and cultural matters. Under Harvard's auspices, the country's first printing press was established in 1640.

OPPOSITE: The towers of Eliot House and Lowell House at Harvard University.

In the nineteenth century, Harvard took its place as one of the world's premier universities with the establishment of its schools for the study of law, dentistry, and divinity, and its graduate school of arts and sciences. The faculty has included some of the greatest names in American intellectual life, among them James Russell Lowell, Oliver Wendell Holmes, Louis Agassiz, William James, and Henry Wadsworth Longfellow. In the 1870s, the law school pioneered the casebook approach—the study of actual cases rather than theoretical principles. Charles William Eliot, during his long tenure as Harvard's president, from 1869 to 1909, supervised a tremendous expansion in the number of students, faculty, and facilities. He raised academic standards and tightened discipline, instituted the elective system by which students could choose the courses they wished to study, and advocated free high school education as a way to social and economic progress. Eliot also encouraged the establishment of Radcliffe College for women.

The university's historic buildings are located in Harvard Yard, a shady enclave of dormitories, offices, classrooms, and libraries, many in the red brick that defines the image of Harvard. There are five eighteenth-century buildings in what is known as the Old Yard, and they demonstrate the gracefulness and elegance of the pre-Revolutionary Georgian style. A clapboard building by an entrance from Harvard Square is **Wadsworth Hall,** built in 1726. It served as the home of Harvard's presidents until 1849, and it may have been in this building that Washington actually took command of the Continental Army in 1775. The oldest building in the Yard is **Massachusetts Hall,** built in 1720 as a dormitory and laboratory. Troops of the Continental Army were housed here in 1775 and 1776. **Harvard Hall,** erected in 1764, was also a barracks at this time. Next to it is **Hollis Hall,** built in 1763.

Charles Bulfinch designed **University Hall,** which was completed in 1815 and acts as a sort of point of demarcation between the Old and New Yards. In front of the hall is the well-known statue of John Harvard by Daniel Chester French. No portrait of the college's namesake existed upon which French could base his likeness, so he chose a student for his model—one of the statue's "three lies." The inscription refers to John Harvard as the founder, which he was not, and gives the incorrect date for the founding of the school. University Hall and **Holworthy Hall** broke with tradition in that they were built of granite. **Stoughton Hall,** virtually identical to Hollis, was erected in 1804 to designs by Bulfinch.

Dunster House, Harvard University.

Holden Chapel was built in 1742 with funds from the Holden family, whose elaborately decorated crest appears in the pediments of the building. It has served a variety of nonreligious purposes, and is now occupied by offices.

Even though the school's original library burned in 1764 and only one volume of John Harvard's bequest survived, Harvard now possesses the third largest collection of books and other printed matter in the country, after the Library of Congress and the New York Public Library. The university's main library is **Widener Library,** a broad, colonnaded building at the south side of the New Yard. The library was completed in 1915 with funds donated by the family of Harry Widener, class of 1907, who died in the *Titanic* disaster. Three dioramas show Harvard Square in 1667, 1775, and 1936. Two treasures which are frequently on display are a copy of the Gutenberg Bible and a First Folio of Shakespeare, published in 1623. Adjacent to Widener is **Houghton Library,** the repository of the university's rare books and where representative items from the collection are exhibited.

Sever Hall, an 1880 building on the east side of the Yard, is one of the finest examples of Henry Hobson Richardson's version of Romanesque architecture. Richardson designed a second building for Harvard, **Austin Hall,** which is located in the Law School north of the Yard. Another architectural landmark just north of the Yard is **Memorial Hall,** a tribute to the Harvard men who died in the Civil War. Completed in 1878, the vast, cathedral-like building in the Anglo-Ruskinian Gothic style, with its steep, multi-colored roof, provokes varied opinions. Some call it a great beauty of the Victorian age, while others agree with the architectural historian, G. E. Kidder Smith, who called it a "piquant pile. . . . Though not lovely [it] is loved, a mammoth ugly duckling, an almost fanatic statement of the taste of its time."

Harvard's Museums

Harvard University administers a total of twelve museums; eight on the Cambridge campus, the others in Boston, Washington, DC, and Florence, Italy.

The Harvard University Art Museums (617–495–9400) include three museums, all in Cambridge, with separate buildings and collections under one administration. Together they house one of the finest university art collections in the world.

The **Fogg Art Museum** (32 Quincy Street) houses collections of European and American paintings, drawings, prints, and sculpture from the middle ages to the present day. Particularly excellent collections are the drawings and watercolors, French nineteenth-century painting, late medieval painting and sculpture, the work of Ingres, British pre-Raphaelite painting, and eighteenth- and nineteenth-century American painting.

The **Arthur M. Sackler Museum** (485 Broadway) displays ancient, Near Eastern, and Oriental art. It contains the world's finest collection of ancient Chinese jades and ceramics, as well as outstanding collections of Persian and Indian miniature paintings, Japanese prints, and important Greek vases, sculpture, and coins.

The **Busch-Reisinger Museum** (Kirkland Street), devoted to paintings, drawings, prints, and sculpture from northern and central Europe, is the only museum of its kind in the Western Hemisphere. Its most important collection is of works from the Expressionist period of the early twentieth century, the best in America, including masterpieces by Beckmann, Nolde, Kandinsky, and Klee.

The **Peabody Museum of Archaeology and Ethnology** (617–495–2248), founded in 1866, has extensive collections of prehistoric, ancient, and pre-Columbian artifacts. A new (1989) **Hall of the North American Indian** displays a portion of their comprehensive holdings. Other Harvard museums in Cambridge include the **Botanical Museum** (with the world-famous Glass Flowers), the **Museum of Comparative Zoology,** the **Mineralogical Museum,** and the **Semitic Museum.**

CHRIST CHURCH AND OLD BURYING GROUND

The oldest church in Cambridge, Christ Church was built in 1761 because the Anglican community of Cambridge found it inconvenient to travel to King's Chapel in Boston for services. The architect who had designed King's Chapel, Peter Harrison of Newport, provided the plans. During the Revolution, Christ Church suffered greatly when it served as a barracks for American troops, and it was vandalized by a mob after a funeral service for a British officer, one of the prisoners taken at the Battle of Saratoga; the officer is buried below the church. In the vestibule is a bullet hole, presumably from a shot fired as the British marched by on their way to Lexington. Adjacent to the church is the Old Burying Ground, with the graves of many Harvard and Cambridge notables.

LOCATION: Zero Garden Street. HOURS: 9–5 Daily. FEE: None. TELEPHONE: 617–876–0200.

RADCLIFFE COLLEGE

Radcliffe was founded in 1879 to permit Harvard professors to teach women, who were not allowed admission to Harvard as students. The college was named in honor of a seventeenth-century British benefactor of Harvard, Lady Anne Radcliffe Mowlson, who gave £100 to establish the college's first scholarship. Alice Longfellow, daughter of the poet, was one of the prime movers behind the foundation of Radcliffe.

Gilman Gate (8 Garden Street) is the entry to Radcliffe Yard. The oldest building in the Yard is the 1807 **Fay House,** the administrative center, and the building in which Radcliffe's first classes were held. The **Schlesinger Library** specializes in the history of American women. Its archives hold papers of Julia Ward Howe,

Susan B. Anthony, Harriet Beecher Stowe, Elizabeth Cady Stan-
ton, Amelia Earhart, and others prominent in American history.

The college president's residence is **Greenleaf House,** a mansion built in 1859 by James Greenleaf, the son of a Harvard Law
School professor who made his fortune in cotton before the Civil
War. He was the cousin of the poet John Greenleaf Whittier, and
he married Longfellow's sister, Mary. East of Greenleaf House, in
the courtyard of the Cronkhite Graduate Center, is a monument
honoring Helen Keller, Radcliffe class of 1904, and Anne Sullivan,
who taught Keller from the age of six.

HENRY WADSWORTH LONGFELLOW HOUSE

This elegant pre-Revolutionary mansion on Brattle Street was built
in 1759 and abandoned by its Tory owner in 1774, when Patriot
mobs made life dangerous for Loyalists in Boston and Cambridge.
In 1775 and 1776 the house was George Washington's residence.

From 1837 until his death in 1882, this was the home of
America's most famous nineteenth-century poet. When he was a
professor of modern languages at Harvard, Longfellow rented
rooms here. In 1843 he married Fanny Appleton, daughter of the
wealthy Nathan Appleton of Beacon Hill, who bought the house
and the land across the street as a wedding gift for the couple.
Longfellow wrote many of his best-known works here, including
Evangeline (1847), *The Song of Hiawatha* (1855), and *The Courtship of
Miles Standish* (1858). The publication of *Hiawatha* brought fame
and financial success, enabling him to command fees of thousands
of dollars for the publication of his poems. His house was elegantly
furnished, and it was among the first in the country to be equipped
with indoor plumbing. Fanny Longfellow died in the house in 1861
after a tragic accident: Her dress caught fire, burning her entire
body despite Longfellow's frantic efforts to snuff out the flames.
She died the day after the accident.

The house is furnished virtually as it was in Longfellow's time,
with a host of historical and literary mementoes. In the dining
room hangs a painting by Albert Bierstadt, the famed landscape
painter, that depicts a scene from Longfellow's enormously successful poem, *The Song of Hiawatha.* The parlor, with its mid-
Victorian-era furnishings, is an interesting example of the tastes of
the time. Longfellow's study on the first floor preserves his desk
and writing implements: He used quill pens and an inkstand given

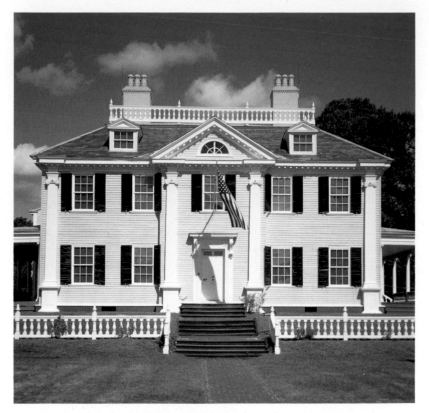

Henry Wadsworth Longfellow House, built in 1759.

to him by the British poet Samuel Taylor Coleridge. On the walls are portraits and photographs of some of his closest friends— Ralph Waldo Emerson, Nathaniel Hawthorne, Oliver Wendell Holmes, Louis Agassiz, and Senator Charles Sumner—as well as photographs of Longfellow himself. Also in the study is a chair presented to Longfellow by the schoolchildren of Cambridge, made from the "spreading chestnut tree" described in his poem, *The Village Blacksmith.* (The blacksmith made famous in that poem was Dexter Pratt, who lived at 56 Brattle Street.) The house remained in the Longfellow family until 1973, and is now under the jurisdiction of the National Park Service.

LOCATION: 105 Brattle Street. HOURS: 10–4:30 Daily. FEE: Yes. TELEPHONE: 617–876–4471.

BOSTON   ENVIRONS

BROOKLINE

Since the mid-nineteenth century, Brookline has been one of the wealthiest suburban enclaves in the Boston area. The noted landscape architect Frederick Law Olmsted made his home in Brookline from 1883 until his death in 1903. His farmhouse and design office are being restored as the **Frederick Law Olmsted National Historic Site** (99 Warren Street, 617–566–1689). On display are drawings, photographs, and models of Olmsted projects from across the nation. Guided tours also include the "Fairsted" grounds which Olmsted landscaped as a model for suburban residential design. Brookline was the birthplace, in 1917, of President John F. Kennedy. The house where his parents, Joseph P. and Rose Kennedy, lived from 1914 to 1921 is now the **John F. Kennedy National Historic Site** (83 Beals Street, 617–566–7937). Tours include

Gore Place, built in 1807.

rooms that have been restored with family mementoes and period pieces. There is also a taped narrative prepared by Rose Kennedy.

WALTHAM

Waltham was a quiet farming town until 1812, when Francis Cabot Lowell's Boston Manufacturing Company built cotton mills here along the Charles River. In the late nineteenth century the name of Waltham was known throughout the country as the source of watches. The American Waltham Watch Company, founded in 1854, produced millions of watches in its century of operation. The **Charles River Museum of Industry** (154 Moody Street, 617–893–5410), housed in a 1911 mill building, chronicles the various industries of eastern Massachusetts. The museum displays antique machinery used to make watches, textiles, computers, and other items including antique cars manufactured in Massachusetts.

Gore Place

One of the most sumptuous nineteenth-century residences in New England, Gore Place is a twenty-two-room country mansion built in 1806 for Christopher and Rebecca Gore. Rebecca Gore designed the house with the aid of a French architect, Jacques Guillaume Legrand, when the Gores were living in Europe. It is one of the earliest American houses which can be proved to have been designed largely by a woman. Rebecca Gore inherited a substantial insurance fortune, which her husband enlarged through a legal practice and currency trading. Christopher Gore served as Massachusetts governor and U.S. senator.

The facade of the two-and-a-half-story brick house is over two hundred feet wide with a bowed center. In the center of the house is an oval salon, one and a half stories high, with an oval family parlor above it. The house offered comforts very advanced for the time: hot and cold running water, flush toilets (among the first in the country), and a system for circulating air. The first floor was designed for public entertaining—the Gores once had 450 guests for breakfast; the second floor held the family's living quarters.

The house preserves more than one hundred items that belonged to the Gores, including furniture, textiles, silver, and paintings by John Trumbull, Gilbert Stuart, and John Singleton Copley.

It is believed that some of the family portraits painted by a youthful Copley were done for Gore's father, a dealer in colors, in exchange for paint. The estate has forty acres of woodlands, fields, and gardens. A 1793 carriage house on the grounds has been attributed to Samuel McIntire, who was designing the nearby Lyman Estate.

LOCATION: 52 Gore Street. HOURS: Mid-April through mid-November: 10–5 Tuesday–Saturday, 2–5 Sunday. FEE: Yes. TELEPHONE: 617–894–2798.

Lyman Estate

The Boston merchant Theodore Lyman hired Salem's architect Samuel McIntire to design this house in the early 1790s. It was substantially enlarged and altered in the late nineteenth century— only the ballroom and the oval parlor remain as McIntire designed them. The house, owned by the Society for the Preservation of New England Antiquities, is open only to groups by advance appointment. The grounds, open on a regular basis, are of note by themselves. The Lyman family was interested in horticulture and landscape design in the English style. An early nineteenth-century greenhouse, one of the oldest in the country, holds grape vines from England's Hampton Court, and a century-old camellia tree.

LOCATION: 185 Lyman Street. HOURS: House: by appointment. Grounds: 10–4 Thursday–Sunday. FEE: Yes. TELEPHONE: 617–227–3956.

DEDHAM

Dedham, located on the Charles River, was settled 1635. The first residents envisioned "a loving and comfortable society," which they wished to name Contentment. One of these settlers built the **Jonathan Fairbanks House** (511 East Street, 617–326–1170) in 1636, framing it from the timbers of the ship *Griffin*, on which Fairbanks sailed from England. It contains only those household goods, tools, and furniture the family brought with them or made and used here, and is the oldest surviving frame house north of Florida.

OPPOSITE: Bedroom at the Jonathan Fairbanks House, built in 1636 by one of the first settlers of Dedham.

ARLINGTON

On April 18 and 19, 1775, Arlington, then known as Menotomy, was on the British route to and from Concord. On the night of the 18th, Paul Revere and William Dawes galloped through Menotomy on their midnight ride. The bloodiest combat along the retreat took place here. In a celebrated episode, the "old men of Menotomy" ambushed eighteen British soldiers bringing supplies to the battered column. Samuel Whittmore, aged eighty, picked off three Redcoats before he was bayoneted. He recovered from his wounds and lived another eighteen years. The elderly Patriots gathered up the supplies, and six fleeing British soldiers were captured by an old woman, Mother Batherick, at **Spy Pond.** A plaque at Medford Street and Massachusetts Avenue marks the site of **Cooper Tavern,** where two men were killed by British soldiers firing wildly through the tavern's windows.

Massachusetts Avenue and Linwood Street was the site of **Black Horse Tavern** where, on April 18, the British raided a meeting of the Committee of Safety and Supplies. One of the committee members who fled the tavern and hid in a field was Jeremiah Lee of Marblehead. He died of the effects of exposure. The sharpest fighting took place at the Jason Russell House.

Jason Russell House & Smith Museum

As the British approached Arlington, Jason Russell piled up a barricade in front of his house with the plan of sniping at the British column. Nineteen militiamen, closely pursued by a British patrol, took cover in Russell's house. The British shot Russell dead at his front door and stormed the house, killing eleven other members of the militia. Built in 1680, the house is owned by the Arlington Historical Society, which has restored and furnished it with eighteenth-century items. The Society has its headquarters at the Smith Museum next door, which displays historical exhibits.

LOCATION: 7 Jason Street. HOURS: mid-April through October: 2–5 Tuesday–Saturday. FEE: Yes. TELEPHONE: 617–648–4300.

MEDFORD

Situated on the Mystic River, Medford was a center of trade in the eighteenth century and an important shipbuilding center in the early nineteenth century.

The **Old Ship Street Historic District,** located along Pleasant Street from Riverside Avenue to Park Street, includes more than thirty houses from the first half of the nineteenth century. The **Hillside Avenue Historic District,** along Hillside and Grand View avenues, reflects Medford's late-nineteenth-century prosperity with a score of substantial homes. The 1872 Gothic Revival **Grace Episcopal Church,** at 160 High Street, was one of the first churches designed by the architect Henry Hobson Richardson.

Isaac Royall House

This imposing fourteen-room mansion was built in 1732 by Isaac Royall, Sr., a wealthy trader in slaves and rum who owned a large sugar plantation in Antigua. He died shortly after the house was completed, and it passed to his son, Isaac, Jr. The house was built around a small 1637 farmhouse, the silhouette of which can be seen in the southern wall. The walls of the farmhouse form the walls of the mansion's dining room. On the grounds are the only surviving slave quarters in the state. Royall, Sr., brought twenty-seven slaves when he moved here from Antigua. The house's two parlors feature elaborately carved woodwork with rosettes, acanthus leaves, and columns. The rooms have been restored with antiques of the period. Architecturally, the house remains unchanged since the 1730s.

Isaac, Jr., a Tory, fled to England at the outbreak of the Revolution and never returned. In the spring and summer of 1775 the house was the headquarters of Colonel John Stark, whose New Hampshire regiment camped on the lawn. Some of the planning for the Battle of Bunker Hill, in which Stark and his men played a critical role, may have taken place here.

LOCATION: 15 George Street. HOURS: May through September: 2–5 Tuesday–Thursday and Saturday–Sunday. FEE: Yes. TELEPHONE: 617–396–9032.

CHAPTER TWO

LEXINGTON
AND
CONCORD

OPPOSITE: North Bridge in Concord, site of "the shot heard round the world."

L exington and Concord, suburbs just west of Boston, were the first battlefields of the Revolutionary War. On the night of April 18, 1775, a column of seven hundred British regulars set out from Boston to seize military supplies gathered at Concord by the Patriots—powder, musketballs, flints, cannon, flour, salt beef, dried fish, and other foodstuffs. The British believed the raid had been kept secret, but American spies knew of the intended sortie and, when the British left Boston Common, Paul Revere and William Dawes galloped off to spread the alarm through the countryside.

Well-trained Minute Men and militia, who had been preparing for just such a raid, sprang into action: The British were met at Lexington Green by about seventy-seven Minute Men, and by hundreds more at Concord. After the battle at Concord, one thousand reinforcements joined the British column, but they had to retreat back to Boston through a gauntlet of 3,500 colonials. The day-long fight along Battle Road claimed more casualties than the two fights at Lexington and Concord. The total casualties for the day were 247 killed or wounded on the British side, 89 on the American. Each year, on the third Monday in April (Patriots' Day in Massachusetts), the Battle of Lexington is re-created by uniformed Minute Men and Redcoats.

This chapter is presented in five main sections: Paul Revere's Route; Lexington; Battle Road; Revolutionary Concord; and Literary Concord. The major battle sites are presented in geographical order, proceeding from Lexington to Concord. All of the major battle sites in Concord and along Battle Road are within the boundaries of Minute Man National Historical Park. The Park Service maintains a visitor center in Concord by the North Bridge, and a Battle Road Visitor Center on route 2-A, just west of Lexington. The centers have excellent exhibits and programs. At the end of the chapter are entries for other sites in the area. Although it is not included in the National Park, Arlington has several important sites associated with the retreat.

PAUL REVERE'S ROUTE

Paul Revere's ride took him along present-day Broadway and Massachusetts Avenue through Cambridge, Somerville, Arlington, and Lexington. The British took the same road several hours after

OPPOSITE: Detail from Ralph Earl painting of British troops searching Concord for hidden supplies, as Colonel Smith and Major Pitcairn scan the hills for Minute Men.

Revere's passage. The route has not been maintained as a historic site, and today it runs through heavily traveled commercial districts. Nevertheless, Revere's midnight ride is re-created every year on Patriots' Day.

Paul Revere was not the only one to carry the alarm that night. William Dawes set out from Boston along a different route. Dr. Samuel Prescott was heading home after a tryst with his fiancée when he ran into Revere and Dawes just outside of Lexington and he alerted Concord after Revere was detained by a British patrol.

From town to town, the alarm was spread by booming signal cannons and frantically pealing church bells, prearranged signals for which the militia had been waiting. Men all over eastern New England left their beds, took up their muskets, and marched toward Lexington. Many did not arrive at Lexington or Concord in time to fight in those battles, but they were on hand for the running battle that took place along the British march of retreat.

LEXINGTON

The Battle of Lexington took place on the town Green, a triangle of grass surrounded by houses that still stand from the time when the battle was fought. At its eastern point is the well-known statue of *The Minute Man* holding his musket, which was sculpted by Henry Hudson Kitson and dedicated in 1900. The figure stands upon boulders taken from stone walls from behind which the militia shot at the British. The **Visitor Center,** facing the Green, contains an excellent diorama of the battle.

Buckman Tavern (617–861–0928) also faces the Green. Here the Minute Men, who had first mustered about midnight in response to Paul Revere's alarm, waited through the night for the Regulars to arrive. A bullet hole can be seen in a door preserved inside the tavern, and displays of eighteenth-century muskets, cooking equipment, and furniture are inside.

When a scout rushed into the tavern to report that the British were within a half mile of the Green, Captain John Parker ordered William Diamond to beat a drum, and about seventy-seven men (the exact number is not known) formed a line on the Green. The spot where they stood is marked by a boulder, inscribed with the command Parker may have called out to his men: "Stand your ground. Don't fire unless fired upon, but if they mean to have a war, let it begin here." The quotation is based upon the recollections of a veteran, recorded in 1826.

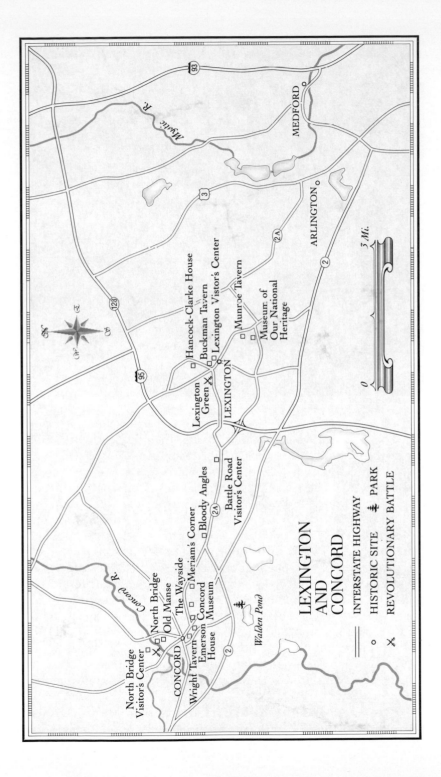

LEXINGTON
AND
CONCORD

— INTERSTATE HIGHWAY
o HISTORIC SITE   ⚔ PARK
✕ REVOLUTIONARY BATTLE

MEDFORD

ARLINGTON

Mystic R.

Munroe Tavern
Museum of
Our National
Heritage

Lexington Vistor's Center
Buckman Tavern
Hancock–Clarke House
Lexington
Green ✕
LEXINGTON

Battle Road
Visitor's Center
Bloody Angles
Meriam's Corner
The Wayside
Old Manse
North Bridge ✕
North Bridge
Visitor's Center
CONCORD
Wright Tavern
Emerson
House
Concord
Museum

Concord R.

Walden Pond

3 Mi.

0

Buckman Tavern, where Parker's Minute Men awaited the arrival of the British.

The British formed a line of battle, their backs to Buckman Tavern, facing the Americans. Major Pitcairn, on horseback, rode forward and shouted, "Lay down your arms, you damned rebels, and disperse!" There are conflicting accounts of what happened next. The Minute Men may have been dispersing when someone (British or American, his identity is not known) fired a shot. The British soldiers, exhausted and angry after a sleepless night of marching, defied their orders and fired volley after volley. They then leveled their bayonets and charged. Eight Americans were killed and ten wounded. Jonathan Harrington, Jr., struck in the chest by a musketball, managed to drag himself to the steps of his house on the Green, where he died with his arms outstretched to his wife. She had watched the shooting from a second-floor window with their young son, and raced down the stairs to reach her husband as he died. The **Harrington House** remains, but it is private. The British did not suffer any casualties, and continued on their way to Concord.

Across the Green is the **Marret and Nathan Munroe House** (private), built in 1729. Nathan Munroe was one of the Minute

Men on the Green, and he took a potshot at the British from behind a stone wall after the shooting had started.

At the western end of the Green is an **obelisk** commemorating the battle. Erected in 1799, it was the nation's first Revolutionary War monument. A plaque on the base bears an inscription that begins with the stirring declaration: "Sacred to Liberty & the Rights of Mankind!!! / The Freedom & Independence of America. / Sealed & defended with the blood of her sons." In 1835 the remains of the Minute Men who died on the Green were unearthed from the Old Burying Ground and buried at the monument. The **Old Burying Ground,** just west of the Green, contains the graves of Captain Parker and a British soldier who was wounded during the retreat from Concord and died at Buckman Tavern.

Overlooking the Green from a hill is a replica of the **Old Belfry,** with the bell that pealed the midnight alarm. The original belfry collapsed in a storm in 1909.

Buckman Tavern's tap room, with muskets displayed on a wall.

Hancock-Clarke House

About a quarter of a mile north of the Green on Hancock Street is the Hancock-Clarke House, where John Hancock and Samuel Adams were staying on the night the British marched to Lexington. They were there to attend meetings of the provincial congress at Concord. Sergeant William Munroe of the Minute Men (the owner of Munroe Tavern) was standing guard at the house when Revere galloped up and shouted for Hancock to come out. Munroe told him to stop making noise. "Noise?" yelled Revere, "You'll have noise enough before long. The Regulars are out!" Hancock wanted to take up a musket and join the Minute Men, but Adams persuaded him that his services were more urgently required in the congress.

The Hancock-Clarke House is maintained as a museum by the Lexington Historical Society. The house exhibits items relating to the battles, including the drum on which William Diamond beat the signal summoning the Lexington Minute Men for the encounter with the British, and the pistols carried that day by Major Pitcairn, who lost them on the retreat from Concord.

LOCATION: 36 Hancock Street. HOURS: Mid-April through October: 10–5 Monday–Saturday, 1–5 Sunday. FEE: Yes. TELEPHONE: 617–862–5598.

Amos Doolittle's engraving, based on eyewitness accounts, of the shooting on Lexington Green. OPPOSITE: *First Parish Church, facing the Green.*

Doolittle's view of the retreat along Battle Road. The militia, behind stone walls, are seen firing

Munroe Tavern

In the chaotic retreat from Concord, Lord Percy, the commander of a one-thousand-man relief column sent out from Boston, briefly set up a field headquarters here, and it was here that his wounded were brought for tending. After pouring drinks for British officers, the bartender bolted out a door and was shot in the back. A bullet hole can be seen in the tavern ceiling. The tavern has been maintained as it was in the 1770s and 1780s and there are mementoes of a 1789 visit by George Washington.

LOCATION: 1332 Massachusetts Avenue. HOURS: Mid-April through October: 10–5 Monday–Saturday, 1–5 Sunday. FEE: Yes. TELEPHONE: 617–862–1703.

on the British, who have brought up cannon and set fire to houses.

A half mile east of the Munroe Tavern is the **Museum of Our National Heritage** (Route 2-A off Massachusetts Avenue, 617–861–6559), founded by the Scottish Rite masons. The museum features changing exhibits on American history.

BATTLE ROAD

Route 2-A between Concord and Lexington follows the general line of the eighteenth-century road, but the modern roadway is a good deal straighter than the original. A five-mile stretch of Battle Road, from Route 128 to Old Bedford Road, is within Minute Man National Historical Park.

Battle Road Visitor Center

This unit of the Minute Man National Historical Park shows a twenty-two-minute film depicting the events leading up to battles, and an animated map illustrates British and American movements. Adjacent to the parking lot is a section of Battle Road that has been restored to its eighteenth-century appearance. A trail forms a half-mile loop around **Fiske Hill,** where the British officers attempted to regroup their panic-stricken troops but did not succeed. The trail leads to the site of the **Ebenezer Fiske farmhouse,** of which a portion of the foundation has been unearthed. Here a Minute Man, pausing for a drink from a well, was met by a British soldier who called out, "You are a dead man!" "And so are you!" the American responded, as they both leveled their muskets and fired. Both men were killed.

LOCATION: Route 2-A, Lexington. HOURS: Mid-April through November: 8:30–5 Daily. FEE: None. TELEPHONE: 617–862–7753.

A boulder on Route 2-A marks the place where Paul Revere was detained by a British patrol after he had alerted Lexington and was

Meriam's Corner, where the fighting along Battle Road began.

on his way to Concord. At about 1 AM, Revere, William Dawes, and Samuel Prescott were stopped by two officers. Dawes and Prescott escaped, but when Revere spurred his horse toward the woods, six other officers stopped him. Interrogated with a pistol at his head, Revere boldly informed his captors that the entire countryside was in arms against them. The officers released Revere an hour and a half later. He returned to the Hancock-Clarke House to hurry Adams and Hancock out of Lexington. A few moments after he had carried a trunk of papers across Lexington Green, passing through the ranks of Minute Men, he heard "a continuous roar of musketry," the sound of the British attack.

Meriam's Corner, about a half mile east of Concord, was the starting point of the battle along the British retreat. The rear guard of the retreating British column turned and fired a volley without provocation. Militiamen, who had been watching the retreat from the cover of stone walls, houses, and trees, returned the fire. Farther east, at **Bloody Angle,** the British had to slow their march where the road takes a sharp turn. The Americans took full advantage of the delay and poured musketfire into the column with deadly effect: Eight British soldiers fell here.

C   O   N   C   O   R   D

Concord is doubly famed: as the site of the second engagement of the Revolution, and as the home of the great literary flowering in the first half of the nineteenth century. Three giants of American literature—Ralph Waldo Emerson, Nathaniel Hawthorne, and Henry David Thoreau—lived and wrote in Concord. Walden Pond is as widely known as the old North Bridge. Louisa May Alcott lived and wrote here as well. The historic sites in this section will be treated in two parts: Revolutionary Concord, and literary Concord.

REVOLUTIONARY CONCORD

Elated by their easy victory at Lexington, the British entered Concord at about 7 AM on April 19th. The officers set up a field headquarters at **Wright's Tavern** (Lexington Road), which now houses shops and, in the basement, an information center (508–369–6219) for the city's sites.

Hill Burying Ground, on a gently rolling slope across from Wright's Tavern, contains the town's oldest burials. Upon their

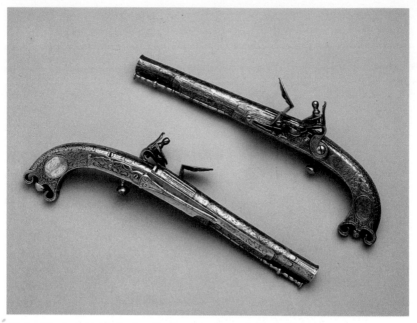

Major Pitcairn's pistols, in the collection of the Hancock-Clarke House.

arrival in Concord, Major Pitcairn and Colonel Smith walked up
the hill among the gravestones to survey the surrounding countryside, only to witness swarms of militiamen converging on Buttrick's
farm on the other side of the North Bridge. At the center of
Concord is **Monument Square,** where a British sergeant, burning a
pile of captured supplies, inadvertently set fire to a building. Pitcairn led a fire brigade to douse the flames, but the Americans
massing on the other side of the Concord River saw the smoke and
assumed that the British were burning the town. As a council of
militia officers debated what to do next, Joseph Hosmer of Concord demanded: "Will you let them burn the town down?" The
officers decided to march into Concord to defend it, "or die in the
attempt." The colonials then advanced upon a British detachment
guarding the North Bridge.

From Monument Square, Monument Street leads to the Old
Manse and the North Bridge.

North Bridge

Immortalized by Ralph Waldo Emerson as "the rude bridge that
arched the flood," the North Bridge was the site of "the shot heard

e*l Hadley, Jonathan Harrington J
uxxy, Caleb Harrington and John Bro
xington, & Asahel Porter of Woburn.
lI on this field, the first Victims to t
d of British Tyranny & Oppressio
e morning of the ever memorab
eteenth of April, An. Dom. 1775.
The Die was cast!!!
The Blood of these Martyr's,
e cause of God & their Country
ement of the Union of these States,
& gave the spring to the spirit, Firm
esolution of their Fellow Citizer
e as one man, to revenge their bretl
d at the point of the sword, to ass

Inscription on Lexington Green's Revolutionary War monument, erected in 1799.

round the world." Here British troops fired upon advancing militiamen, killing two. Major John Buttrick called out, "Fire, fellow soldiers, for God's sake, fire!" The resulting fusillade—considered to be the first American shots of the Revolution—killed two British soldiers outright and wounded nine others, including four officers. The British fell back to the center of town, but the Americans did not pursue. Two hours later the British column began to retrace its route to Lexington and Boston. They had failed to locate and destroy the bulk of colonial supplies, and had succeeded in providing the spark that ignited the New England countryside.

The original North Bridge was torn down in 1793, but a commemorative bridge was constructed on the site in 1875 and the present bridge was built in 1956. A few steps from the bridge is the gravesite of the two British soldiers who fell here. The western end of the bridge is the location of the famous statue of a Minute Man by Daniel Chester French (his first important commission). At the eastern side is a granite memorial obelisk erected in 1836.

The North Bridge is part of the **Minute Man National Historical Park.** The park maintains a **Visitor Center** (508–369–6944) on Liberty Street, near the **Major John Buttrick House** (private).

Buttrick is honored by a statue near the Visitor Center. Liberty Street also runs by Punkatasset Hill, the high point where the militia gathered as the British entered the town.

Near the bridge are the Old Manse, from which Emerson's grandfather watched the battle, and the **Bullet Hole House** (private) where, it is said, a British soldier fired at Elisha Jones as he looked out a window. A "bullet hole" has been preserved, but it is questionable whether the story has any truth to it.

LITERARY CONCORD

The Old Manse

Built about 1770 by the Reverend William Emerson, who died of camp fever while serving as a chaplain in the Continental Army, the Old Manse is rich in literary associations. Emerson's grandson, the writer Ralph Waldo Emerson, lived in the house in 1834 and 1835. He wrote his first book, *Nature,* in a second-floor study.

Nathaniel Hawthorne and his wife, Sophia, who was a painter, rented the house for two years. The first night they spent there was their wedding night, July 9, 1842. In Emerson's old study, Hawthorne wrote *Mosses from an Old Manse,* a collection of stories that secured the house a place in literary history. Scratched on the window of the study is a message by Hawthorne and Sophia— "Man's accidents are God's purposes"—and, on the window of the dining room, where she painted, Sophia recorded, "Endymion painted in this room—finished January 20, 1844." On March 3, 1844, the Hawthornes' first child, Una, was born in the upstairs bedroom. They left the house in 1846 and returned to Salem, where Hawthorne took a job at the Custom House. The Old Manse has been restored with Emerson and Hawthorne memorabilia.

LOCATION: Monument Street. HOURS: Mid-April through October: 10–4:30 Thursday–Saturday and Monday, 1–4:30 Sunday. FEE: Yes. TELEPHONE: 508–358–7615.

Orchard House

The Alcott family lived here from 1858 to 1877. Louisa May Alcott wrote her first novel, *Moods,* at Orchard House in 1860 and 1861. In 1862 she went to Washington to serve as a nurse, and almost immediately contracted typhoid. She returned to Orchard House,

OPPOSITE: *Entrance of the Old Manse, with bull's-eye panes above the door.*

gravely ill, just several weeks after she had left. Medication left Alcott with mercury poisoning, which afflicted her for the rest of her life. Despite being in pain, she was able to edit a series of her letters into a book, *Hospital Sketches*. A few years later she wrote *Little Women* and *Little Men,* both of which enjoyed great success and solved the family's financial problems. The Alcotts left the house in 1877 and later moved to Louisburg Square in Boston. The house displays many Alcott family items and manuscripts.

LOCATION: 399 Lexington Road. HOURS: April through mid-September: 10–4:30 Monday–Saturday, 1–4:30 Sundays; mid-September through October: 1–4:30 Daily. FEE: Yes. TELEPHONE: 508–369–4118.

The Wayside

The Wayside is associated both with the Alcotts and with Hawthorne. The Alcotts lived here from 1845 to 1848. Louisa May Alcott based her novel *Little Women* on some of her girlhood experiences in this house. Hawthorne bought the house in 1852, just after his book, *The Blithedale Romance,* had been published. While living here he wrote a campaign biography of Franklin Pierce, a friend from Bowdoin College. After Pierce was elected president, he appointed Hawthorne U.S. Consul at Liverpool, England. Hawthorne and his family spent the next seven years in Europe (where he wrote his last complete novel, *The Marble Faun*), returning to the Wayside in 1860. The following years at the Wayside were not productive ones: Hawthorne started and put aside several novels, and turned to travel writing to earn money. The tower Hawthorne added to the house as a study proved too uncomfortable for working, and he said he would be happy if the house just burned down.

LOCATION: 455 Lexington Road. HOURS: Mid-April through October: 9:30–5:30 Friday–Tuesday. FEE: Yes. TELEPHONE: 508–369–6975.

Emerson House

When he was not traveling across the country giving the lectures that brought him his income, Ralph Waldo Emerson lived here from 1835 until his death in 1882. Thoreau, Hawthorne, and the Alcotts often visited, and Thoreau performed odd jobs at the house. It is said that he made the dollhouse in the nursery for one of Emerson's daughters. All of the furnishings in the house are original except those in the library, which are replicas.

LOCATION: 28 Cambridge Turnpike. HOURS: Mid–April to mid–October: 10–5 Thursday–Saturday, 2–5 Sunday, 1–5 holidays. FEE: Yes. TELEPHONE: 508–369–2236.

Concord Museum

This fine, small museum displays a wealth of Revolutionary artifacts, literary relics, furniture, and other items associated with the history of Concord. Emerson's library was removed from his house across the road and reconstructed here. The Thoreau Room preserves the simple, handmade furniture the writer fashioned for his retreat at Walden Pond. The museum owns the largest collection of Thoreau artifacts in the country. Fifteen period rooms and galleries display furniture and decorative items from Concord houses of the eighteenth and nineteenth centuries. The Revolutionary War collection includes one of the lamps hung from the Old North Church, and musket flints scattered on the first field of battle.

LOCATION: 200 Lexington Road. HOURS: 10–4 Monday–Saturday, 1–4 Sunday. FEE: Yes. TELEPHONE: 508–369–9609.

The **Thoreau Lyceum** (156 Belknap Street, 508–369–5912) headquarters of the Thoreau Society, maintains a research library and sponsors lectures about the writer. On the Lyceum's grounds is a replica of the cabin Thoreau built on Walden Pond.

Sleepy Hollow Cemetery (Bedford Street) is the final resting place of the Concord literati—Hawthorne, the Alcotts, Thoreau, Emerson—and the sculptor Daniel Chester French.

In the center of the town, on Sudbury Road, is the **Concord Free Public Library,** with a Concord Alcove displaying the works of the town's famed writers. A statue of Ralph Waldo Emerson by Daniel Chester French shows the author in his favorite dressing gown. There are portrait busts of Concord's other writers, and dioramas of Concord as it looked at the height of its literary flowering in the middle of the nineteenth century.

Walden Pond Reservation

A cairn of stones marks the site where, for two years and two months, from 1845 to 1847, Henry David Thoreau lived in a one-

OVERLEAF: *Walden Pond.*

room cabin he built on land owned by Emerson. His years in the woods at the edge of town were an experiment in self-sufficiency. He wished to separate himself—somewhat—from a society in which "the mass of men lead lives of quiet desperation," and to immerse himself in nature. He wrote that "I went to the woods because I wished to live deliberately, to front only the essential facts of life, and see if I could not learn what it had to teach, and not, when I came to die, discover that I had not lived." He recounted his experience in *Walden*, published in 1854.

While living at Walden Pond, Thoreau was jailed for one night for refusing to pay a poll tax that, he said, indirectly supported slavery. He explained his action and described his night in jail in the widely influential essay, "Civil Disobedience." One person profoundly influenced by the essay was Gandhi. Ironically, after observing ice harvesters cutting ice from his pond for shipment to India, Thoreau wrote, "The pure Walden water is mingled with the sacred water of the Ganges."

Today, Walden Pond is a busy state park that preserves little of the solitude that Thoreau found. A trail leads to the site of the cabin, and park staff provide year-round programs about Thoreau's life and his stay at Walden.

LOCATION: Walden Street (Route 126). HOURS: 5 AM–Dusk. FEE: Yes. TELEPHONE: 508–369–3254.

SUDBURY

One of the prettiest of the state's eighteenth-century towns, Sudbury was a Patriot stronghold during the Revolution. With a population of only 2,100, Sudbury sent 500 men to the fighting. The **Sudbury Center Historic District** includes the graceful **First Parish Church** (1797), the Greek Revival **Grange Hall** (1846), and **Loring Parsonage** (1723) with its small museum. The **Center Cemetery** holds more graves of Revolutionary War soldiers than any Revolutionary cemetery in the United States. Three sites and monuments mark the last battles of King Philip's War.

Longfellow's Wayside Inn

The Wayside, built about 1700, claims to be the oldest operating inn in the country. Sudbury's militia gathered here before march-

OPPOSITE: The Old Barr Room at the Wayside Inn, Sudbury.

Codman House. OPPOSITE: *Interior of the Codman House.*

ing to the Battle of Lexington. The inn was made famous by Henry Wadsworth Longfellow's cycle of poems entitled *Tales of a Wayside Inn.* Longfellow created characters who told verse tales by the inn's hearth, and the most celebrated of these narrative poems remains "Paul Revere's Ride." Henry Ford purchased the inn in 1923, restored it, and moved several other historic structures to the site, including a reconstructed eighteenth-century gristmill, a general store, and a red schoolhouse associated with the poem "Mary Had a Little Lamb."

LOCATION: Off Route 20. TELEPHONE: 508–443–8846.

CODMAN HOUSE

A showplace of eighteenth- and nineteenth-century architecture, furniture, and decorative arts, Codman House stands on sixteen acres of landscaped grounds in Lincoln. Originally built about

Shaker barn, Harvard.

1740, the house was acquired by the merchant John Codman in the 1790s and was enlarged by him into a grand country seat, a three-story mansion. Boston architect Charles Bulfinch may have helped with the design, although the evidence is not conclusive. The house was further enlarged by Codman's grandson in the 1860s, who added eighteenth-century style embellishments to the exterior and a back parlor with robust butternut paneling in emulation of the Elizabethan period. The southeast parlor retains its 1741 paneling.

> LOCATION: Codman Road (between Route 117 and Route 126), Lincoln. HOURS: June through mid-October: 12–5 Wednesday–Sunday. FEE: Yes. TELEPHONE: 617–259–8843.

FRUITLANDS MUSEUMS

In 1843 this farm, fifteen miles northwest of Concord, was the site of a short-lived experiment in communal living, carried out by the premier dreamer of nineteenth-century Massachusetts, Amos Bronson Alcott. Alcott and an English friend, Charles Lane, envi-

Cast-iron markers in the Shaker cemetery, Harvard.

sioned a pure and self-sufficient life of vegetarianism, celibacy, philosophizing, and freedom of expression. Alcott brought along his wife and four daughters, including the future author, Louisa May Alcott, who was then ten. Lane's son and a handful of other followers made up the rest of the commune. The men talked and went on lecture tours while the women did the farm work. After raising little food and less money, and with winter already upon them, the Fruitlands commune disbanded in January 1844, just seven months after they had started.

The Fruitlands farmhouse has been restored as a museum to the Alcotts and other members of the Concord circle of thinkers. There are three other museums on the grounds: an art gallery displaying nineteenth-century paintings; a Shaker museum; and a museum of Indian culture. A large network of nature trails winds through the old farmlands.

LOCATION: 102 Prospect Hill Road, Harvard. HOURS: 10–5 Tuesday–Sunday. FEE: Yes. TELEPHONE: 508–456–3924.

THE
SOUTH SHORE
AND
CAPE COD

OPPOSITE: Edgartown Harbor, Martha's Vineyard.

The coastal region of Massachusetts between Boston and Cape Cod, known as the South Shore, has been an important maritime area since the days of the Pilgrims. At Cohasset, to quote Samuel Eliot Morison, "the granite skeleton of Massachusetts protrudes for the last time." South of Cohasset the shore is sandy, in contrast to the rockbound North Shore, and is punctuated by the salt marshes so valuable to the region's farmers.

Within a decade of their settlement at Plymouth, the Pilgrims had managed to stabilize their precarious existence, and had gone on to establish satellite communities in Duxbury, Marshfield, Hingham, and north as far as Quincy. The harbors of the South Shore were the bases for fishing fleets that pursued the cod, and later mackerel, on a small scale. As early as the seventeenth century, however, shipbuilding had become a more remunerative industry. The early shipyards had a modern successor in the enormous yards at Quincy, where many of the navy's vessels were built during World War II. In the nineteenth and twentieth centuries Quincy and Brockton grew into important industrial centers, and the "Old Colony" at Plymouth also developed mills and factories. But generally the South Shore, in the assessment of Timothy Dwight, who toured it in the early nineteenth century, "wears remarkably the appearance of stillness and retirement; and the inhabitants seem to be separated, in a great measure, from all active intercourse with their country."

This chapter begins at Quincy and proceeds south along the shore to Plymouth, thence to the great old whaling port, New Bedford, and the industrial city of Fall River. It then surveys Cape Cod and the islands of Nantucket and Martha's Vineyard.

T H E   S O U T H   S H O R E

QUINCY

Quincy calls itself "the City of Presidents," being the birthplace of two—John Adams and his son John Quincy Adams. Quincy was originally named Wollaston, after Captain Thomas Wollaston, who arrived in 1624. A year later one of the original settlers, Thomas Morton, established an outpost of jollity called Merrymount. Morton and his followers outraged the Plymouth Pilgrims by trading

OPPOSITE: The King Caesar House, Duxbury.

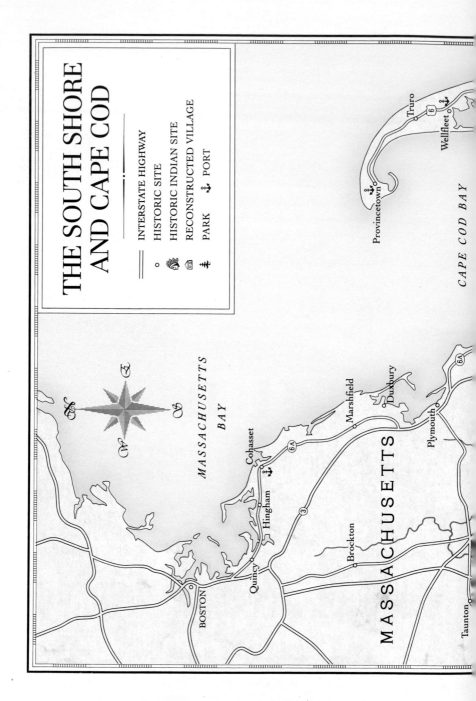

THE SOUTH SHORE
AND CAPE COD

━━━ INTERSTATE HIGHWAY
○   HISTORIC SITE
🌿   HISTORIC INDIAN SITE
🏛   RECONSTRUCTED VILLAGE
⚓   PARK   ⚓ PORT

N

W   E

S

MASSACHUSETTS
BAY

Cohasset
Hingham ⚓

Marshfield
Duxbury
Plymouth

Quincy

BOSTON

Brockton

MASSACHUSETTS

Taunton

6A
3

6A

Provincetown ⚓

Truro
6
Wellfleet ⚓

CAPE COD BAY

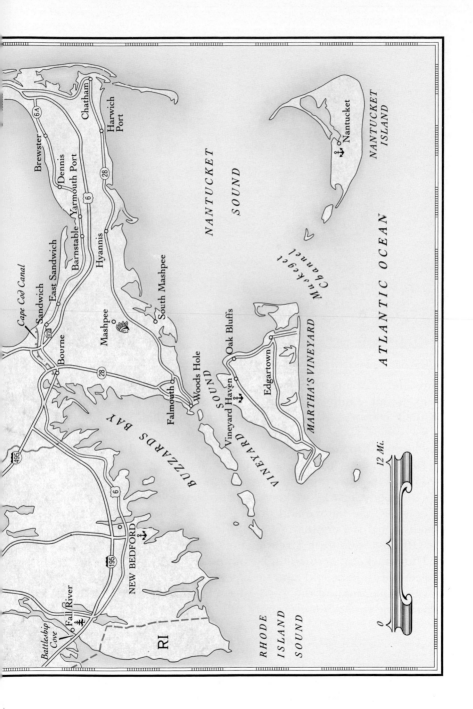

The eighteenth-century John Quincy Adams House. OPPOSITE: *The Stone Library.*

liquor and firearms to the Indians and by celebrating May Day in drunken and scandalous fashion: ". . . inviting the Indian women for their consorts, dancing and frisking together like so many fairies . . . and worse practices." To put an end to the carrying on, the Pilgrims dispatched Myles Standish, who arrested Morton and put him on a boat for England. Undaunted, Morton returned to Merrymount, only to be once again arrested and sent home, this time for good. Since all we know of Morton comes down to us from his enemies, the nature and degree of this "consorting" with the Indians remains a mystery.

Off East Squantum Street facing Quincy Bay is the **Moswetuset Hummock,** an arrow-shaped mound marked by a stone. The Moswetuset Indians sold land to the Pilgrims, and their tribal name provided the origin of the word Massachusetts. Quincy has several sites relating to the Adams family and to the Quincy family.

Adams National Historic Site

Over a 140-year period, this spacious clapboard house was home to four generations of the Adams family. Both of the Adams presidents, John and John Quincy, used the house while in office.

President Monroe dined here in 1817, and Lafayette visited in 1824. When John and Abigail Adams acquired the house in 1787 it had only seven rooms, which the family eventually increased to twenty. The house contains a rich trove of furniture, paintings, and decorative objects collected by the family. The magnificent Stone Library in the garden, built in 1870, houses presidential books and manuscripts.

LOCATION: 135 Adams Street. HOURS: April 19 through November 10: 9–5 Daily. FEE: Yes. TELEPHONE: 617–773–1177.

East of the Adams National Historic Site is the **Dorothy Quincy Homestead** (1010 Hancock Street, at Butler Road, 617–472–5117). Four generations of the family lived in the house, the oldest portion of which was built in 1686. Dorothy Quincy married the eminent Patriot, John Hancock, who was also born in Quincy; one of his coaches is displayed on the grounds.

Hancock's birthplace no longer exists, but on its site is the **Adams Academy** (intersection of Adams and Hancock streets, 617–773–1144), founded by John Adams. The imposing granite-and-brick Gothic Revival building, erected in 1872, is now the home of the **Quincy Historical Society.** Here, exhibits document the city's industrial history; also included is a portion of the tree around which Morton and his followers reputedly frolicked.

At the center of the city is the **United First Parish Church** (1306 Hancock Street). This beautiful church of local granite, with a four-columned, broadly pedimented portico, was designed by Alexander Parris and built in 1828. John Adams, John Quincy Adams, and their wives are buried here in a crypt. Another architectural landmark is across the street: the 1844 **City Hall,** designed in the Greek Revival style by Solomon Willard. Adjacent to City Hall is the **Hancock Cemetery,** opened about 1640. John Hancock's father is buried here, as are Quincy and Adams forebears. The **Thomas Crane Public Library** (Coddington and Washington streets, in Quincy Center), built in 1881, is one of the finest works by Henry Hobson Richardson.

John Adams and John Quincy Adams Birthplaces

These modest salt-box houses, built on adjacent sites on the old Boston–Plymouth highway, were much beloved by the Adams families. Abigail Adams wrote that she preferred the charms of "my little cottage" to the grandeur of the London court. The John

Quincy Adams birthplace was erected in 1663, the John Adams house in 1681. When John and Abigail lived at the 141 Franklin Street house, she managed the family farm while he busied himself with his law practice and public affairs. They moved into the house at 135 Adams Street in 1787.

> LOCATION: 133 and 141 Franklin Street. HOURS: April 19 through November 10: 9–5 Daily. FEE: Yes. TELEPHONE: 617–773–1177.

Farther south on Franklin Street (Penn's Hill at Faxon Park), the **Abigail Adams Cairn** marks the place where she and seven-year-old John Quincy Adams watched the British shell Charlestown during the Battle of Bunker Hill.

Josiah Quincy House

Built in 1770 by Colonel Josiah Quincy, this elegant home exhibits furnishings and memorabilia of the Quincy family. Josiah Quincy II was a noted Patriot but, with John Adams, undertook the task of defending the British soldiers who had done the shooting in the Boston Massacre. Josiah III served as mayor of Boston and president of Harvard. Benjamin Franklin, Daniel Webster, and President Monroe were among the house's distinguished visitors. One of the most interesting exhibits in the house is a pane of glass upon which Colonel Quincy scratched, "October 10th 1775 Governor Gage saild for England with a fair wind." From his third-floor windows, the colonel had been keeping a close watch on the activities of the British fleet in Boston Harbor.

> LOCATION: 20 Muirhead Street. HOURS: June through mid-October: 12–5 Tuesday, Thursday, Saturday, and Sunday. FEE: Yes. TELEPHONE: 617–227–3956.

Quincy Quarries and Granite Railway

In the 1820s Solomon Willard, architect of the Bunker Hill Monument, inspected granite deposits in Massachusetts and chose Quincy granite for the monument. Willard then began the task of large-scale quarrying, virtually inventing the industry as he designed jacks, hoists, and other equipment for maneuvering huge blocks. Meanwhile, the engineer Gridley Bryant (father of the Boston architect Gridley J. F. Bryant) was inventing the railroad: He designed and built the Granite Railway, America's first commercial railway, whose initial customer was the Bunker Hill Monument

The General Sylvanus Thayer Birthplace, Braintree.

Association. Granite blocks were gently rolled down an inclined railway on four-wheeled cars to the Neponset River, and horses pulled the empty cars back to the quarry. Bryant's inventions—the two-truck, eight-wheeled car, the switch, turntable, and frog, where rail lines cross—became the standard equipment of later railroads. Although the hard Quincy granite was costly to quarry, its proximity to the Atlantic made it cheap to transport. From New England to Texas custom houses and other harbor structures were built of granite from Quincy's fifty-four quarries. The Metropolitan District Commission (617–698–1802) offers tours of the **railway incline** (Mullin Avenue in West Quincy), the **railway terminus** (Bunker Hill Lane), a **quarry** (Ricciuti Drive), and a **turning mill.**

In **Braintree,** just south of Quincy, the **General Sylvanus Thayer Birthplace** (786 Washington Street, 617–848–1640) has been restored to the style of the last quarter of the 1700s. General Thayer (1785–1872), known as the "Father of the Military Academy," was the superintendent of West Point from 1817 to 1833, where he greatly raised the standards of scholarship and discipline. The house, built by Thayer's great-great-grandfather in 1720 a mile from its current location, features its original panelling.

BROCKTON

Settled in 1700, Brockton was a quiet farming town until the invention of a machine for sewing shoes made their mass production economical. Large factories rose in Brockton, and it became one of the most important industrial centers in New England. William Cullen Bryant said that, "the whole place resounds, rather rattles with the machinery of shoe shops." The Civil War created an enormous demand for shoes, and Brockton grew rich shodding the Union army. In 1865 alone, the city produced a million shoes. The **Brockton Historical Society** (617–583–1039) has exhibits relating to the history of the shoe industry.

HINGHAM

Hingham, settled in 1635, contains a large number of early American homes and public buildings. Main Street is lined with historic homes from the eighteenth and nineteenth centuries, and downtown three historic buildings are open to the public.

Old Ship Church

The oldest building in continuous ecclesiastical service in the United States, the Old Ship Church is located near the site of the original Hingham Meetinghouse, and its congregation gathered in

Old Ship Church, built in 1681.

Cemetery of Old Ship Church, Hingham.

1635. Built in 1681, with the addition of side galleries in 1730 and 1755, architecturally it reflects the Elizabethan Gothic of the builders' homeland. Great curved frames, like the knees of a ship, support the roof, which was cut from oak grown on neighboring hillsides. The familiar name "the Old Ship," most likely came from the unusual roof structure, which resembles an inverted ship's hull.

Behind the church, the cemetery offers a fine view of Hingham's harbor, and the adjacent **Memorial Bell Tower** is one of the few places in the United States where one can hear the bells played in either the European style (as a chime ringing a hymn tune) or in the English change-ringing style (a series of constantly shifting mathematical patterns).

LOCATION: Lower Main Street. HOURS: Summer only: 12–4 Tuesday–Friday, and by appointment. FEE: None. TELEPHONE: 617–749–1679.

Derby Academy

Derby Academy is the oldest coeducational day school in New England. Founded by Madam Sarah Derby in 1784, the original 1818 academy building still stands and serves as the headquarters of the Hingham Historical Society.

LOCATION: 34 Main Street. HOURS: By appointment. FEE: None. TELEPHONE: 617–749–7721.

The Old Ordinary

The Old Ordinary is the Historical Society's house museum, with fourteen rooms containing an extensive collection of period furniture, export porcelain, glass, paintings, textiles, tools, and artifacts of local history. The periods of the rooms range from the seventeenth to the nineteenth century as does the structure itself. At various times in its history its owners have been tavernkeepers, thus the name the Old Ordinary. The garden's design may have been that of Frederick Law Olmsted, Jr.

LOCATION: 21 Lincoln Street. HOURS: Mid June through Labor Day: 1:30–4:30 Tuesday–Saturday, or by appointment. FEE: Yes. TELEPHONE: 617–749–0013.

COHASSET

This coastal suburb has a long maritime history. Captain John Smith landed here in 1614 during an exploratory voyage. In the eighteenth and nineteenth centuries the town prospered from maritime pursuits, especially fishing and shipbuilding. On Elm Street, at Cohasset Center, the **Cohasset Historical Society** (617–383–6930) maintains a **Maritime Museum,** which displays ship models, carvings, equipment, photographs, documents, and artworks relating to the town's seafaring history. A general historical collection of artifacts from the town's early years is also on display. Adjacent is the **Captain John Wilson House,** where eighteenth- and nineteenth-century furnishings are displayed. The society also operates the **Caleb Lothrop House** on Summer Street, an 1821 Georgian home holding a library and archives of local and area history. **First Parish Meeting House,** on the common, dates to 1747. Jerusalem Road runs from the town common along the shore, with views of the Atlantic.

In November 1849 Cohasset was the scene of the tragic wreck of the *St. John,* which was carrying Irish immigrants to Boston. During a storm, the ship foundered on Grampus Ledge, a mile and a half from shore, and sank. The town's volunteer lifeboat crew heroically attempted to reach the vessel, but in vain. The next day Henry David Thoreau, on his way to Cape Cod, stopped at Cohasset. In his journal of the trip, he vividly described the aftermath of the wreck, when grief-stricken relatives came from Boston to identify and bury the dead.

In the preceding fifty years the waters off Cohasset had had an appalling record for shipwreck and loss of life, prompting the construction of **Minot's Light.** Not yet operational at the time of the *St. John* disaster, it was completed in 1850. One year later a storm swept away the iron tower and its two lighthouse keepers. In 1860 a replacement was built, two-and-a-half miles offshore, which stands today. The construction of the second Minot's Light, a 114-foot granite tower, was an engineering triumph; the two-ton foundation stones could be laid on Minot's Ledge only at low tide in a dead calm.

Kendall Whaling Museum

The collections in this compact nine-gallery museum concern the history of whaling worldwide, not solely the industry in America. It displays a wide variety of scrimshaw, including purely decorative pieces and such items as clothespins and pie-crust crimpers made from whalebone. There is a fine collection of prints, paintings, and figureheads.

LOCATION: 27 Everett Street (off Route 27, north of Sharon). HOURS: 10–5 Tuesday–Saturday. FEE: Yes. TELEPHONE: 617–784–5642.

MARSHFIELD

Located on the North River, the town was settled in 1632, but the marshes that gave it its name were drained in the nineteenth century to cultivate cranberries and strawberries. **Winslow House** (corner of Careswell and Webster streets, 617–837–5141), built in 1699 and rebuilt in 1750, has been restored with furniture of the Pilgrim era and of the eighteenth century. On its grounds are an eighteenth-century blacksmith shop and the **Daniel Webster Law Office.** The great orator and statesman spent the last twenty years of his life in Marshfield, and is buried in nearby Winslow Cemetery. The office displays his books on nature and a variety of Webster memorabilia. Across the street from the Winslow House is a restored nineteenth-century schoolhouse. The **Hatch Mill** (Union Street, 617–834–7329, by appointment only) is a restored nineteenth-century sawmill.

OPPOSITE: Cohasset Harbor, and Minot's Light, two and one-half miles offshore.

DUXBURY

An outgrowth of the settlement at Plymouth, Duxbury was settled
after 1627 by John Alden, Myles Standish, Elder Brewster, and
other Pilgrims who needed land to pasture their cattle. The **John
Alden House** (105 Alden Street, 617–934–6001), built in 1653, was
the home of John and Priscilla Alden, the romantic figures in
Longfellow's poem, "The Courtship of Myles Standish." Two restored houses in Duxbury were built by prosperous families in the
early nineteenth century. The **Captain Gershom Bradford House**
(931 Tremont Street, 617–934–6106) was the home of a sea captain, and today houses the furnishings of four generations of the
family. The **King Caesar House** (Powder Point, 617–934–2378) is
the mansion built by shipbuilder and merchant Ezra Weston II,
whose sizable fortune caused him to be dubbed "King Caesar." The
house displays period furnishings and has exhibits on local history;
Weston's old stone wharf is adjacent. The **Art Complex Museum**
(189 Alden Street, 617–934–6634) contains two art galleries for
traveling collections, shows by well-known artists, special loan exhibits, and items from the museum's permanent collection; it also
maintains a Japanese tea hut on the grounds.

PLYMOUTH

In December 1620, one hundred and two Pilgrims disembarked
from the cramped quarters of the *Mayflower* at Plymouth to begin
their heroic settlement. Plymouth was not their expected destina-
tion. They had intended to settle farther to the south, but the
Mayflower was blown off course. Nor was Plymouth their first
landfall in the New World: A small party had landed at Provincetown and surveyed the Cape. In a small boat, the advance group
sailed around Cape Cod Bay until they found Plymouth, which had
a good harbor, high ground that could be defended in case of
attack, fresh water and, luckily, fields that had been cleared and
abandoned by Indians.

The Pilgrims landed in the dead of winter with inadequate
supplies, no horses or cows, and no heavy farming equipment. On
Christmas Day, to them a popish holiday not requiring any special
observance, the men set about building a common house. During
the construction the colonists had to remain on board the *Mayflower*, where many suffered from scurvy and other diseases. There

OPPOSITE: The King Caesar House, overlooking Duxbury harbor.

were deaths every day. Shortly after they completed the house it caught fire early on a Sunday morning, destroying the thatched roof. Preferring to shiver through a sleet storm rather than repair the roof on the Sabbath, the Pilgrims paid a heavy price. Pneumonia and influenza swept through the weakened settlers: about half their number died before the first winter was over.

The entire colony might have perished had they not received help from the Indians, who gave them food and taught them how to plant corn. They harvested their first crop in the autumn of 1621, and celebrated with a harvest feast. But Plymouth's claim to the first Thanksgiving is disputed by Virginia scholars, who say, with some justification, that the honor belongs to the settlement at Berkeley Plantation on the James River.

Plymouth Rock

According to tradition the landing place of the Pilgrims was Plymouth Rock, located on the beach at Water Street. It is certainly among the most famous landmarks in the world, enshrined beneath a columned monument designed in grand style by the firm of McKim, Mead & White. During the 1920s and 1930s, historians cast doubt on the authenticity of the Plymouth Rock story, however. In their view it was a charming legend and nothing more. More recent scholarship tends to support the original idea that this rock was indeed the Pilgrims' stepping stone from the *Mayflower*'s small landing boat to the New World. It was so identified by ninety-five-year-old Elder Faunce in 1741. According to a history of Plymouth published in 1832, "it was represented to Elder Faunce that a wharf was to be erected over the rock, which impressed his mind with deep concern, and excited a strong desire to take a last farewell of the cherished object. . . . Having pointed out the rock directly under the bank of Cole's Hill, which his father had assured him was that which had received the footsteps of our fathers on their first arrival, and which should be perpetuated to posterity, he bedewed it with his tears, and bid to it an everlasting adieu."

Adjacent to Plymouth Rock is an accurate, full-size replica of the vessel that brought the Pilgrims to the New World. The *Mayflower II* (State Pier, 508–746–1622) measures a mere 104 feet in length. Its cramped quarters vividly convey the hardships suffered on the sixty-six-day crossing. Costumed interpreters on the ship portray actual historical figures.

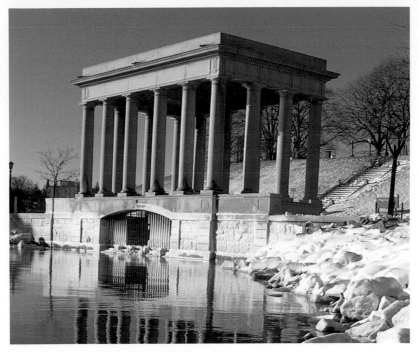

The Neoclassical monument sheltering Plymouth Rock.

Across the street from Plymouth Rock is **Coles Hill,** where the settlers buried the victims of disease during their first winter on these shores. The early graves were not marked "lest the Indians know how many were the graves." Over the centuries erosion revealed some of these unmarked graves. In 1921 a granite sarcophagus was placed atop the hill to hold remains that had been recovered. Another monument on the hill commemorates Chief Massasoit of the Wampanoag, who befriended the Pilgrims, gave them food, and taught them how to plant. **Burial Hill,** on School Street, also has seventeenth-century graves, including that of Governor Bradford. This hill is the site of the Pilgrims' first meetinghouse, fort, and watchtower. From this height they could scan the bay for arriving friends or foes.

Three seventeenth-century houses that have been restored and furnished with items from the Pilgrim era are open to the public. The **Richard Sparrow House** (42 Summer Street, 508–747–1240), Plymouth's oldest surviving house, was built in 1640 and today is occupied by the Plymouth Pottery Guild, which offers demonstrations of pottery-making techniques. The **Jabez Howland House** (33 Sandwich Street, 508–746–9590) was built in 1667 by the son of one of the original Pilgrims. The **Harlow Old Fort House** (119 Sandwich Street, 508–746–3017) dates to 1677 and may have been constructed with oak timbers salvaged from a fort erected in 1622. Of later date is the 1749 **Spooner House** (27 North Street, 508–746–0012). It displays the furnishings and personal items of the Spooner family, who lived here for two centuries.

The **Mayflower Society Museum** (4 Winslow Street, 508–746–2590), headquarters of the General Society of Mayflower Descendants, has nine period rooms with furnishings from the seventeenth to nineteenth centuries, all contained in a house built in 1754. The early days of the settlement are dramatized with sound-and-light demonstrations at the **Plymouth National Wax Museum** (16 Carver Street, 508–746–6468).

Pilgrim Hall Museum

The nation's largest collection of Pilgrim artifacts is displayed in this, the oldest public museum in the country, dating to 1824. (Salem's Maritime Museum is older, but it began as a private collection.) This collection of furniture, household items, weapons, books, and paintings includes swords owned by Myles Standish, Governor Bradford's Bible, and the cradles that rocked the Fuller children and Peregrine White, who was born on the *Mayflower*.

LOCATION: 75 Court Street. HOURS: 9:30–4:30 Daily. FEE: Yes. TELEPHONE: 508–746–1620.

Plimoth Plantation

A cluster of primitive wooden houses surrounded by a stockade comprise this authentic re-creation of the 1627 Pilgrim village. Costumed interpreters portray Pilgrims such as Governor William Bradford, John and Priscilla Alden, Bridget Fuller, and Myles Standish, all of whom recount their adventures using the accents of the seventeenth century. They reenact the life of the plantation with musket drills, baking bread in a clay oven, shearing sheep, making clapboards, salting fish, weaving wattle, playing nine pins and walking on stilts, and conducting trials and punishments. The Plantation attempts authenticity down to the breeds of livestock— the proprietors have "back-bred" livestock to re-create the animals the Pilgrims would have had: lineback cattle, a Dartmoor pony, and

Seventeenth-century life at Plimoth Plantation. OVERLEAF: *Plimoth Plantation, a re-creation of a Pilgrim village ca. 1627.*

several old breeds of chicken. The adjacent **Wampanoag Summer Campsite** re-creates the life of the Indians who lived at Plymouth before the Europeans arrived.

LOCATION: Off Route 3 on Plimoth Plantation Highway. HOURS: April through November: 9–5 Daily. FEE: Yes. TELEPHONE: 508–746–1622.

NEW BEDFORD

New Bedford was one of America's largest whaling ports in the nineteenth century. In the 1840s some ten thousand seamen were at work on New Bedford vessels, which gathered more than half a million barrels of oil and three million pounds of whalebone in the year 1847 alone. In *Moby Dick,* Herman Melville described the town as "perhaps the dearest place to live in all New England. . . . Nowhere in America will you find more patrician-like houses." Some of the mansions to which he referred are still to be seen today along **County Street,** on a high ridge overlooking the waterfront on the Acushnet River. The street's centerpiece is the **Rotch-Jones-Duff House and Garden Museum** (396 County Street, 508–997–1401), which is undergoing restoration. Designed by Richard Up-

john, it was built in the 1830s for a whaling merchant. Walking tours of the area leave from the museum. The city's **Visitor Center** is located at North Second Street (508–991–6200).

New Bedford is still the most active fishing port in the country, although whales are no longer the quarry. The nineteenth-century houses and commercial buildings of the **Waterfront District,** including two notable landmarks, have been restored. The **Seaman's Bethel,** on Johnny Cake Hill, is described in Melville's *Moby Dick* as the church where sailors destined for distant seas would be certain to visit. It has a prow-shaped pulpit and memorials to lost seamen on the walls. The Greek Revival **U.S. Custom House** (corner of Second and William streets), built in the mid-1830s, was probably designed by Robert Mills.

In the late nineteenth century, the city was a major glass-making center. The **New Bedford Glass Museum** (50 North Second Street, 508–994–0115) contains almost two thousand pieces of American glassware, along with antique lamps, and copper and brass objects made in New Bedford. The museum is housed in the 1821 Benjamin Rodman mansion.

The prow-shaped pulpit at the Seaman's Bethel. OPPOSITE: *The world's largest ship model, the eighty-nine foot* Lagoda, *in the New Bedford Whaling Museum.*

New Bedford Whaling Museum

Although the museum displays a large collection of scrimshaw, figureheads, logbooks, marine paintings, and tools of the whaler's trade, perhaps the most impressive exhibit is an enormous panorama, originally over a quarter of a mile long, that depicts a whaling voyage. The pride of the museum is a half-scale replica of a fully rigged whaling ship, the *Lagoda;* at eighty-nine feet in length, it is the largest ship model in the world. Also on display is the roster of the whaler *Acushnet,* listing Melville as a member of the crew.

LOCATION: 18 Johnny Cake Hill. HOURS: 9–5 Monday–Saturday, 1–5 Sunday. FEE: Yes. TELEPHONE: 508–997–0046.

Ernestina

The schooner *Ernestina,* built as a fishing vessel in Essex, Connecticut in 1894, was originally named the *Effie M. Morrissey.* After twenty-five years of service on the Grand Banks, she carried explorers and cargo into the Arctic where she also saw wartime service for the navy. Rechristened *Ernestina,* she transported immigrants from the Cape Verde Islands. A museum across from the dock documents the history of the ship.

LOCATION: 30 Union Street. HOURS: 9–2 Daily. FEE: None. TELEPHONE: 508–992–4900.

The **New Bedford Fire Museum** (Bedford and South Sixth streets, 508–992–2162) has an excellent collection of antique fire trucks, uniforms, and fire-fighting equipment.

FALL RIVER

From the 1870s to the late 1920s Fall River was one of the most important textile-producing centers in the country, thanks to its fine harbor, Mount Hope Bay, and the waterpower provided by the Quequechan River. The old cotton mills, some five and six stories high, still line the center of the city along Interstate 195, which was built over the bed of the Quequechan. Mills were most often brick but, because Fall River is situated on a ridge of granite, the builders also made good use of that handsome stone. The lower walls were made three feet thick to withstand the vibrations of the looms. The city has large populations of Irish, Portuguese, and

French-Canadians, the grandparents of whom came here to work in the mills. The **Fall River Heritage State Park** (Battleship Cove, 508–675–5758) has its headquarters in a new building designed to resemble the massive nineteenth-century mills, and displays historical photographs of the city and a twenty-minute film on Fall River's industrial past.

The **Fall River Historical Society Museum** (451 Rock Street, 508–679–1071), in an 1843 mansion built for a mill owner, has exhibits about the city's manufacturing history, while the **Marine Museum** (70 Water Street, 508–674–3533) has a superb collection of more than 150 ship models including transatlantic liners, coastal ferries, fishing vessels, and tallships.

Battleship Cove

The four ships and the submarine docked at Battleship Cove form a floating museum of naval history.

The battleship USS *Massachusetts*, commissioned in 1939, was the flagship for the 1942 invasion of North Africa and then saw two years of action in the Pacific. The ship is the length of more than two football fields, and had a crew of 2,300. Armaments included sixteen-inch guns, and she was equipped with two catapults for launching scout planes. A Japanese suicide submarine is exhibited on the deck. Below decks is a warren of crew's quarters and the support shops needed to support this floating town. It is the official memorial to the 13,000 Massachusetts men and women who lost their lives in World War II.

The destroyer USS *Joseph P. Kennedy, Jr.*, launched in 1945, saw long and varied service during the Korean War, for training exercises, during the Cuban Blockade, and as a NASA recovery ship. She was named for the oldest of the Kennedy brothers, an airman killed in Europe in 1944, and is the Massachusetts memorial to the state's citizens who died in the Korean and Vietnam wars.

The USS *Lionfish*, launched in 1943, is an example of the standard submarine used by the navy during World War II. The PT 796 and PT 617 were both fast, highly maneuverable boats used for the hazardous mission of launching torpedoes at enemy ships from relatively close range.

LOCATION: Battleship Cove. HOURS: 9–5 Daily. FEE: Yes. TELE-PHONE: 508–678–1100.

CAPE COD AND THE ISLANDS

It was Henry David Thoreau who called Cape Cod "the bared and bended arm of Massachusetts: The shoulder is at Buzzard's Bay; the elbow, or crazy bone, at Cape Mallebarre; the wrist at Truro; and the sandy fist at Provincetown." This sturdy appendage was formed by the edge of a glacier that deposited sand upon a spine of bedrock. From the Cape's bicep at Falmouth to its fist, the sandy beach, backed by dunes as high as one hundred feet, is one of the most spectacular in the world. The cape was named in 1602 by Bartholomew Gosnold for "the great store of cod-fish" he noticed when he explored the region.

Before the Pilgrims arrived on the Cape in 1620 (their first landfall in the New World was not at Plymouth, but at Province-town, where they lingered for about a month), the Cape had been the homeland of the Wampanoag Indians for over 3,500 years. The Wampanoag lived by fishing and farming, and by catching whales that washed up on shore or ventured close enough to be captured in small boats. The interior of the Cape was covered with thick hardwood forests that European settlers entirely stripped away to build and heat their settlements. By the middle of the nineteenth century, when Thoreau took his two long walks, the Cape was virtually bare of wood but for scrawny shrubbery. In the century and a quarter since, scrub pines have been planted throughout, and have flourished.

The Cape was settled by emigrants from Plymouth which, by the 1630s, already seemed overcrowded to its inhabitants. The Pilgrims' first venture on the Cape was the establishment of the Aptucxet Trading Post at modern-day Bourne. At that location, Scusset Creek (which flowed into Cape Cod Bay) almost met the Manomet River (which flowed into Buzzard's Bay). Boats could navigate either stream and the cargo could be portaged three miles to the other stream. On this route the Pilgrims traded with the Dutch at New Amsterdam, and they immediately realized that it was an ideal place for a canal—but it would take almost three centuries for that vision to be realized in the Cape Cod Canal. The trading post at Aptucxet spawned the town of Sandwich, with Barnstable and Yarmouth both following in 1639.

Every inlet and tidal creek had its own small fishing fleet. Cape Codders pursued the cod and mackerel, but only Provincetown

OPPOSITE: Race Point Beach, Provincetown, is among a string of beaches that form the Cape Cod National Seashore.

had a harbor deep enough for whaling ships, and the lead in whaling was easily taken by Nantucket. Wellfleet became famous for its oysters, some brought up from the Chesapeake and bedded down in Wellfleet to attain the distinctive local flavor. The Cape's mariners did not prosper on the scale of Salem's or Boston's, and there is no corresponding cluster of magnificent mansions to compare with those on the North Shore. Though Cape Cod had no Bulfinch or McIntire, it did have legions of ship's carpenters who created the Cape cottage, built, as Samuel Eliot Morison wrote, "with that nice sense of proportion that a ship-carpenter instinctively absorbs." The Cape cottage was described by Agnes Edwards, in 1918, as "a story and a half, shingled, gray, and weather-beaten, nestled in a nook, across a meadow, or half hidden under trees . . ."; as for inside, "[there is] no luxury, nor elegance, nor superfluity." They can be seen in every town on the Cape.

CAPE COD CANAL

Opened in 1914 after three and a half decades of on-and-off construction, the canal represents the fruition of a long-cherished dream, the idea of digging a canal here having been first raised by Myles Standish, in 1624, to "avoyd the compasing of Cape-Codd." During the Revolution George Washington ordered an engineering survey, and plans were drawn up but never acted upon. The final success of the project was thanks to the New York financier August Belmont II, who took over the project in 1909, pushed it to conclusion, and ultimately lost millions of dollars on it. The seven-mile canal saves mariners the one-hundred-mile voyage around the Cape, through hazardous waters that have brought many a sailor to grief. The Sagamore and Bourne bridges were built in the 1930s.

SANDWICH

Sandwich was the first settlement on the Cape, dating to 1627 when the Pilgrims established the Aptucxet Trading Post in Bourne. Permanent settlement began ten years later when Edmund Freeman arrived from Saugus with a small group of followers. Farming and shore whaling brought Sandwich a quiet prosperity, but the lack of a large natural harbor kept the town from becoming a major maritime center.

The town's main nineteenth-century industry was the manufacture of glass. The Boston & Sandwich Glass Company, founded

A selection of the Sandwich Glass Museum collection.

in 1825, produced a range of glass items prized by collectors for their subtle colors. The **Sandwich Glass Museum** (129 Main Street, 508–888–0251) displays some of the works of the factory's artisans as well as a diorama, built in 1940 by students from the Massachusetts Institute of Technology, showing the factory as it looked in 1850. When the factory closed, after a bitter labor dispute in 1888, Sandwich went into an economic decline.

Slow growth has helped the center of the town retain its old character. The focus of the **Town Hall Square Historic District** is the 1834 Greek Revival Town Hall, and the district includes forty-seven houses ranging in date from the late 1600s to the nineteenth century. One of the Cape's most picturesque spots is the cluster of historic sites around Shawme Pond, an artificial lake created by the early settlers to provide power for milling. These include the **Hoxie House** (508–888–1173), dating to the 1630s, which may be the oldest house on the Cape; it has been restored with authentic seventeenth-century furnishings. Adjacent is the **Dexter Mill** (508–888–1173), in use from the 1650s until the late nineteenth century; demonstrations of old milling techniques are given here. Also by

Shawme Pond is the town cemetery, where the oldest headstone reads 1680. The **First Church of Christ** (136 Main Street, 508–888–0434) dates to 1847 but the congregation itself is considerably older: It was gathered in 1637 from the area's first settlers.

In a pine grove on Wilson Road (off Tupper Road) is an unusual **gravesite** of a husband and wife. The town founder, Edmund Freeman, who died in 1677, is buried under a stone saddle, and his wife, Elizabeth, under a pillion—a seat that was attached to a saddle, thereby allowing two people to ride the same horse.

Heritage Plantation

Located on seventy-six acres of gardens, Heritage Plantation displays a wide variety of Americana in a complex of buildings that reproduce different architectural styles. A replica of the round Shaker Barn at Hancock Shaker Village houses an impressive collection of antique cars from 1899 to 1937. The Old East Mill is a restoration of a mill built in Orleans in 1800, while the Military Museum displays a notable collection of firearms, two thousand miniature military figures, flags, and Indian artifacts. The Plantation's other collections, housed in an art museum, encompass crafts, folk art, Currier & Ives lithographs, and tools. The gardens of the Plantation feature rhododendrons bred by Charles O. Dexter and over a thousand varieties of trees, shrubs, and flowers.

LOCATION: Pine and Grove streets. HOURS: Mid-May through late October: 10–5 Daily. FEE: Yes. TELEPHONE: 508–888–3300.

East Sandwich, a section of farms and cranberry bogs, was settled by Quakers. Its present **meetinghouse** (off Quaker Meeting House Road) was built in 1810; the first meetinghouse on the site was erected in 1658. Behind it is the **Wing Fort House** (69 Spring Hill Road, 508–888–3591), the oldest section of which dates to 1641 and was designed, according to tradition, as a stronghold in case of Indian attack. This Quaker home was enlarged and remodeled in the eighteenth century. Also historic is the **Benjamin Nye Homestead** (Old Country Road, 508–888–4213). Built in 1685, it has been restored and furnished with period items.

BOURNE

Originally part of Sandwich, Bourne is where in 1627 the Plymouth Pilgrims established a post to trade with the Indians of the Wampanoag Federation and the Dutch from New Amsterdam (later New York). In the 1930s, that outpost was re-created on the stone foundation of the original building as the **Aptucxet Trading Post & Museum** (Aptucxet Road, 508–759–9487). It includes a salt works, gristmill, and a tiny railroad station built for the visits of President Grover Cleveland, who summered in the area.

On Herring Pond Road, off Route 6, a plaque marks the site of **Indian Burial Hill,** a cemetery used by the Wampanoag until 1810. A meetinghouse for Christian Indians once stood here. **Cataumet Methodist Church** (Old County Road, north of Shore Road) was built in 1765 for the Indian congregation.

FALMOUTH

Falmouth was settled in 1660 by Isaac Robinson, a Congregational minister, and his followers who had aroused the ire of their Barnstable neighbors by becoming Quakers. There was widespread persecution of Quakers in Massachusetts, but the area of West Falmouth became a refuge for them. The **Friends Meetinghouse** here on Route 28-A, was built in 1842 on the site of a meetinghouse built in 1755. Nearby is a Quaker cemetery, established in 1720.

Falmouth Green was set aside as a common in 1749, and today it is still surrounded by eighteenth- and nineteenth-century houses. The Falmouth Historical Society (508–548–4857) maintains two historic properties on the Green—the **Julia Wood House** and the **Conant House Museum.** The Wood house, built in 1790, displays nineteenth-century furnishings and items of local historical interest. The Conant House Museum features exhibits of whaling items. The **First Congregational Church** facing the Green has a bell cast by Paul Revere, installed in 1797. During the Revolution and the War of 1812, Falmouth's men battled the British to save the town from destruction. In 1814, British ships bombarded the town after a demand to surrender a pair of cannon was refused, but little damage was done.

The **Katharine Lee Bates Birthplace Museum** (East Main Street) has a small display of Victorian furniture and memorabilia relating to Bates, a poet and professor of English at Wellesley College who wrote the lyrics to "America the Beautiful."

MASHPEE

The center of a 1682 land grant to the Wampanoag, the town was named for one of the tribes in the federation, the Massipee. As white settlement expanded, Mashpee became the refuge for the Cape's Indians, and today it is the site of an annual powwow held in the second week of July, when Indians from all over the country gather here for ceremonies, dancing, and demonstrations of crafts. The **Mashpee Wampanoag Indian Museum** (Route 130, 508–477–1536) has a small collection of artifacts and a diorama of a Wampanoag encampment. It was King Philip, a Wampanoag leader, who launched a war against the English intruders in 1675. The Indians lost, and the frightened settlers forbade them to carry on their traditional lifestyle, thereby sapping their strength. The **Old Indian Meetinghouse** (Route 130, 508–477–0208) is the oldest surviving church building on the Cape, dating to 1684. It marks one of the first attempts by the settlers to convert the land's natives to Christianity. Adjacent to the church is an eighteenth-century cemetery that has tombstones inscribed with Wampanoag names.

BARNSTABLE

The second town founded on the Cape, Barnstable was settled in 1639 by the members of a separatist parish who landed in Scituate in 1634. The **West Parish Congregational Church,** founded in that year, is probably the oldest Congregational parish in America. In the church building in West Barnstable (Route 149, 508–362–4445), erected in 1717, the entrance and pulpit are situated on the broad side of the building, in keeping with the custom of the time. The bell, weighing almost half a ton, was cast by Paul Revere.

Barnstable flourished in its early years thanks to the abundant supply of salt hay in the Great Marshes. But the town's farmers soon realized that a more profitable commodity was washing up on their shores—dead and stranded whales. Sandy Neck, a barrier beach that stretches for eight miles, is where the early settlers

OPPOSITE: The interior of the 1717 West Parish Congregational Church, West Barnstable.

captured whales and set up try-pots for boiling blubber. Later they pursued whales in small boats just off shore, and thus became expert seamen. In the nineteenth century Barnstable was home to hundreds of sea captains. Its harbor carried on a brisk trade, evidenced by the substantial **Custom House** built in 1855 which is now the location of the **Donald G. Trayser Museum** (Main Street, 508–362–2092) of Barnstable history. Wealth from the sea trade also gave the town the **Sturgis Library** (3090 Main Street, 508–362–6636), named for William Sturgis who made a fortune trading with China and the Northwest. A portion of the library is a house built in 1644 for the Reverend John Lothrop, minister of the congregation that founded Barnstable; his Bible is on display.

On Route 6-A, just east of Barnstable, a marker stands on the site of the **grave of Sachem Iyanough,** for whom Hyannis was named. Chief of the Cummaquid Indians, he died while hiding from a punitive raid led by Myles Standish. His grave was discovered by accident in 1860 when a farmer was plowing his field.

The town of Barnstable includes the quiet resort villages of Cotuit, Santuit, Osterville, and Centerville as well as Hyannis, the bustling tourist hub of the Cape. The **Santuit-Cotuit Historical Society** (1148 Main Street, 508–428–0461) has a small display of local historical items. Adjacent is the **Dottridge Homestead,** a small house built by a carpenter in the early nineteenth century, now filled out with period furnishings. The **Centerville Historical Society Museum** (West Bay Road, 508–775–0331), in an 1840 house, has eleven rooms exhibiting ship models, logs, antique clothing, glass, toys, dolls, and quilts, along with a large collection of antique clothing. The **Osterville Historical Society Museum** (West Bay Road, 508–428–5861), housed in a 1795 building with some later additions, displays furniture from the Colonial to Victorian periods, china, Sandwich glass, and historical photographs. A restored boathouse on the grounds has exhibits about the invention in the 1840s of the Crosby Cat—a fishing boat preferred by the sport and professional fishermen of the era for its speed and stability.

YARMOUTH PORT

Yarmouth was the third town on the Cape, founded in 1639 by a minister from Lynn. Myles Standish negotiated with the Wampanoag on behalf of the new settlers, persuading the Indians to accept a reserve around Long Pond and Bass River. Near Long Pond is an **Indian burial site,** marked by a boulder. Both Yarmouth Port and Dennis were seafarers' towns in the nineteenth century, and many of their older private homes once belonged to sea captains.

The **Winslow-Crocker House** (Route 6-A, 617–227–3956), originally built in West Barnstable around 1780, was taken apart, moved, and reassembled here in 1935. Now under the auspices of the Society for the Preservation of New England Antiquities, the house displays a fine collection of American furniture.

Across the street is the headquarters of the Yarmouth Historical Society, in the Greek Revival **Captain Bangs Hallet House** (508–362–3021). Captain Hallet, whose voyages took him to many ports in the Far East, occupied the house from 1863 to 1893. The oldest section of the house dates to the 1740s. Walking tours of the **Botanic Trails of Yarmouth,** which wind through fifty-three acres of preserved lands, begin at the Hallet house.

DENNIS

The town of Dennis, established in 1783, was named for a popular minister whose house, the **Josiah Dennis Manse** (Nobscusset Road and Whig Street, 508–385–2232), has been restored and furnished with period items, including the minister's portable pulpit and writing desk. A plaque on Sesuit Neck Road marks the site of the old **Shiverick Shipyards,** where clipper ships and schooners were built in the early 1800s. Dennis ships plied the Far East trade.

East of Dennis, on Route 6-A, a boulder marks the **burying ground** of the Nobscusset Indians. At **Scargo Lake,** named for a Nobscusset princess, a stone observation tower, built in 1902, affords an eighty-mile view. From East Dennis, Route 134 leads to South Dennis, another mariner's town. The **South Parish Congregational Church,** erected in 1835, has a plaque listing the names of the town's sea captains. Many sailors are buried in the adjacent cemetery, while the stones for other mariners are inscribed, "Lost at Sea." The nearby **Jericho House Museum** (508–385–2232), built in 1801 and restored in the 1950s and 1960s, contains a sizable collection of nineteenth-century furnishings. The barn on the property displays Victorian tools and household items as well as equipment used for cultivating cranberries.

BREWSTER

Although it lacked a harbor, Brewster was the home of a large number of sea captains, reputedly more masters and mates than any other town of its size. Their homes line the streets off Route 6-A, and their graves can be seen in the cemetery next to the **First Parish Church** (Main Street, 508–896–5577), built in 1834 and known as "the Captains' Church." One of the gravestones is the subject of a local legend: It bears two names, those of Captain David Nickerson and his adopted son, Captain René Rousseau, both of whom were lost at sea. Nickerson was handed the infant René in Paris, during the French Revolution, by a mysterious veiled woman. The townspeople remain convinced René was actually the dauphin—the child of King Louis XVI and Marie Antoinette—spirited out of France to save him from the revolutionaries.

    Stony Brook Mill (Main Street), built in 1873, was originally part of a small manufacturing complex that included a tannery and wool and cotton mills. Demonstrations of nineteenth-century milling techniques are given here. The **Dillingham House** (Stony Brook Road, private) may be the second oldest house on the Cape, dating to about 1660. Built by the ship captain John Dillingham,

Gravestone in the First Parish Church cemetery, Brewster.

the house is typical of the Cape's early domiciles. The **New England Fire and History Museum** (Route 6-A, 508–896–5711) has a large collection of antique fire trucks and equipment. The **Drummer Boy Museum** (Route 6-A, 508–896–3823) dramatizes the events of the Revolution in twenty-one life-size scenes with light-and-sound effects. The museum overlooks Cape Cod Bay, and there is also a mill, built in 1795, on the grounds.

HARWICH PORT

Harwich boasts an architecturally distinguished central area. The streets running into Main have been designated a historic district with some thirty architecturally notable homes and public buildings, including the 1880 **Brooks Block Public Library,** with ornate shingle detailing; the **Franklin Dodge House** (1836) in the Greek Revival style; and the 1832 **First Congregational Church,** which was remodeled in 1854. The **Harwich Historical Society,** located in the 1804 Brooks Academy Building (Sisson Road, 508–432–8089), displays a small collection of nautical items, equipment for raising cranberries—a major Harwich enterprise—and a powder house used during the War of 1812.

CHATHAM

In 1606 the French explorer Samuel de Champlain dropped anchor at Stage Harbor to repair a broken rudder and had a violent brush with the Indians. The rest of Chatham's history is peaceful, however. The historical society's museum, in the 1752 **Atwood House** (347 Stage Harbor Road, 508–945–2493), displays household implements, equipment from the Chatham Light, and literary memorabilia relating to the author Joseph C. Lincoln, whose sea tales were enormously popular at the turn of the century. The **Chatham Railroad Museum** (Depot Road, 508–945–0783), located in a station built in 1887, displays a caboose from 1910.

    Chatham Light (Main Street, 508–945–0164), built in 1877, stands on a bluff that has seen many tragic wrecks and heroic rescues. In the 1870s the surf carved away more than 230 feet of land, toppling the twin lighthouses. A monument by the present lighthouse pays tribute to Captain Elmer Mayo and Seth Ellis, who nearly lost their lives in a daring rescue here. Nearby is a graveyard of unknown seamen whose bodies washed up at Chatham.

EASTHAM

Eastham, founded in 1647, originally included all the land from modern Eastham on out to the tip of the Cape. In the **Old Cove Cemetery** (Route 6), three *Mayflower* Pilgrims are buried. The **Eastham windmill** (Route 6), the oldest on Cape Cod, was built in Plymouth in 1680, moved to Truro, then finally to this location. The **Swift-Daley House** (Route 6, 508–240–1247), built in 1741, exhibits eighteenth- and nineteenth-century furniture.

The **Fort Hill Preserve** (off Route 6) includes a two-mile nature trail that passes through remnants of early settlement, such as stone walls and house sites. The Second Empire–style **Captain Edward Penniman House** (Fort Hill Road), built, with an octagonal cupola, for a New Bedford whaling captain in 1867, is also on this site.

A **plaque** (Samoset Road) marks the site of the first encounter of the Pilgrims with Native Americans: The third exploring party led by Myles Standish, while the *Mayflower* was anchored at Provincetown, was attacked by Indians on this site. They were hostile because in 1614 an English slave trader had kidnapped some Indians and sold them in Spain. (Among those kidnapped Indians had been Squanto, who made his way to England, and then back to

Site of the first encounter of Pilgrims and Native Americans, Eastham.

America, where he aided the Pilgrims.) The Indians loosed a barrage of arrows, which Standish and his men met with musketfire. The Indians retreated, with no injuries on either side. Subsequent relations between the Wampanoag of Cape Cod and the English settlers were generally peaceful.

The **Eastham Schoolhouse Museum** (Route 6, 508–255–2170), in a one-room schoolhouse opened in 1869, displays a small collection of whaling, life-saving, and farming artifacts.

The **Salt Pond Visitor Center** (Nauset Road, 508–255–3421) is a unit of the Cape Cod National Seashore, which preserves 27,000 acres of uplands in the outer Cape. The center has exhibits on the Cape's history and an orientation film.

WELLFLEET

Famed for its oysters as early as 1606, when Champlain savored them and named the harbor Oyster Port, Wellfleet prospered from its oyster beds and from whaling. It is still an active fishing port. The clock in the **Congregational Church** on Main Street, built in 1850, strikes "ship's time" on the half hour. Nautical items are displayed at the **Wellfleet Historical Society Museum** (Main Street, 508–349–9157), which also exhibits farm implements, household items, and weapons. The society administers the **Samuel Rider House** (Gull Pond Road, 508–349–3876), a farmhouse built in the late eighteenth century. At the end of this road is **Newcomb Hollow** beach, where Thoreau stopped on his first walk along the Cape, spending the night at the house of an old oysterman.

An old pirate ship, the *Whidah*, has recently been discovered lying off the Wellfleet shore. On the beach south of Wellfleet is the **Marconi Area,** the site chosen in 1901 by Guglielmo Marconi to build radio towers. He sent the first radio signal across the Atlantic from this spot on January 18, 1903.

TRURO

The Pilgrims nearly settled in Truro after Myles Standish explored the area. Standish and his men stumbled upon Indian graves and houses, both of which they plundered along with an Indian's cache of corn, which they paid for a year later when Standish encountered the owner. The site of the corn theft is marked by a **plaque** at Corn Hill. The area where Standish found a spring is marked as **Pilgrim Heights,** with maps and walking trails.

Farmers arrived in the area in 1697, but in the eighteenth and nineteenth centuries the main occupations were whaling and fishing. The waters off Truro constitute some of the most hazardous stretches of the Cape, thus, in 1797, Truro was chosen by the federal government as the site for the Cape's first lighthouse, **Cape Cod Light,** (Lighthouse Road), also known as Highland Light. Fifty-seven Truro fishermen lost their lives in a storm in 1841. The lighthouse seen today was built in 1857 on the site of the first one. Thoreau visited the spot and commented on the ferocious winds here. The nearby **Museum of the Truro Historical Society** (Lighthouse Road, 508–487–3397), housed in an inn built around 1900, has a collection of furniture, household implements, and items salvaged from shipwrecks.

PROVINCETOWN

Provincetown is a colorful enclave of fishermen, artists, and writers packed tightly along the western coastline at the tip of the Cape. The bustling town stands in sharp contrast to its immediate surroundings—long stretches of beautiful, empty moors and desolate sand dunes. The moors and dunes are preserved as the **Province Lands** area of the National Seashore. At the Province Lands **Visitor Center** (off Route 6), an observation tower offers panoramic views of dunes and sea, and whales can often be seen just off shore.

This is the place where the Pilgrims first landed, on November 21, 1620. As the *Mayflower* rode at anchor in the shelter of Provincetown Harbor, Myles Standish explored the Cape in a small boat, looking for a suitable spot for settlement. Aboard the *Mayflower* the Pilgrims, under the leadership of Governor William Bradford, drew up the "Mayflower Compact," a landmark document in which the Pilgrims agreed to govern themselves according to democratic principles. At the tip of the Cape, by a traffic rotary on Commercial Street, a **plaque** memorializes the Pilgrims' first landing in America. A more imposing memorial to the Pilgrims is found in town.

Pilgrim Monument and Provincetown Museum

The Pilgrim Monument, a granite tower over 250 feet high, was erected in 1907. Ramps and stairs lead to an observation deck 352 feet above sea level. The walls of the stairway are set with memorial plaques from associations of Pilgrim descendants and from Massachusetts towns, giving the date when each town was founded. At the foot of the tower is a small but superb museum of Provincetown history. The displays include a diorama of the *Mayflower*, ship models, whaling equipment, scrimshaw, and other seafaring artifacts as well as manuscripts and photographs documenting Provincetown's literary and artistic history.

LOCATION: High Pole Hill, off Route 6. HOURS: 9–5 Daily. FEE: Yes. TELEPHONE: 508–487–1310.

Provincetown flourished in the nineteenth century as a fishing port, and the wealth of the sea captains is evident from the many fine houses that survive from that period. Most are located on Commercial Street, one of the two main routes (the other is Bradford Street) that run the length of the town from east to west, and they range in style from the simple Cape Cod to the fancier Italianate. Captain Samuel Soper's house at 74 Commercial Street is an octagon, built in 1834. At the center of town is Provincetown's **Heritage Museum** (356 Commercial Street, 508–487–0666), which displays a fishing boat, a large model of the schooner *Rose Dorothea*, and other maritime items. The museum is housed in the old Center Methodist Church, built in 1861 — its tall octagonal belfry a prominent landmark both in town and from the sea.

Aerial view of Provincetown and the tip of Cape Cod.

MARTHA'S VINEYARD

The English explorers John Brereton and Bartholomew Gosnold landed on Martha's Vineyard in 1602. Brereton extolled "the incredible store of vines and the beautie and delicacie of this sweet soil," and Gosnold named it after his daughter Martha. In 1641 Thomas Mayhew of Watertown, Massachusetts purchased Martha's Vineyard, Nantucket, and the Elizabeth Islands from two English noblemen and then, with his son, Thomas, Jr., proceeded to establish missions to convert the Wampanoag Indians. Today there is an Indian community at Gay Head, at the western tip of the island. **Mayhew Chapel,** a memorial to the missionaries, is located in West Tisbury off Christiantown Road. Near the chapel is an Indian cemetery.

VINEYARD HAVEN

Vineyard Haven, officially named Tisbury, was an important port in the eighteenth and nineteenth centuries, until the 1914 opening of the Cape Cod Canal changed the shipping lanes. During the Revolution, a huge British fleet—eighty-three ships—arrived at the port and plundered the island. A fire destroyed much of the town in 1883; but many white clapboard houses along **William Street** survived. The 1796 **Ritter House Museum** (Beach Street, 508–693–5353) has exhibits about nineteenth-century life on the island.

The **Old Schoolhouse Museum** (Colonial Lane and Main Street, 508–627–4441) is located on the site where three girls destroyed the town's flagpole to keep it from falling into the hands of the British, who intended to make a warship's spar of it. Operated by the Daughters of the American Revolution, the museum exhibits crafts, scrimshaw, primitive paintings, spinning wheels, clothing, exotic items brought home from far-flung ports by the Vineyard's whaling ships, and an old stele with an indecipherable inscription, which may have been left on the island by Vikings.

The **Seaman's Bethel,** which opened in 1892, is one of the few waterfront buildings that survives from whaling days. The purpose of the bethel was to provide a refuge for seamen in a Christian atmosphere, away from the temptations of the taverns and streets. The building's chapel has been restored, and nautical memorabilia is displayed in the common room.

OPPOSITE: Gay Head Cliffs, Martha's Vineyard.

OAK BLUFFS

A Methodist minister selected this site in 1835 to be a meeting ground. Thousands of people came here every summer and lived in tents in order to attend religious services. The visitors began to construct cottages, with exuberant carved decorations, until about a thousand houses were built and a charming Victorian village had been created. Every August since 1869, a festival—called Illumination Night—has been held, during which thousands of Oriental lanterns are strung from the houses.

EDGARTOWN

Founded in 1642 by the Mayhews—who called it Great Harbor—Edgartown became a busy, prosperous port and the home of many of the island's captains. Their houses remain, overlooking the harbor along North and South Water streets. Presiding over Main Street are the massive columns of the **Whaling Church,** built in 1843. Adjacent to the church is the **Daniel Fisher House** (now offices, private), built in 1840. Fisher amassed a fortune dealing in whale oil: He held the contract to supply many of the federal

A Cape Cod cottage, Nantucket.

government's lighthouses with it. Behind the Fisher house is the oldest residence on the island, the **Vincent House,** built in 1672.

The **Dukes County Historical Society** (Cooke and School streets, 508–627–4441) includes the 1765 Thomas Cooke House, a research library and maritime museum, displaying the lens that was used in the Gay Head Lighthouse from 1856 to 1952.

In the western part of the island, the cemetery in **Chilmark** has many graves of early Vineyard families. South Road leads from Chilmark to the spectacular **Gay Head Cliffs,** the terminus of the glaciers that formed the island.

N   A   N   T   U   C   K   E   T

The historical course of Nantucket was set in 1712 when strong winds blew the ship of Captain Christopher Hussey out to sea and he harpooned a passing sperm whale. Nantucketers had learned to catch right whales close to shore, but Hussey's capture of a sperm whale, which yielded more valuable oil than that of a right whale, inspired the islanders to fit out larger ships for longer voyages. In the next century and a half whaling brought great riches to Nantucket. In the town of Nantucket, the waterfront bustled with every kind of nautical industry—shipbuilding, rope making, sail making—and the air was heavy with the smell of the candle factories. Above the waterfront, along Main Street, rose the houses of the wealthy ship owners.

The Revolution, the Embargo of 1807, and the War of 1812 all brought severe economic depressions to Nantucket. In the 1780s and the 1810s the islanders were literally starving. In order to get food through the British blockade during the War of 1812, Nantucket proclaimed itself neutral. After the war the islanders rebuilt their fleet and set about discovering new whaling grounds in the Pacific. Then a fire in 1846 devastated the waterfront, the California Gold Rush lured crewmen away, and the discovery of petroleum in 1859 ended the great days of the whaling industry. Nantucket went into a slow decline, until vacationers discovered the island's beaches and moors in the late nineteenth century.

The town of Nantucket has been well preserved. Its historic district contains hundreds of eighteenth- and nineteenth-century houses, most of them private residences. The narrow, winding, cobblestoned lanes remain much as they were one hundred years ago, with fourteen historic sites being maintained by the Nantucket

Historical Association. Information on all of the sites in this section may be obtained from the Association (508–228–1894).

A walking tour of Nantucket might begin at the wharves, then to the Peter Foulger and Whaling museums, and then up Main Street, where many of the town's finest historic houses can be seen.

Two museums stand side by side on Broad Street. The **Whaling Museum,** in an 1846 building that was originally a candle factory, displays a superb collection of scrimshaw, the forty-three-foot-long skeleton of a whale, and equipment used to capture whales and process the blubber, such as an enormous oil press. The **Peter Foulger Museum** documents homelife ashore through photographs, drawings, and exhibits of the riches brought to the island by whalers and traders, such as silks, carpets, and porcelain from the Orient.

On Main Street Square, the **Pacific Club** (private) was founded in the 1850s. The building bought for the club was constructed by William Rotch in 1772 as a warehouse for the candles and oil he was shipping to London. By the door a sign carries the names Dartmouth, Beaver, and Bedford—three of Rotch's ships that earned places in nautical history: The *Dartmouth* and *Beaver* were emptied of their cargoes of tea in the Boston Tea Party, while the *Bedford* was the first American ship to fly the American flag in a British port after the Revolutionary War.

Main Street, west from Main Street Square, is the architectural showplace of Nantucket, a parade of mansions built by Coffins, Starbucks, Macys, and other prosperous whaling families. The **Three Bricks** (private), a trio of identical houses at 93–97 Main, were built in the 1830s by Joseph Starbuck for his sons. Across the street is **Hadwen House,** the 1844 Greek Revival mansion of William Hadwen, who owned the factory that houses the Whaling Museum. This imposing house, with a massive portico, preserves elegant Regency, Empire, and Victorian furnishings. Just off Main Street, at Walnut and Liberty, is the **Nathaniel Macy House.** Built in 1723, the modest house is furnished with eighteenth- and nineteenth-century items.

Pleasant Street, with several interesting nineteenth-century houses, leads to Mill Street, the location of the **1800 House.** The house has been restored and furnished with items from the late 1700s and early 1800s, including a chair that was tossed overboard from the *Beaver* during the Boston Tea Party. This was the home of the county sheriff, and the furnishings reflect the life of an islander

Jethro Coffin House, Nantucket.

of modest means. Also off Pleasant Street is Summer Street (site of a Baptist church built in 1840), which leads to Moor's Lane and Fair Street. On Fair Street is a **Quaker Meetinghouse,** built in 1846.

On Vestal Street, just beyond the end of Main, is the **Maria Mitchell Birthplace** (508–228–2896). America's first woman astronomer, Mitchell discovered a comet in 1849 as she studied the skies over Nantucket from the roof of her father's bank. Nearby is the **Old Gaol,** built in 1805, complete with an iron-walled cell for especially dangerous prisoners.

The **Old Mill** (South Mill Street) was built in 1746; its wooden milling machinery still functions.

On the north side of the town is the **Jethro Coffin House** (Sunset Hill). Built in 1686, it is believed to be the oldest surviving house on the island.

SALEM
AND THE
NORTH SHORE

OPPOSITE: Thacher Island lighthouse, Cape Ann.

The name Salem is inextricably linked to the witchcraft hysteria of the 1690s, and this connection is the lure that brings thousands of visitors every year. But Salem also has a glorious maritime history and splendid architecture. Some of the finest eighteenth-century houses in America can be found here, evidence of the enormous wealth amassed by Salem's ship captains. John Adams, visiting Salem in 1766, wrote, "the houses are the most elegant and grand that I have seen in any of the maritime towns." In the late eighteenth and early nineteenth centuries, Salem's premier architect was Samuel McIntire, who worked in the Federal style and was responsible for many of the town's supremely graceful and elegant homes. The architectural historian William H. Pierson spoke of McIntire's "exquisite sense of beauty and . . . deep poetic feeling for the qualities of wood."

Salem was first settled in 1626 by Roger Conant and a group of fishermen who had abandoned Cape Ann. Here they found a cove suitable for a fine harbor, with a high ridge overlooking the cove on which they built their houses. Their settlement has been re-created at Pioneer Village.

In the 1690s Salem was gripped by the infamous witchcraft hysteria. Tituba, the West Indian slave of a minister, told stories of the supernatural to the minister's young daughter and her friends. The girls' later fits of convulsions and babbling were diagnosed as the effects of a bewitching and, under interrogation, the girls accused Sarah Good and Sarah Osborne as well as Tituba. Good was tried and hanged as was another innocent woman, 70-year-old Rebecca Nurse of Danvers. In all, nineteen people were hanged and one was crushed to death under heavy stones. The witch hunt ended when the governor's wife fell under suspicion, and the governor ordered the release from jail of all accused witches.

By 1770 Salem had made itself into one of America's most prosperous towns by means of fishing and trading with Britain, Spain, the Netherlands, France, and the West Indies. During the Revolution, Salem privateers captured more than four hundred British ships. After the war, the town's seafarers sailed beyond the Atlantic trading American goods for exotic Asian luxuries—spices, fabrics, china, tea, and coffee—and fetching enormous profits. So many ships came from this one town that in some parts of Asia

OPPOSITE: Custom House at Salem Maritime National Historic Site.

CUSTOM HOUSE.

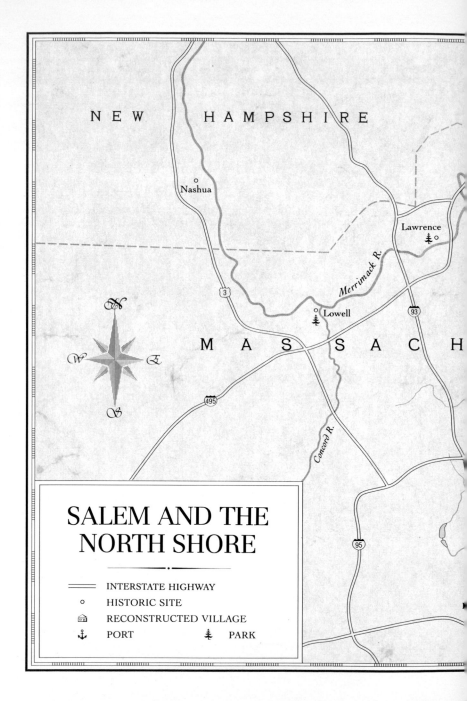

NEW HAMPSHIRE

Nashua

Lawrence

Merrimack R.

Lowell

3

93

M A S S A C H

495

Concord R.

95

SALEM AND THE NORTH SHORE

═══════ INTERSTATE HIGHWAY
○ HISTORIC SITE
⌂ RECONSTRUCTED VILLAGE
⚓ PORT ⚘ PARK

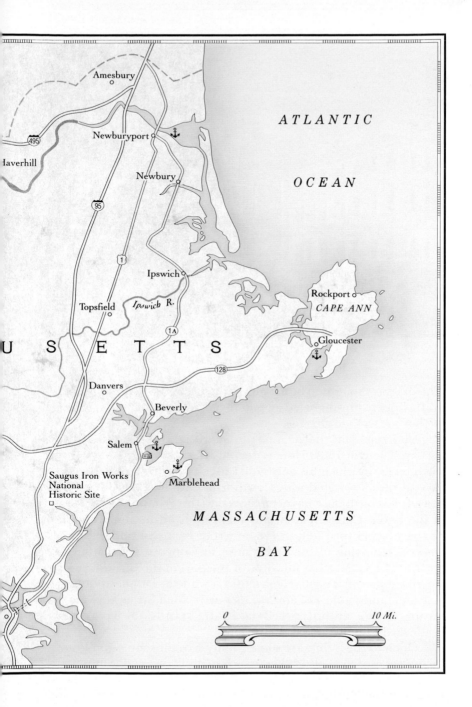

Hawks House (left) and Derby House at Salem Maritime National Historic Site.

"Salem" was thought to be a nation unto itself. The advent of deep-draft clipper ships signaled an end to Salem's trading days, because the harbor was too shallow.

Nathaniel Hawthorne, one of America's greatest authors, was born in Salem in 1804. He was deeply affected by the legacy of the witch trials, in which his ancestor, Judge Hathorne, played a part. Several sites associated with Hawthorne's life here have been preserved: His birthplace has been moved to the grounds of the House of the Seven Gables. For twelve years he lived in obscurity at 10 Herbert Street (private), where he wrote *Fanshawe* and *Twice-Told Tales*. After living at the Old Manse in Concord for a while, he returned to Salem to be surveyor of the port at the Custom House, a political patronage job. He lived for a while at 18 Chestnut Street (private), and wrote *The Scarlet Letter* at 14 Mall Street (private). A statue of the author, by Bela Pratt, stands on Hawthorne Boulevard.

Open to the public are some twenty-five museums and historical houses as well as other sites, which include two major museums: the Peabody Museum and the Essex Institute. Some of the finest houses in the Northeast can be seen along Federal, Chestnut, and

Counting room in the Salem Custom House. OVERLEAF: *The launching of the ship* Fame, *painted by George Ropes in 1802.*

Essex streets, and the atmosphere of Salem's maritime past has been preserved at the Salem Maritime National Historical Site.

This chapter begins with a detailed description of Salem, then proceeds to other sites on Massachusetts's North Shore and in its Merrimack River Valley.

SALEM

Salem Maritime National Historic Site

Embracing several acres along the old waterfront, the site includes the Custom House, Derby House, and the two-thousand-foot-long **Derby Wharf,** once one of the busiest trading depots in the world.

Surmounted by a proud-looking gilded eagle clutching arrows and a shield, the **Custom House** is a sturdy red-brick symbol of Salem's maritime prowess. Nathaniel Hawthorne labored in the Custom House from 1846 to 1849, and described it in the opening pages of *The Scarlet Letter;* his office and desk have been preserved. A brief audio-visual presentation on Salem's history is given here. The **Warehouse** behind the Custom House displays tea chests, barrels, hardtack, and samples of the goods Salem's ships brought

back from all over the world. Also on the grounds is the **Scale House,** with nineteenth-century scales.

Derby House is a brick mansion built for Elias Derby, one of Salem's most successful early merchants as well as a runner of privateers during the Revolution. It was later owned by Henry Prince, captain of the first American ship to call at the Philippines. The Derby House, with its restrained panelling in the mid-eighteenth-century style, contrasts markedly with McIntire's more elegant, Adamesque decoration of the post-Revolutionary period.

The park also includes the three-story **Hawkes House** (private), designed by McIntire, and the small **West India Goods Store,** now operated by a nonprofit organization. It sells items like those one might have found in Salem's nineteenth-century shops—spices, coffee, tea, and porcelain.

LOCATION: 178 Derby Street. HOURS: 8:30–5 Daily. FEE: None. TELEPHONE: 508–744–4323.

House of the Seven Gables

The House of the Seven Gables was the setting for Hawthorne's novel of that name. One of his cousins, Susan Ingersoll, lived here, and Hawthorne visited often. As he described it in his novel, "On every side the seven gables pointed sharply towards the sky, and presented the aspect of a whole sisterhood of edifices." The "venerable mansion," he wrote, "has always affected me like a human countenance, bearing the traces not merely of outward storm and sunshine, but expressive, also, of the long lapse of mortal life, and accompanying vicissitudes that have passed within." The house has been restored to appear as it did in Hawthorne's time.

Also on the grounds are the **Retire Becket House,** built in 1655, for six generations the home of the Becket family of shipbuilders. The **Hathaway House,** built in 1682, is known as "the old bakery," and it has a finely restored kitchen and a collection of Hawthorne memorabilia. The **Hawthorne Birthplace,** moved here from 19 Union Street, has been restored and furnished to the mid-eighteenth century and includes some Hawthorne family pieces.

LOCATION: 54 Turner Street. HOURS: July through Labor Day: 9:30–5:30 Daily; September through June: 10–4:30 Daily. FEE: Yes. TELEPHONE: 508–744–0991.

OPPOSITE: House of the Seven Gables, Salem.

At the center of Salem are the town's two major museums as well as a number of lesser sites. On Charter Street is the entrance to **Burying Point.** Dating from 1637, this cemetery holds the graves of Hawthorne's ancestor, Judge Hathorne, who presided over the witch trials, the architect Samuel McIntire, and a *Mayflower* Pilgrim, Richard More, who arrived at Plymouth when he was twelve. Adjacent is the **Goult-Pickman House** (private), which dates to the 1630s. A block away, at Derby Square, is the **Old Town Hall and Market House,** which was built in 1816 on the site of the Elias Hasket Derby mansion, a house so magnificent that none but Derby could afford to maintain it. After his death it could not be sold and had to be torn down. **City Hall** (93 Washington Street), built in 1837, is a stolid structure with massive pilasters and a fine gilded eagle on the roof.

Peabody Museum of Salem

America's oldest museum in continuous operation, the Peabody was founded by ship captains in 1799—as the East India Marine Society—to exhibit the "natural and artificial curiosities" they brought back from remote parts of the world. The collection now exceeds 300,000 items, which are housed in a complex of seven interconnected buildings, with more than thirty galleries. East India Marine Hall, a stone building with seven tall, arched windows, was built in 1824 and was the museum's first permanent home.

The museum's holdings are divided into four related collections. The maritime-history collection includes scrimshaw, ship models, figureheads, navigational instruments, portraits, paintings, fishing equipment, and a full-sized reconstruction of the master salon from America's first ocean-going yacht, launched in 1816. Important ship models include a seventeenth-century Dutch yacht and the oldest known (1812) model of the *Constitution.*

The Asian Export Art Collection, the largest in the world, comprises objects made in Asia for Western markets between 1500 and 1940, and includes works in porcelain, silver, gold, and ivory as well as furniture and paintings. The ethnology collections include musical instruments, pottery, clothing, jewelry, and weapons from Japan, China, Korea, India, and the Himalayas. The museum has one of the most important collections of Japanese artifacts in the world: The Japanese displays in Weld Hall number some thirty

OPPOSITE: Japanese porcelain decanter ca. 1690, ca. 1786 Hadley Quadrant, and reconstructed yacht salon, at the Peabody Museum, Salem.

thousand items. The Pacific Island collections include carvings, tools, weapons, clothing, and utensils from Polynesia, Micronesia, Melanesia, and Indonesia. There is also a large collection of items relating to the natural history of New England.

LOCATION: East India Square, 161 Essex Street. HOURS: 10–5 Monday–Saturday, 12–5 Sunday. FEE: Yes. TELEPHONE: 508–745–9500.

Essex Institute

Salem's second major historical organization was founded in 1848 when two earlier historical societies were joined. The institute's headquarters are in two buildings—Plummer Hall (1857), and the John Tucker Daland House built in 1852 by the Boston architect Gridley J. F. Bryant—both in the Italian Revival style. The research library is in the Daland House. Plummer Hall has a portrait gallery and collection of paintings (including works by Copley, Trumbull, and Stuart), decorative arts, military artifacts, tools, and furniture.

The institute has also restored three major historic houses, all of which can be entered through 132 Essex Street:

The **John Ward House** was built from 1684 to 1685 and restored in 1912 to its late-seventeenth-century appearance. The house reflects the modest means of its original owner, who made his living from softening leather. A weaving room, with spinning wheels and an eighteenth-century loom, an early nineteenth-century apothecary shop, and a "scent shop," are housed in a lean-to.

The **Crowninshield-Bentley House** was moved to its present location and restored in 1960. The oldest portion of the house, built by Captain John Crowninshield, dates to 1727. The best-known occupant of the house was not an owner but a boarder, the Reverend William Bentley, who took rooms here from 1791 to 1819. Bentley's meticulous diary, in which he described life in Salem and recorded the reminiscences of the town's old-timers, has proved to be a valuable chronicle of the period.

The **Gardner-Pingree House,** designed by Samuel McIntire for the well-to-do merchant John Gardner, reflects the wealth and sophistication of Salem society at its zenith, and has been called McIntire's masterpiece. The hall and double parlor, with lavish detailing in the wood and plaster, is a beautiful interpretation of the Adamesque style. It was completed in 1805, but Gardner had to

OPPOSITE: The Crowninshield-Bentley House Drawing Room.

leave it in 1815 after suffering financial reverses. The house was the scene of a murder in 1830, when Joseph White was killed in his bedroom. David Pingree purchased the property in 1834, and it remained in his family until 1934. It has been extensively restored to reflect the lives of Salem merchants during the prosperous Federal period.

The institute's complex also includes the **Lye-Tapley Shoe Shop** (1830), the **Gardner-Pingree Carriage House** (ca. 1860), the **Derby-Beebe Summer House** (1799), the **Louise duPont Crowninshield Garden,** and the **Quaker Meetinghouse** (1688).

LOCATION: 132 Essex Street. HOURS: June through October: *Museum* 9–5 Monday-Saturday, 1–5 Sunday; *Houses* 9:30–4 Monday–Saturday, 1:30–4:30 Sunday. November through May: *Museum* 9–5 Tuesday–Saturday, 1–5 Sunday; *Houses* closed. FEE: Yes. TELEPHONE: 508–744–3390.

Washington Square is a triangular, nine-acre park also known as Salem Common. The **Witch Museum** (19½ Washington Square North, 508–744–1692), located in a church built in the 1840s, dramatizes the events of the witch hunt of the 1690s with a half-hour sound-and-light show. Many of the private residences lining the sides of the Common were built by Salem's well-to-do captains and merchants. The monumental, three-story **Andrew-Safford House** (13 Washington Square West, private), reputedly the most expensive house built in New England at the time, impressed Salemites with its four tall columns on the side of the house facing the garden. It was constructed in 1819 for John Andrew, who had made a fortune trading in Russia from 1809 to 1816.

West of the Peabody Museum and Essex Institute are the elegant homes on Essex, Federal, and Chestnut streets.

Essex Street

The historic section of Essex Street begins at the corner of North Street, with the gabled **Witch House** (310½ Essex Street, 508–744–0180), the home of Jonathan Corwin, one of the judges in the witch trials. The house was built in 1642, and has been restored and furnished in accordance with its appearance in the 1690s. Judge Corwin questioned some two hundred accused witches at the house. Next door is the **Lindall-Gibbs-Osgood House** (private), a

OPPOSITE: Statue of Roger Conant, Salem's founder, in front of the Witch Museum.

The porcelain collection at Ropes Mansion, Salem.

gambrel-roofed, three-story house built in 1743. It was the childhood home of Benjamin Thompson, later Count Rumford, who
invented the Rumford stove, oven, and fireplace to use heat more
efficiently. The **Unitarian First Church** at number 316 was built in
1835, in the Gothic Revival style, by Gridley J. F. Bryant.

Ropes Mansion

Built after 1727 for the merchant Samuel Barnard, the mansion
was later home of Judge Nathaniel Ropes, a Loyalist who was
besieged here by a mob of Patriots in 1774. It remained in the
Ropes family until 1907, when it became a museum. Its furnishings, all original to the house, include Irish glass and a rare double
service of Canton export porcelain purchased by Joseph Orne and
Sally Ropes at the time of their wedding in 1817. The house and its
fine formal garden are administered by the Essex Institute.

LOCATION: 318 Essex Street. HOURS: June through October: 10–4
Tuesday–Saturday, 1–4:30 Sunday. FEE: Yes. TELEPHONE: 508–
744–0718.

The **Loring-Emmerton House** (private) at 328 Essex Street is a substantial brick mansion with a grand carriage entrance topped by a balustrade and an outsized, scrolled pediment. At number 339 is the **Salem Athenaeum,** a private library dating to 1810. Hawthorne used the library often, and its collection includes a book with his notes in the margins. The **Salem Public Library** (370 Essex Street) was built in 1855 as the home of ship captain John Bertram. **Grace Church,** at number 381, was built in 1927 in the English Gothic style. Its Federal-style parish house dates to the early nineteenth century. Many beautiful houses line the **Federal Street** historic area, west of North Street.

Peirce-Nichols House

Built in 1782 for Jerathmiel Peirce, an India trader, the house was remodeled in 1801 by Samuel McIntire for the wedding of Sally Peirce and George Nichols. It may have been his first major project. The East Parlor includes furniture designed by McIntire for the wedding; he also designed the delicate Adamesque woodwork and plaster ornamentation. The rear of the house once offered a view of the docks, over which Peirce undoubtedly kept close watch.

LOCATION: 80 Federal Street. HOURS: By appointment only. FEE: Yes. TELEPHONE: 508–744–3390.

Assembly House

Built in 1782 as a venue for balls, concerts, plays, and other types of public entertainment, the Assembly House was also the site of receptions for George Washington and the Marquis de Lafayette. The musical events apparently sparked some generational disagreements, as noted by the Salem diarist William Pynchon: "Musick at the Assembly Room: 2 fiddles, [French] horn, and drum. These and the assembly engross the conversation of the young and gay; the elders shake their heads with, what are we coming to?" In 1796 Samuel McIntire remodeled the building to make it into a private residence. The interior has been restored to reflect eighteenth- and nineteenth-century styles, and the furniture on display includes Salem pieces from the nineteenth century as well as items imported from Zanzibar, India, and China.

LOCATION: 138 Federal Street. HOURS: By appointment only. TELE-PHONE: 508–744–2231.

Chestnut Street Area State Historic Landmark

This well-preserved district of houses between Summer and Flint streets dates to 1796, when Chestnut Street was first laid out; it was then a quiet refuge far from the bustling dock area. Only one building in the district is open to the public.

Hamilton Hall (9 Chestnut Street, private), designed by Samuel McIntire and built in 1805, was named after Alexander Hamilton, who was very popular among the Federalist merchants of Salem. The hall was the center of the town's social life: Lafayette was honored here at a ball in 1824. Construction of the building was opposed by the minister of the church, now gone, that was across the street. He sermonized: "Back to back, and breast to breast, they are dancing their souls down to hell."

The **Stephen Phillips Memorial Trust House** (34 Chestnut Street, 508–744–0440), built in the early nineteenth century, displays bounty brought back from around the world by Salem's traders and exhibits furniture, paintings, and Chinese porcelain. **Number 18 Chestnut Street** (private) was the home of Nathaniel Hawthorne in 1847.

Two other houses in Salem are open by appointment: The **Pickering House** (18 Broad Street, 508–744–1647) dates to the mid-1600s and is still occupied by descendants of its builder. **Gedney House** (21 High Street), built in the 1660s, is a study house of the Society for the Preservation of New England Antiquities and appointments may be made through their office (617–227–3956).

Pioneer Village

A re-creation of the first settlement by Roger Conant and his band of fishermen, the village displays dugouts, wigwams, and small thatched houses. It was built in 1930, on the 300th anniversary of the arrival of the *Arbella,* which brought Governor John Winthrop to Salem. A two-story re-creation of the governor's house, one-room log houses dug into hillsides for protection against the winter winds, basins where sea water was evaporated to extract the salt for curing food, and brick kilns can all be seen here.

LOCATION: Forest River Park, south of Salem. HOURS: Mid-June through October: 9–4 Daily. FEE: Yes. TELEPHONE: 508–745–0525.

OPPOSITE: The 1782 Peirce-Nichols House, Salem.

THE   NORTH   SHORE

The North Shore of Massachusetts is a region of seaports—Marblehead, Gloucester, Newburyport—and well-preserved seventeenth-century houses. The town of Ipswich has a remarkable number of historic houses in a setting that summons up the atmosphere of the prosperous New England communities that followed the first temporary, rude habitations of settlement.

The later buildings of the Merrimack Valley are a world apart, however. Lowell and Lawrence, two cities on the Merrimack, both played a large role in the American Industrial Revolution. Their huge mills helped make New England one of the great manufacturing centers in the world. One of the country's oldest industrial sites is at Saugus, south of Salem.

SAUGUS IRON WORKS NATIONAL HISTORIC SITE

In the 1640s John Winthrop, Jr., the son of the governor of the colony, established an iron works on the Saugus River, where there were deposits of iron ore and a good supply of wood for fueling the furnace and forge. Several buildings have been reconstructed on the original site of the works, including the furnace, forge, blacksmith shop, and slitting mill, and museum exhibits demonstrate the technology that was used at the works. Waterpower pumped a bellows that forced air into the furnace, and drove a large hammer that pounded out wrought iron. The Iron Works House, built about 1646 with steep gables and an overhanging second floor, is the only surviving structure of the original complex. Now somewhat reconstructed, it was the home of one of the owners.

LOCATION: 244 Central Street, Saugus. HOURS: April through October: 9–5 Daily; November through March: 9–4 Daily. FEE: None. TELEPHONE: 617–233–0050.

MARBLEHEAD

The old shipbuilding and fishing port of Marblehead stands on a series of rocky ledges overlooking a fine harbor. Its inhabitants have been as rugged as the setting. Settled by fishermen in 1629,

OPPOSITE: Choate House, on Hog Island off Ipswich. OVERLEAF: Saugus Iron Works, founded in the mid-1600s by John Winthrop, Jr.

Marblehead made its living from the sea, by fishing, shipbuilding, and trading. Its seamen played important roles in the Revolution, under the leadership of General John Glover. A Marblehead vessel owned by Glover, the *Hannah*, was the first American warship: The Continental Congress rented it from Glover, and Washington ordered it to sea to capture British supplies. When Washington's army was in danger of annihilation after the Battle of Long Island, Glover's men evacuated them from Brooklyn to Manhattan. Marblehead boatmen rowed Washington's assault force at night across the ice-clogged Delaware River to attack Trenton. At the end of the Revolution, there were 468 widows in Marblehead. The graves of 600 Revolutionary War veterans are in **Old Burial Hill.**

At the town's highest point is **Washington Square,** the town common where Glover gathered his men before marching off to Boston. It is surrounded by the mansions (private) built by sea captains and merchants, and fronted by **Abbot Hall.** This town hall, built in 1876, has a clock tower that is a landmark easily visible from anywhere in Marblehead. The hall displays Archibald Willard's famous painting, *The Spirit of '76.*

Jeremiah Lee Mansion

This sixteen-room mansion, completed in 1768, is one of the finest houses of pre-Revolutionary America. The exterior, like that of George Washington's Mount Vernon, is "rusticated," made of wood cut to look like stone. A grand entrance hall, wallpaper, original panelling, and elegant furnishings distinguish the interior; the drawing room has an imposing fireplace. Jeremiah Lee, who made his fortune in shipping, was one of the organizers of the Massachusetts Committee of Safety before the outbreak of the Revolution. On the night of April 18, 1775, he was attending a meeting at the Black Horse Tavern in Arlington when the British passed on their way to Concord. He hid in a cornfield and died a month later from exposure.

LOCATION: 161 Washington Street. HOURS: Mid-May through mid-October: 10–4 Monday–Saturday. FEE: Yes. TELEPHONE: 617–631–1069.

In **Danvers,** northwest of Salem, are two houses of historic interest. The **Rebecca Nurse Homestead** (149 Pine Street, 508–774–8799)

OPPOSITE: Rebecca Nurse Homestead, Danvers. OVERLEAF: Whipple House, Ipswich.

was the home of a seventy-two-year-old woman hanged as a witch in 1692. She was buried on the grounds of the house. **Glen Magna** (Ingersoll Street, 508–774–9165) is a late-nineteenth-century mansion, behind which is a summer house designed by Samuel McIntire. Frederick Law Olmsted landscaped the grounds.

In **Beverly,** across the harbor from Salem, the Beverly Historical Society (117 Cabot Street, 508–922–1186) administers three restored houses: **Balch House** (448 Cabot Street), built in 1636; **John Hale House** (39 Hale Street), the residence of a minister who aided in the prosecution of witches until his own wife was accused; and the **John Cabot House** (110 Cabot Street), built in 1781 for a successful merchant and privateer. The exhibits in these houses include restored period rooms, clothing, and maritime artifacts.

GLOUCESTER

Founded in 1623, Gloucester is the state's oldest fishing port, and today fishing continues to be the town's main enterprise. Rudyard Kipling's 1897 novel *Captains Courageous,* about a Portuguese fisherman who rescues a rich boy who fell off an ocean liner, was set aboard the Gloucester fleet. The **Cape Ann Historical Association** (27 Pleasant Street, 508–283–0455) displays a collection of marine paintings, notably works by Gloucester-born Fitz Hugh Lane (1804–1865), ship models, furniture, silver, pewter, fishing equipment, and historical photographs of Cape Ann. The nearby **Sargent-Murray House** (49 Middle Street, 508–281–2432) has been restored to its late-eighteenth-century appearance. John Murray established the first Universalist church in the country, located across the street from his house. South of downtown Gloucester is Eastern Point, an exclusive enclave of summer houses and the location of Beauport.

Beauport

This unusual house museum was built and furnished between 1907 and 1934 by Henry Davis Sleeper, a decorator and collector of American art and antiquities. Beauport grew to become a forty-room mansion by 1934, as Sleeper added rooms to accommodate his ever-growing collections. The Pembroke Room incorporates

OPPOSITE: Eighteenth-century wallpaper in the China Trade Room—one of some forty beautiful rooms—in Beauport, Gloucester.

panelling acquired from an early seventeenth-century Massachusetts house; the China Trade Room (refurnished by a later owner
as a Chippendale parlor) displays eighteenth-century Chinese wallpaper; and the Strawberry Hill Room was Sleeper's tribute to the
English Gothic style. Many American collectors and decorators of
the day—Isabella Stewart Gardner, Elsie De Wolfe, Nancy McClel-
land, John D. Rockefeller, and Henry Francis duPont—visited
Sleeper's house, which had considerable impact on their tastes.

LOCATION: 75 Eastern Point Boulevard. HOURS: Mid-May through
mid-October: 10–4 Daily; mid-September through mid-October: 1–4
Weekends. FEE: Yes. TELEPHONE: 508–283–0800.

Hammond Castle Museum

John Hays Hammond, Jr., an inventor who held more than four
hundred patents in the fields of radio, television, and radar, constructed this enormous castle between 1926 and 1929, using portions of European chateaux. The castle was his home and laboratory, and the gallery for his art collection. He included a Roman bath,
secret passageways, and a 100-foot-long hall for his 8,200-pipe
organ. The castle stands on a bluff overlooking the sea and Norman's Woe, a surf-pounded rock that was the setting of Henry
Wadsworth Longfellow's poem "The Wreck of the Hesperus."

LOCATION: 80 Hesperus Avenue. HOURS: Mid-May through December: 10–4 Daily; January through mid-May: 10–4 Thursday–Saturday, 1–4 Sunday. FEE: Yes. TELEPHONE: 508–283–7673.

IPSWICH

Ipswich, founded in 1633, has been well preserved and retains the
atmosphere of the earliest New England settlements. **Choate
Bridge,** which crosses the river at South Main Street, was built in
1764. Ipswich was the home of America's first woman poet, Anne
Bradstreet, in the 1630s and 1640s. Her husband, Simon, was the
secretary of the Massachusetts Bay Colony and later the governor.
In the house at 33 High Street (private) she wrote some of the
poems published in England in the 1650 book *The Tenth Muse Lately
Sprung Up in America.*

The town's historic houses can be seen along South Main,
High, and East streets near the Green. Two houses are open to the
public: The **John Whipple House** (53 South Main Street, 508–
356–2811), built in 1640, is one of the finest surviving examples of

the early Puritan homes. It has been restored and furnished with items owned by the Whipple family. Adjacent to the house is a colonial herb garden. The **John Heard House** (40 South Main Street, 508–356–2641), built in 1795 by a sea captain, displays items brought back from the Far East. There is also a collection of antique carriages.

The **Choate House,** built about 1725, is situated in tranquil isolation on Hog Island off Crane's Beach, and is accessible only by boat. The house was occupied by the Choate family until 1916. The exterior remains almost exactly as it was in the 1720s. It is not open for tours, but a visit to the island conveys a strong sense of the North Shore landscape as it was in the eighteenth century. The house and island are administered by the Trustees of Reservations (508–921–1944).

In **Topsfield,** another early house of great interest to the "colonial revival" architects of the late nineteenth century is the 1683 **Parson Capen House** (1 Howlett Street, 508–887–8845). On the first floor, seventeenth-century furnishings are displayed.

Parson Capen House, Topsfield.

NEWBURYPORT

Newburyport, an old shipbuilding town at the mouth of the Merrimack River, is one of the best places to see historic houses in a wide range of styles, including Georgian, Federal, Greek Revival, and Victorian. The town's prosperity after the Revolution created the row of mansions along **High Street. Cushing House** (98 High Street, 508–462–2681) was built in 1808 for John Cushing, a sea captain whose son Caleb was the first U.S. ambassador to China. The 21-room mansion is elegantly furnished, with an excellent collection of furniture, silver, clocks, china, toys, needlework, and glassware. A garden includes plants that are over a century old. The **Market Square Historic District** preserves Newburyport's handsome waterfront commercial buildings. The **Custom House** (25 Water Street, 508–462–2681), built in 1835, now serves as a museum devoted to the town's maritime history, with ship models, navigational gear, and artifacts gathered by Newburyport's captains.

Newburyport was an offshoot of the town of **Newbury.** The **Coffin House** (14–16 High Street, Route 1-A, 617–227–3956) in Newbury was occupied by the Coffin family continuously from the 1650s until 1929, when it was acquired by the Society for the Preservation of New England Antiquities. Architectural and decorative features of the house reveal changes in New England home life across four centuries. The house is especially interesting for its two kitchens, one dating to the 1600s, the other to the 1700s; the north parlor still has its early nineteenth-century wallpaper.

In **Amesbury,** across the Merrimack River from Newburyport, is the **Rocky Hill Meetinghouse** (4 Portsmouth Road, 617–227–3956), a study property of the Society for the Preservation of New England Antiquities. Built in 1785, the meetinghouse was little used and has survived entirely unchanged from the day it was built. It has a severe appearance outside and in: There is no steeple, and inside the pews are unpainted and the wooden floor is bare; the only hint of ornament is marbleizing on the columns.

John Greenleaf Whittier Home

The abolitionist writer and poet John Greenleaf Whittier—one of the most popular American poets of the nineteenth century—lived

OPPOSITE: 1872 bank building (above) and Federal-period house in Newburyport.

here from 1836 until his death in 1892, where he wrote and edited abolitionist articles, and wrote poetry. He became nationally famous late in life with the 1866 publication of his poem, *Snow-Bound*, which earned him $10,000 in royalties. Whittier never married, but was devoted to his mother, Abigail, whose Quaker principles were responsible for the poet's hatred of slavery. The Garden Room remains the way it was when Whittier wrote here, with his desk, books, and portraits of literary friends he admired. He is buried at **Union Cemetery** on Haverhill Road, not far from the house. His birthplace in nearby Haverhill has also been restored.

LOCATION: 86 Friend Street, Amesbury. HOURS: May through October: 10–4 Tuesday–Saturday. FEE: Yes. TELEPHONE: 508–388–1337.

MERRIMACK RIVER VALLEY

The waterpower of the Merrimack River attracted the attention of Boston's industrialists in the first half of the nineteenth century, causing the factory cities of Lowell and Lawrence to be created from scratch. Haverhill, a shipbuilding port in the early decades of the nineteenth century, lost its livelihood when ocean-going ships grew too large to navigate the river, causing the town's investors to look to manufacturing. By the end of the century, Haverhill had become a leading producer of shoes.

JOHN GREENLEAF WHITTIER BIRTHPLACE

Whittier was born in this farmhouse on December 17, 1807, and lived here until he was twenty-nine. The house has been restored to this period, with his writing desk and the fireplace he described in *Snow-Bound*. Many of his poems, including "The Barefoot Boy," and "The Sycamores," were inspired by the people and places of this area.

LOCATION: Whittier Road off Route 110, East Haverhill. HOURS: Mid-April through mid-October: 10–5 Tuesday–Saturday, 1–5 Sunday. Mid-October through mid-April: 1–5 Tuesday–Friday, 10–5 Saturday, 1–5 Sunday. FEE: Yes. TELEPHONE: 508–373–3979.

LAWRENCE

Lawrence was founded in 1845 at Bodwell's Falls on the Merrimack. From the start is was purely an industrial center. In contrast to the situation at Lowell, its founders—including Abbot Lawrence, for whom it was named—gave little thought to providing adequate housing or safe working conditions for the population of workers. As a result, a poorly built factory collapsed in 1860, killing eighty-eight workers; women and children worked long hours for small wages. Finally, discontent over ten-hour workdays, high rents, and overcrowding culminated in the famous "Bread and Roses" strike in 1912, marked by murder and mass arrests. Some thirty thousand textile workers struck the mills for two months, thereby winning wage increases for textile workers throughout New England. The history of the city is chronicled at the **Lawrence Heritage State Park** (1 Jackson Street, 508–794–1655), housed in an 1847 boarding house. Exhibits trace the arrival of immigrants from Europe and the city's labor movement. The park sponsors tours of the city's old mills, canals, and the Great Stone Dam on the Merrimack.

LOWELL

Lowell was founded in the 1820s by a group of Boston investors, led by Francis Cabot Lowell. They had seen the terrible industrial slums of England and were determined to build a factory city that would be free of the social evils that manufacturing had wrought in the Old World. Not wishing to create a permanent underclass of wage slaves, the founders decided to hire farmgirls as well as men to work in the factories, believing that female workers would get married and leave their jobs in a few years. To make life as safe and as pleasant as possible, the founders built dormitories for the workers and provided for educational, recreational, and religious activities. The owners' generosity was not boundless or evenhanded, however: They paid women half the wages they paid men.

The result, for a while, was one of the wonders of the industrialized world. British visitors to Lowell, notably Charles Dickens, were amazed at the cleanliness and good order of the city, and at the apparent contentment of the workers. As Lowell grew to be one of the biggest textile-manufacturing centers in the world, the mills required more and more labor. An influx of European immigrants, poorly housed in congested quarters, changed the city's utopian character. By the end of the nineteenth century, Lowell faced the same social problems that other, less nobly intentioned industrial centers, such as Lawrence, were struggling with. In the 1920s Lowell's companies lost business to Southern mills, and the

Depression forced the closing of many remaining factories. In the 1970s and 1980s the mills and canals underwent restoration.

Lowell National Historical Park

The park sponsors a variety of guided tours (advance reservation required) on foot, by trolley, and on barges through the city's streets and canals, examining the history, architecture, and technological developments that made large-scale milling possible. The park's visitor center is in the Market Mills, built in 1828.

LOCATION: 246 Market Street. HOURS: 8:30–5 Daily. FEE: None. TELEPHONE: 508–459–1000.

At the **Lowell Heritage State Park** (25 Shattuck Street, 508–453–1950), exhibits demonstrate the technologies of waterwheels, turbines, and canal locks. The **Whistler House Museum and Parker Gallery** (243 Worthen Street, 508–452–7641), a house built in 1823 for a mill manager, was the home of the father of James Abbott McNeill Whistler. Etchings by the artist are displayed in a first-floor gallery.

OPPOSITE AND ABOVE: Lowell National Historical Park.

CHAPTER FIVE

THE
BERKSHIRES
AND THE
CONNECTICUT
RIVER
VALLEY

OPPOSITE: Williamstown, near the Massachusetts-Vermont border.

B erkshire County has been a favored refuge for writers, artists, and the wealthy for over a century. Just after the Revolution, however, the area was the scene of the short-lived
Shays' Rebellion, in which disgruntled Revolutionary War veterans
and other local men rose up against the area's aristocrats, and
threatened to seize the armory at Springfield. The veterans and
farmers did have legitimate grievances. The property of many
veterans, for example, was being seized for nonpayment of loans
and back taxes. Meanwhile lenders who bought up state government loans at a discount were being helped to collect by the government brought to power through the sacrifices of those veterans.
The rebellion ended in drunkenness and violence at Stockbridge
and Great Barrington.

For the most part, however, the sites to be seen in this area are
neither battlefields nor crude homes of colonial settlers, but rather
elegant summer "cottages" (actually enormous mansions) of the
rich and studios where writers and artists worked. No less impressive are the natural wonders of Berkshire County, such as the
Mohawk Trail, Monument Mountain, and Bartholomew's Cobble.

The mountain ranges that give the region its picturesque character are the Taconic, which runs along the New York-Massachu-
setts border, and the Hoosac, dubbed the "Berkshire barrier" because it was an obstacle to pioneers from the Connecticut River
Valley. Between the two ranges flows the Housatonic River. The
entire region is actually a plateau, fitting to an area long possessing
the sense of being a place apart.

The landscape has continually enchanted visitors, including
Henry Ward Beecher who wrote in 1855: "The endless variety of
such a country never ceases to astonish and please. At every ten
steps the aspect changes; every variation of every atmosphere, and
therefore every hour of the day, produces new effects . . . bold,
tender, deep, various!" Herman Melville said the rolling hills gave
him the feeling of the sea: "I look out of my window in the morning
when I rise as I would out of a porthole of a ship in the Atlantic."
And Oliver Wendell Holmes was fond of quipping, "The best tonic
is the Housatonic."

In 1722 a group of investors "bought" ninety-eight square
miles of land from the Housatonic Indians—a swath fifteen miles

*OPPOSITE: Chesterwood, the summer "cottage" of sculptor Daniel Chester French, designed by
Henry Bacon. The gardens are French's creation.*

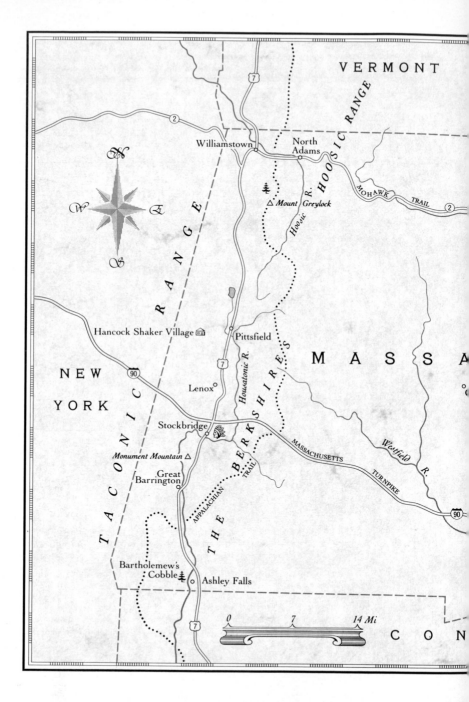

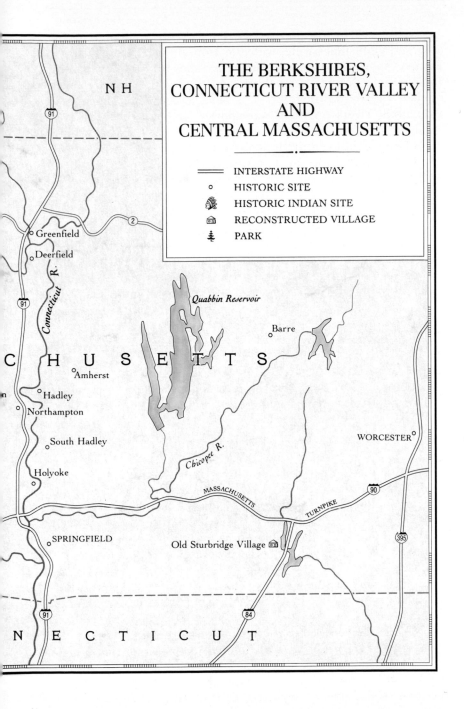

THE BERKSHIRES,
CONNECTICUT RIVER VALLEY
AND
CENTRAL MASSACHUSETTS

INTERSTATE HIGHWAY
HISTORIC SITE
HISTORIC INDIAN SITE
RECONSTRUCTED VILLAGE
PARK

N H

91

2

Greenfield

Deerfield

Connecticut R.

91

Quabbin Reservoir

Barre

C H U S E T T S

Amherst

Hadley

Northampton

South Hadley

Chicopee R.

WORCESTER

Holyoke

MASSACHUSETTS

TURNPIKE

90

395

SPRINGFIELD

Old Sturbridge Village

91

84

N E C T I C U T

long and eight miles wide, with the Housatonic River as its axis. Farmers soon began to move into the valley and the Housatonic Indians were granted a patch of land of about six square miles, dubbed Indian Town; today it is Stockbridge. The Hoosic and Housatonic rivers provided waterpower, and mills were built at Pittsfield, Adams, and North Adams, where the brick factory buildings of nineteenth-century industry can still be seen.

In the late nineteenth century, the Berkshires attracted wealthy people from New York, Boston, and Philadelphia whose community of cottages near Lenox and Stockbridge became known as "the inland Newport." Today, many of the great houses survive as museums—such as Naumkeag and The Mount—or as inns, restaurants, medical or educational facilities, or as private homes.

The Berkshires' literary history is also impressive, with such luminaries as Nathaniel Hawthorne, Herman Melville, William Cullen Bryant, Edith Wharton, Henry James, and Catherine Sedgwick, among other writers, included in the roster of those who lived and found inspiration in Berkshire County.

This chapter follows Route 7 as it runs north through the Berkshires. Although the southern region of the county remains largely farmland (in the area of Ashley Falls, Egremont, and Great Barrington), the central-Berkshires area—specifically Stockbridge and Lenox—has remained a prime resort area since the late 1800s.

ASHLEY FALLS

Ashley Falls is the site of the oldest house in Berkshire County. The **Ashley House** (Cooper Hill Road, 413–229–8600) was built in 1735 by Colonel John Ashley, one of the townsmen who drafted the 1773 Sheffield Declaration, a document which stated that men were equal and had inalienable rights to property. Ashley's slave, known as Mum Bet, remembered all the talk of personal rights and, with the aid of Judge Theodore Sedgwick, won her freedom from slavery in 1783, citing Massachusetts state law. Ashley House has been restored with some original family furnishings and other period items.

Adjacent to Ashley House, **Bartholomew's Cobble** (413–229–8600) is a nature preserve with rambling walks along the Housatonic which, here, is lazy and serpentine. The paths wind around the "cobble," a knob of quartzite and limestone that rises up from the floor of the river valley. Noted for its large variety of ferns, some of them rare, the preserve also has a small museum devoted to the flora and fauna of the Berkshires.

GREAT BARRINGTON

During the Revolution, Colonel Henry Knox hauled through Great Barrington the 43 cannon and 16 mortars Ethan Allen had captured at Fort Ticonderoga. An epic feat of logistics in which 60 tons of matériel were transported 300 miles on ox-drawn sledges in the dead of winter, it gave George Washington the firepower he needed to drive the British from Boston. Then, after the Revolution, this town was the scene for the final episode in Shays' Rebellion. After a night of looting and drinking in Stockbridge, 100 rebels and their hostages were confronted at Great Barrington by the Sheffield militia. Shooting erupted and one of the hostages, the Stockbridge schoolmaster, fell dead. Two rebels and two militiamen met the same fate before the militia won the skirmish and took Shays' men into custody.

This small farming and resort town was also the first American locality to be illuminated by electricity. Inventor William Stanley experimented with the electrical transformer here, testing it by wiring the downtown area for lights in 1886. W. E. B. Du Bois, the black writer, editor, and educator known for his pioneering contributions to the civil rights movement, was born in Great Barrington on Church Street in 1868.

MONUMENT MOUNTAIN

According to local legend, an Indian girl hurled herself from a cliff here when her love for a man was not returned. William Cullen Bryant used the legend as the basis for his poem "The Story of the Indian Girl." The mountain was also the site of a notable literary encounter in August, 1850, when David Dudley Field, Jr., introduced Nathaniel Hawthorne to Herman Melville during an afternoon's climb. Caught in a thunderstorm, the climbers, ten in all, passed the time by drinking champagne as one of them recited Bryant's tragic poem, with lightning cracking around them. Later, at the summit, Melville scrambled onto a dangerous ledge and demonstrated how sailors haul in a sheet. Hawthorne and Melville became close friends.

The view remains as spectacular today as it was in their time.

LOCATION: Route 7, north of Great Barrington.

Nathaniel Hawthorne (above left) and William Cullen Bryant (above right) both drew inspiration from the Berkshire landscape, epitomized by Monument Mountain (opposite). OVERLEAF: Detail from Norman Rockwell's 1967 painting of Stockbridge.

STOCKBRIDGE

Today a tranquil center of leisure and the arts and an enclave of great wealth, Stockbridge began as Indian Town, a curious experiment in "Englishing" the Housatonic Indians. When investors purchased the stretch of land along the Housatonic River in 1722, they set aside six square miles at present-day Stockbridge as the new home for the Housatonic Indians. Under sponsorship of the London Society for the Propagation of the Gospel in Foreign Lands, the Reverend John Sergeant, fresh from Yale, established a social experiment: The Indians would live in close companionship with a small group of English settlers in the hope that the savages would adopt English and Christian ways.

Many Indians did convert to Christianity, but the premature death of John Sergeant (who was succeeded by the famed preacher, Jonathan Edwards) removed their protector and left the Indians open to the sharp dealings of the English. As the local historian, Willard Hanna, wrote: "Within the next several decades the white settlers . . . had set such a matchless example of land-grabbing and devious entrepreneurship that the Indians sought shelter in distant reservations." The migration took place after the Revolution, in which the Indians had loyally served the American cause as scouts (their aged chief having been killed in action in New

York along with seventeen of his braves). Feeling distinctly unwelcome in their ancestral home, the Stockbridge Indians moved to New York, then to Wisconsin, where their descendants live today.

Stockbridge's picturesque Main Street is the location of several historic sites of the colonial period and the nineteenth century, and the town's quaintness was captured on canvas by Norman Rockwell (1894–1978), who spent the last twenty-five years of his life here. The **Norman Rockwell Museum** (Main Street, 413–298–3822) owns about six hundred of his works.

Red Lion Inn

The original Red Lion, built in 1773 on the stagecoach route from Boston to Albany, burned in 1896. The building seen today, still an operating inn, was erected shortly thereafter. Thus although the inn may have a colonial past, it is thoroughly Victorian in appearance. On the night of February 26, 1787, during Shays' Rebellion, some 100 rebels looted Stockbridge houses, took the occupants hostage, and descended on the inn. As their prisoners waited outside in the wintry air—and the sheriff hid in a closet—Shays' men enjoyed liquid hospitality and plotted their next move. In the morning, they rambled on to their defeat in Great Barrington.

LOCATION: Main Street. TELEPHONE: 413–298–5545.

Mission House

The Reverend John Sergeant began building this house in 1739 to be his residence and the headquarters for his missionary work. The restored house, which was moved from its original site on Eden Hill, has a fine Connecticut River Valley doorway and many eighteenth-century furnishings.

LOCATION: Main Street. HOURS: Memorial Day Weekend through Columbus Day: 11–4 Tuesday–Sunday. FEE: Yes. TELEPHONE: 413–298–3239.

The **Merwin House** (39 Main Street, 413–298–3039) was built in the Federal style around 1825. Maintained today by the Society for the Preservation of New England Antiquities, the brick house exhibits American and European furniture. The **First Congregational Church,** founded by the Reverend John Sergeant in 1734, is the parish's third church building (the previous two having been razed) and dates to 1824. The four-story tower in front of the church houses the **Children's Chimes,** a carillon dedicated by David Dudley Field to his grandchildren in 1878.

Across Main Street is the **town cemetery.** John Sergeant is buried here, near some of the Indians he converted, as are many of Stockbridge's better-known citizens including numerous members of the Sedgwick family, whose graves are arranged in a circle. There is a monument to Mum Bet, the slave freed with Judge Sedgwick's help. Down the street is the **Indian Burial Ground.**

Naumkeag

Designed by Stanford White for the New York lawyer and diplomat Joseph Hodges Choate, this twenty-three-room mansion was completed in 1886. The house and its grounds provide a fine example of the tastes of the Berkshires' well-to-do of the late nineteenth and early twentieth centuries. Choate's daughter Mabel's notable collection of Chinese porcelain and ceramics is displayed in the house, along with a sixteenth-century Flemish tapestry, depicting a hunt. A Chinese tea garden, and an outdoor

Naumkeag, designed by Stanford White for Joseph Hodges Choate.

The studio at Chesterwood, summer home of Daniel Chester French, included a segment of railroad track (opposite) *used to view his sculptures in natural light.*

stairway flanked by stands of birch trees, were both designed for her by the landscape architect Fletcher Steele.

LOCATION: Prospect Hill. HOURS: Memorial Day Weekend through third week of June: 10–5 Saturday–Sunday; Last Tuesday of June through Labor Day: 10–5 Tuesday–Sunday; Labor Day through Columbus Day: 10–5 Saturday–Sunday. FEE: Yes. TELEPHONE: 413–298-3239.

Chesterwood

Chesterwood was the summer home and studio of the sculptor Daniel Chester French from 1897 until his death in 1931. Both were designed for French by his friend Henry Bacon, architect of Washington, DC's Lincoln Memorial, and it was here that the sculptor completed the clay and plaster models of his famous statue of the seated Lincoln. The studio includes a railroad track upon which French could roll his sculptures outside to see how they looked in natural light. The 130-acre estate includes gardens and trails designed by the sculptor. The house, occupied by his daughter, Margaret, until 1973, retains many original family possessions.

LOCATION: Off Route 183. HOURS: May through October: 10–5 Daily. FEE: Yes. TELEPHONE: 413–258–3579.

LENOX

The small village of Lenox, like Stockbridge, suddenly found itself raised to the height of fashion in the late nineteenth century, when the social and financial elite of New York arrived in force to enjoy the climate and the scenery. Even around 1850, when actress Fanny Kemble proposed giving a reading for the benefit of the village poor, she was told, "but we have no poor."

Some one hundred stately cottages arose in the glens and meadows around the town. Shadow Brook, which burned down in 1956, had one hundred rooms. Built in 1893 for Anson Phelps Stokes, it was bought in 1917 by Andrew Carnegie, who died there two years later. Tours of the score of surviving Lenox cottages—all converted to a variety of uses—are offered on weekends from late July to October (413–637–1899).

The Mount

The Mount was home to novelist Edith Wharton from 1902 until 1911. Although the house and its fifty acres of grounds are undergoing extensive restoration, and the mansion has few furnishings, The Mount still embodies the architectural and design principles Wharton set forth in her 1897 book, *The Decoration of Houses*, co-written with Ogden Codman. She insisted on symmetry, even if it meant installing mirrors and false windows and false doors to attain it. The arrangement of stairs, halls, and doorways reveals her great concern with privacy. The grounds were landscaped by Wharton and her niece, the great garden designer, Beatrix Jones Farrand. While living here, Wharton wrote *Ethan Frome* and entertained numerous prominent guests, including Henry James.

LOCATION: Southern junction of Routes 7 and 7-A. HOURS: June through October: 10–5 Tuesday–Sunday. FEE: Yes. TELEPHONE: 413–637–1899.

OPPOSITE: Edith Wharton's home, The Mount.

Hawthorne Cottage

This cottage is a reproduction of the small, red farmhouse that Nathaniel Hawthorne and his family rented for eighteen months in 1850 and 1851. His wife, Sophia, called the house "the little red shanty," and the author himself remarked that it was "as red as the Scarlet Letter." Hawthorne loved the scenery of Berkshire County, and found it to be both inspiration and distraction: "I often find myself gazing at Monument Mountain, broad before my eyes, instead of at the infernal sheet of paper under my hand." During his stay here, he wrote *A Wonder Book for Girls and Boys* and *The House of the Seven Gables*. In the summer of 1850, Hawthorne met Herman Melville, who was living at Arrowhead, and the two writers became close friends.

The original cottage burned down in the 1890s, and the current house is a reconstruction based on photographs. Used as a practice studio for the musicians at Tanglewood, it contains some early nineteenth-century furnishings and Hawthorne memorabilia.

LOCATION: Hawthorne Street, part of the Tanglewood Estate. HOURS: July through August, tours given from Main Gate. FEE: None. TELEPHONE: 413–637–1600, ask for Main Gate.

PITTSFIELD

Pittsfield has been a center of paper milling since the nineteenth century. Its **Park Square Historic District** includes the **Berkshire Athenaeum,** built in 1876 in the Gothic Revival style, the Renaissance Revival **Berkshire County Courthouse,** which dates to 1872, and the 1832 Greek Revival **Town Hall.** The holdings of the **Berkshire Museum** (South Street, 413–443–7171) include paintings by artists of the Hudson River School.

Arrowhead

For thirteen years (1850–1863), this eighteenth-century farmhouse was the home of Herman Melville and his family. It was here he finished *Moby Dick* and wrote both *Pierre* and *The Confidence Man.* Melville's years at Arrowhead were not entirely happy. He had written a popular series of romantic tales of the South Seas, but the public's interest in him began to wane with the publication of *Moby Dick.* His father-in-law, Judge Lemuel Shaw, supported him with generous loans but, in 1863, Melville sold Arrowhead to his brother and returned to New York City, where a lowly job as a customs inspector awaited him. He died, virtually forgotten, in 1891.

LOCATION: 780 Holmes Road. HOURS: Memorial Day through October: 10–4:30 Monday–Saturday, 11–3:30 Sunday. FEE: Yes. TELEPHONE: 413–442–1793.

HANCOCK SHAKER VILLAGE

A museum of the Shaker way of life, Hancock Shaker Village has preserved twenty buildings designed in the Shaker style. Demonstrations are presented of Shaker farming methods, cooking, and craftsmanship in making furniture, brooms, and iron and tin ware.

Founded in 1790, this village was one of eighteen Shaker settlements operating as self-supporting communities, separate from "the World." In their architecture, crafts, and way of life, the Shakers promoted the ideals of simplicity and practicality. The furniture they made has become prized for its gracefulness, and the buildings here express this austere beauty. The round barn, built of stone in 1826, is a masterpiece of functional design—one man, standing at the center, could feed fifty-four cows at once. From a peak of some six thousand members in the 1840s, the number of American Shakers has declined to a handful, and the

The round barn at Hancock Shaker Village. OVERLEAF: *A Brethren's bedroom in the Church Family Dwelling.*

Hancock village ceased to be an active Shaker community in 1960.
It has been a museum ever since.

LOCATION: Route 20, five miles west of Pittsfield. HOURS: April
through Memorial Day and November: 10–3 Daily; Memorial Day
through October: 9:30–5 Daily. FEE: Yes. TELEPHONE: 413–443–
0188.

NORTH ADAMS

Originally settled in the 1730s, North Adams became an important
factory town in the nineteenth century. **Beaver Mill,** on Beaver
Street, its oldest portion dating to 1833, has been declared a historic landmark. Downtown, the **Monument Square** district is an area
where residences and commercial buildings from the eighteenth
and nineteenth centuries have been preserved.

Western Gateway Heritage State Park

In this park, historical exhibits detail the construction of the 4.3-
mile-long Hoosac Tunnel (1851–1875), connecting the northern
Berkshire region to the eastern part of the state and opening the
way for development. Its engineers were pioneers in many tunnel-
ing techniques, including the use of nitroglycerine for blasting
rock. Nearly two hundred men lost their lives digging the tunnel.

LOCATION: 9 Furnace Street Bypass. HOURS: 10–4:30 Daily, until 9
Thursdays. FEE: None. TELEPHONE: 413–663–6312.

WILLIAMSTOWN

The town and **Williams College** were both named for Colonel
Ephraim Williams, who wrote into his will a bequest to found a
town and a free school; he then promptly lost his life, in 1755, in
the French and Indian War. The buildings of Williams College
span several centuries of architecture, from the four-story brick
dormitory **West College,** which dates to the 1790s, to the present.

The **Sterling and Francine Clark Art Institute** (225 South
Street, 413–458–9545), one of the finest small museums in the
country, has a strong collection of French nineteenth-century
paintings, English silver, prints, and drawings. Its American holdings include furniture, silver, and paintings by Mary Cassatt, Winslow Homer, Frederic Remington, and John Singer Sargent.

OPPOSITE: *The Sterling and Francine Clark Art Institute at Williams College.*

MOHAWK TRAIL

The sixty-three-mile stretch of Route 2 from the New York–Massachusetts border to Millers Falls, Massachusetts, is called the Mohawk Trail. Opened in 1914, it remains the major access route to the northwestern corner of the state. The road follows an old trail from the Hudson Valley to the Connecticut Valley used during the French and Indian War by the Mohawk Indians as an invasion route. Traversing some of the most scenic areas of the state—with spectacular mountain views from **Whitcomb Summit, Hairpin Turn,** and **Western Summit**—it also passes through picturesque small towns such as **Florida, Charlemont, Shelburne Falls,** and **Greenfield,** just south of which is Deerfield.

CONNECTICUT RIVER VALLEY

Because Massachusetts has always been a maritime state, the Connecticut River did not play as large a role in the state's history and economy as it has in that of Connecticut. Falls and rapids at Enfield formed a barrier to ocean-going ships. The grasslands by the river inspired the town names ending in "-field"—Springfield, Deer-

Bissell Bridge, off the Mohawk Trail in Charlemont.

field, Northfield—and the name of Longmeadow. "The Grassy Banks are like a Verdant Bed," wrote a versifier, "With Choicest Flowers all Enameled. . . ." The rich farmlands along the river valley attracted farmers in the 1600s, but hostile Indians retarded settlement of the region. Springfield, settled in 1636, was burned in an Indian attack, and Deerfield suffered one of the most devastating assaults in colonial history. But the colonists held on, and farms sprouted from Springfield to Northfield. In the nineteenth century, Holyoke, Chicopee, and Springfield became important manufacturing centers for paper, textiles, and weapons.

This valley and the surrounding regions are home to a wide variety of historical sites. Factories and mills from the nineteenth century still stand at Holyoke and Springfield; Deerfield's main street is a time capsule of eighteenth-century America; and to the east and west of the river are many small towns with classic New England commons.

DEERFIELD

Perhaps the best-preserved colonial town in New England, Deerfield has twelve historic houses open to the public. Displaying

The ca. 1743 Sheldon-Hawks House, Deerfield.

superb collections of New England furniture and decorative objects, these houses are among the sixty-five eighteenth- and nineteenth-century dwellings stretching a mile along **The Street,** Deerfield's main thoroughfare.

Settled in 1669, Deerfield was an exposed outpost in the wilderness for decades. In South Deerfield, **Bloody Brook Monument,** an obelisk and tablet completed in 1838, commemorates the deaths of sixty-four men in a fight with the Indians on September 18, 1675, during King Philip's War. An even bloodier encounter awaited Deerfield's settlers, however—one that would give the town an unwanted fame. In February 1704, Frenchmen led about 350 Indians in a dawn raid on the town. A survivor of the attack, the Reverend John Williams, wrote, "not long before the break of day, the enemy came in like a flood upon us; our watch being unfaithful." In five hours they killed forty-nine people and burned about half the town. They rounded up one hundred and twelve prisoners and marched them three hundred miles, in the dead of winter, to Canada. Twenty died on the way. Deerfield managed to survive and settlers returned in 1706, helping to make the town into a small but prosperous agricultural center.

The town's historic properties are maintained by Historic Deerfield, Inc., a nonprofit organization. All museums may be visited by guided tour only and tickets may be purchased at the **Information Center** located in the **Hall Tavern.** A walking tour of the village starts at the north end of The Street at the Wright House and proceeds south.

Across from Hall Tavern are the buildings and campus of **Deerfield Academy,** a preparatory school founded in 1797. A superb collection of Federal furniture and ceramics is displayed in **Wright House,** a Federal style brick house, built in 1824 by Asa Stebbins for his son. Behind it is located the **Boyden Carriage Collection.**

The **Helen Geier Flynt Textile Museum,** in a converted 1872 barn, houses a collection of needlework, textiles, and clothing from the seventeenth, eighteenth, and nineteenth centuries. **The Henry N. Flynt Silver and Metalware Collection** displays American and English silver and pewter, including items by Paul Revere. A re-created silversmith's shop is also in the house. Built about 1720, the **Allen House** displays the furniture, needlework, and household

OPPOSITE: Chippendale chairs in the north parlor, Sheldon-Hawks House.

Deerfield doorways: The Dwight House (above left) *and the Ashley House* (above right).

items collected by the husband and wife who founded Historic Deerfield, Inc., Mr. and Mrs. Henry N. Flynt.

The **Asa Stebbins House** was built in 1799 and enlarged about 1810. The entrance hall is notable for its spiral staircase, elegant New England furniture, and exuberant French wallpaper made by the noted firm of Joseph Dufour, which provided wallpaper to many fashionable American houses in the early nineteenth century. The paper in the Stebbins house depicts the South Sea voyages of Captain Cook. The **Frary House,** built about 1740, displays a collection of furniture, pewter, and ceramics. A tavern was added to it in the 1790s, with a stylish ballroom.

A chronological series of period rooms, which provide fine examples of what life was like in Deerfield houses from 1725 to 1760, can be seen in the **Wells-Thorn House.** The seven rooms contain antique and reproduction furniture, as well as reproduction wallpapers and historically accurate paint colors.

The **Wilson Printing Office,** built in 1816, re-creates an early nineteenth-century printing office and cabinetmaker's studio. The **Dwight House** was originally located in Springfield, where it was built in the 1720s or 1730s. Moved here in 1954, the house today contains a collection of Deerfield-area furniture originally owned by the Williams family of the Connecticut River Valley. The **Indian House Memorial** is a reconstruction of the town's oldest dwelling, with reproductions of period furnishings and artifacts from early Deerfield. (Separate admission fee.)

The **Sheldon-Hawks House,** built about 1743, provides a contrast with the Wells-Thorn house. Built some twenty-five years later, it boasts panelling and plaster. The house displays a fine collection of furniture and a restored kitchen. The **Ashley House** was the home of the Reverend Jonathan Ashley, who came to Deerfield in 1732. His descendants occupied the house until 1869. The house displays a very fine collection of eighteenth-century New England furniture.

LOCATION: Information Center, Hall Tavern. HOURS: 9:30–4:30 Monday–Saturday, 11–4:30 Sunday. FEE: Yes. TELEPHONE: 413–774–5581.

Memorial Hall Museum

Housed in a building designed by Asher Benjamin and erected in 1798, the museum features period rooms and collections of photographs, Indian artifacts, quilts, and musical instruments. The most treasured exhibit is the doorway of the John Sheldon House, a remarkable relic which bears the marks of a ferocious battering by the Indians during the 1704 "Massacre," a large hole having been chopped through its center. The door was salvaged from the 1698 Sheldon house when it was demolished in the 1840s.

LOCATION: Memorial Street. HOURS: 10–4:30 Daily. FEE: Yes. TELEPHONE: 413–774–7476.

NORTHAMPTON

Settled in 1654, Northampton survived Indian attacks to become the seat of Hampshire County and later an important industrial and educational center. The famed minister Jonathan Edwards preached in Northampton for twenty-three years, until 1750, when the congregation dismissed him due to a theological dispute, and he moved to Stockbridge. **Smith College** for women was founded here in 1875. The campus (Elm Street) has some notable buildings in the Gothic Revival style. Calvin Coolidge, governor of Massachusetts and U.S. president, lived in Northampton for most of his life. **Forbes Library** (20 West Street) displays some of his memorabilia in the Coolidge Room. **Northampton Historical Society** (46 Bridge

Street, 413–584–6011) has restored three historic properties—**Parsons House** (ca. 1712), **Shepherd House** (ca. 1798) and its barn, and **Damon House** (1813)—all of which present changing exhibits on local history and have some period rooms.

WILLIAM CULLEN BRYANT HOMESTEAD

Poet and editor William Cullen Bryant was born in 1794 at this 23-room mansion in Cummington, and he spent his early and late years here. After working as a lawyer in Great Barrington, the already well-known poet (from the 1817 publication of "Thanatopsis") moved to New York in 1825, where he edited the *Evening Post.* He bought his old family homestead and its 189-acre grounds in 1865, and it was here that he spent the last years of his life, writing poetry and translating the *Iliad* and *Odyssey.* Today, the house is a preserve for many family items, and it provides a chance to witness the beautiful natural setting that inspired many of Bryant's poems.

LOCATION: Off Route 9 on 112 South, Cummington. HOURS: Last weekend of June through Labor Day: 1–5 Friday–Sunday; Labor Day through Columbus Day: 1–5 Saturday–Sunday. FEE: Yes. TELEPHONE: 413–634–2244.

The study at the William Cullen Bryant Homestead, Cummington.

HADLEY

Housed in a restored barn dating to 1782, the **Hadley Farm Museum** (Route 9) exhibits farm implements, a stagecoach, and broommaking machines. The **Porter-Phelps-Huntington House Museum** (130 River Drive/Route 47, 413–584–4699), also known as Forty Acres, contains a collection of one family's possessions that illustrates the changing ways of life experienced in the Connecticut River Valley over ten generations. The house was built in 1752 and has remained unchanged architecturally since 1799. Neither a restoration nor a reproduction, it has been called the best preserved Colonial house in New England.

AMHERST

Settled in 1703 and named for Lord Jeffrey Amherst, a British general in the French and Indian War, this town is situated on a plateau surrounded by hills. Amherst was a farming village in its early days, but water power provided by two streams led to the development of a papermill after the Revolution, and woolen mills in the 1830s. **Amherst College** was founded in 1821 to train young men for the ministry, Calvin Coolidge and Henry Ward Beecher being among its graduates. Helen Hunt Jackson, who wrote popular novels such as *Ramona* under the pseudonym H.H., lived at 83 Pleasant Street. Amherst was also the home of one of America's greatest poets, Emily Dickinson. There is a tourist information booth on the town common.

Emily Dickinson House

Emily Dickinson (1830–1886) was born and died in this Federal style brick house built by her grandfather, and she wrote most of her poetry here—nearly 1,800 poems. Only ten of these were published in her lifetime, however, and a complete edition did not appear until 1955. She lived as a recluse. After her father's death in 1874, she left the 14-acre grounds only once, when her nephew died next door. Her sister discovered the neatly bound sheafs of poems after Emily's death. Although the bulk of Dickinson's furniture and personal effects are at Harvard, curators have re-created her writing room here with appropriate furniture and photographs of the writers she admired.

LOCATION: 280 Main Street. HOURS: Very limited, appointment required. FEE: Yes. TELEPHONE: 413–542–8161.

Further Dickinson material may be seen at the **Jones Library** (43 Amity Street), which displays a collection of her manuscripts, portraits, and a reconstruction of her writing room in miniature. The library also has a large collection of manuscripts and other items pertaining to the poet Robert Frost, who taught at Amherst. The **Strong House Museum** (67 Amity Street, 413–256–0678) exhibits furniture, clothing, china, and other household items in a 1744 house. There is also an eighteenth-century garden on the grounds. The collections of the **Pratt Museum of Geology** (Amherst College campus, 413–542–2165) contain meteorites, fossils (including an enormous mastodon skeleton), and Indian artifacts, and displays are devoted to evolution, ecology, and geology. The museum's notable collection of dinosaur-track fossils from the Connecticut Valley may be seen by appointment.

SOUTH HADLEY

Settled in the 1650s by farmers, South Hadley is the site of the nation's oldest college for women, **Mount Holyoke College,** founded in 1837. The **Joseph Skinner Museum** (Route 116, 413–538–2085) has eclectic collections of Indian artifacts, farm equipment, stuffed birds, and medieval armor, all exhibited in a church rescued from the town of Prescott, now under the Quabbin Reservoir.

HOLYOKE

For the first century of its existence (it was settled in 1745), Holyoke was a farming community; but its location on the Hadley Falls of the Connecticut River attracted investors from Boston in the 1840s. To harness the river's power, they built a dam—which promptly collapsed—and then another, which held and provided the power for a variety of mills. Four and a half miles of canals still channel water through the city. The **Holyoke Heritage State Park** (221 Appleton Street, 413–534–0909) chronicles the city's industrial history through exhibits, audio-visual presentations, and walking tours of the mills and the housing built for workers. A five-mile train trip through the town can be made on vintage 1920s passenger cars, with a tour guide.

   Wistariahurst Museum (238 Cabot Street, 413–534–2216), once the mansion of silk manufacturer William Skinner, boasts a marble lobby, stained-glass windows by Tiffany & Co., a spacious hall for entertainments, and elegant Victorian furnishings. The Carriage House exhibits Native American artifacts.

SPRINGFIELD

Located on the east bank of the Connecticut River, Springfield has been an important manufacturing center since the federal government established an armory here in 1794. The town had already been a federal arsenal, target of an unsuccessful raid by Daniel Shays and his followers in 1786. In the nineteenth century, Springfield's factories and mills produced textiles, pianos, cigars, jewelry, swords, and leather. Abolitionist John Brown lived here and made it an important station on the underground railroad that aided fugitive slaves.

Architecturally important nineteenth-century residences have been preserved in the **Matoon Street Historic District,** an area of fine rowhouses, and the **Maple Street Historic District,** a stretch of Greek Revival and Second Empire brick homes. The **Court Square Historic District,** a complex of civic and commercial buildings, is notable for the **Old First Church,** which dates to 1819, and the **Hampden County Courthouse,** a granite structure designed by Henry Hobson Richardson. On the north side of the square stands a 300-foot-tall **campanile,** built in 1913.

The Quadrangle

The cultural centerpiece of the city, the Quadrangle is the site of four important museums and a major public library. The **Museum of Fine Arts** (413–732–6092) contains twenty galleries covering fifteen centuries of art, including works by Chardin, Monet, Copley, Frankenthaler, Sargent, and Remington. The **George Walter Vincent Smith Art Museum** (413–733–4214), established in 1899, houses the eclectic collection of the eccentric Victorian entrepreneur whose name it bears. An avid collector of Oriental arms and armor, jade, porcelain, cloisonne, and bronzes, Smith also built a good collection of nineteenth-century American paintings and sculpture. The **Connecticut Valley Historical Museum** (413–732–3080), situated in a stone mansion, documents 350 years of area history with period rooms (some removed intact from houses in the Valley), and exhibits of furniture, arts, household items, and crafts. Folk art is also displayed. The **Science Museum** (413–733–1191)

OVERLEAF: *Thomas Cole's painting* The Oxbow *(detail).*

has the oldest American-built planetarium, dating to 1937, as well as exhibits of dinosaurs and American Indian life.

Springfield Armory National Historic Site

Springfield weapons have played a major part in many American conflicts. The armory opened after the Revolution, but from the late eighteenth century until World War II it produced the shoulder arms American infantrymen carried into battle. The M1903 "Springfield Rifle" was the U.S. Army's standard issue during World War I, and it won a reputation for reliability and accuracy. During World War II, the armory manufactured the M-1 rifle. It was made famous by Henry Wadsworth Longfellow, who visited here on his honeymoon trip and later wrote "The Arsenal at Springfield." The facility closed in 1968 and one building has been converted to a museum displaying firearms and related material.

LOCATION: Armory Square, off Federal Street. HOURS: 8:30–4:30 Daily—undergoing renovation, call to confirm. FEE: None. TELE-PHONE: 413–734–8551.

The **Storrowtown Village Museum** (West Springfield, 413–787–0136), founded in 1929, is a re-created New England village. Thirteen buildings dating to the eighteenth and nineteenth centuries were brought here from other sites. Included are houses, a meeting house, school, herb garden, and shops.

OLD STURBRIDGE VILLAGE

Located on two hundred acres of farmland, forest, and gardens, Sturbridge Village is an authentic re-creation of a rural New England community of the early nineteenth century. Since it opened in 1946, the Village has steadily grown to encompass forty historical buildings, moved to the site from other locations in New England. Along with the 1832 Baptist church in the Greek Revival style are the fine homes of the Center Village families, which face the common, such as the 1704 **Fenno House** from Canton, Massachusetts, and the 1735 **Stephen Fitch House** from Willimantic, Connecticut. Artisans' shops with actual demonstrations of trade include: blacksmith, printer, tinner, cooper, and potter. In addition, a law office, bank, and school are among the Village's "public

OPPOSITE: Baptist church (above) on the common at Old Sturbridge Village, and fenced pastures (below) at the village's Pliny Freeman Farm.

buildings." Galleries exhibit antique timepieces, glass, guns and militia accoutrements, and lighting equipment.

There is real work going on here. Shoe leather is cut and sewn with waxed thread at the shoe shop, while by the common the tinner produces the tinware pails, baking pans, and milkpans sold locally and to villages on the frontier, through peddlers. These vessels competed with the potter's wares—that craft demonstrated at the village kiln, woodshed, clay mill, and pot shop.

Just outside the Center Village proper is the **Pliny Freeman Farm,** where nineteenth-century agricultural processes are practiced today. All the usual tasks of a farming family, such as maple sugaring, weaving cloth, mending fences, gardening, and tending the animals, are done as they were in the early 1800s. The **Mill Neighborhood** has water-powered saw, grist, and carding mills.

The Village has costumed interpreters who carry on the daily activities of 1830s farmers, townsmen and women, artisans, millers, smiths, and other workers. It re-creates the whole rural economy in microcosm, with religious and political events punctuating the daily and seasonal rhythm of village life and farm work.

LOCATION: Route 20. HOURS: May through October: 9–5 Daily; November: 10–4 Daily; December through April: 10–4 Tuesday–Sunday. FEE: Yes. TELEPHONE: 508–347–3362.

WORCESTER

Located in a hilly region at the geographic center of New England, Worcester is the only major industrial city in the United States not situated on a river, lake, or sea coast. In the nineteenth century, steam powered Worcester's mills and factories (which made such products as wire, nails, textiles, and paper), and in the 1820s a group of investors solved the city's transportation problems by digging a canal to Providence. The **Blackstone Canal,** one stretch of which can still be seen at Uxbridge and Northbridge, operated until it was replaced by the railroad in 1848.

Two historic districts preserve the character of Worcester's nineteenth-century life. The **Oxford-Crown Historic District** dates from the 1830s to the Civil War. The more elaborate houses of the **Massachusetts Avenue Historic District** were built in the late 1800s and early 1900s by the city's leading citizens. The **Salis-**

bury Mansion (40 Highland Street, 508–753–8278) was built in 1772 for the merchant, Stephen Salisbury. It has been restored with furnishings dating to the 1830s. The Renaissance Revival **Mechanics Hall** (321 Main Street), completed in 1857, was built as a music hall for the city's laborers, and still holds concerts.

The **Worcester Historical Museum** (39 Salisbury Street, 508–753–8278) contains exhibits on local history. The **American Antiquarian Society** (185 Salisbury Street, 508–755–5221), founded in 1812, maintains a research library of early American history, literature, and culture, and owns one of the country's most important collections of printed matter. The collections include close to three million books, newspapers, pamphlets, prints, broadsides, manuscripts, maps, sheet music, and serials. The Society was founded by Isaiah Thomas, whose newspaper, *The Massachusetts Spy,* championed the patriot cause in the difficult and dangerous years before the Revolution. On July 14, 1776, Thomas gave the first public reading in New England of the Declaration of Independence.

Another Worcester museum established by a private citizen is the **Higgins Armory Museum** (100 Barber Avenue, 508–853–6015). John W. Higgins, president of the Worcester Pressed Steel Company, was fascinated by the metallurgical achievements of armorers in the Middle Ages and the Renaissance. He gathered a large collection of armor and displayed it in this great hall inspired by a medieval Austrian castle.

Worcester Art Museum

Among its comprehensive holdings of fifty centuries of world art, this museum houses one of New England's finest collections of American paintings. The substantial American collection also includes one of the most famous and most frequently reproduced paintings in American art, *The Peaceable Kingdom,* painted in about 1833 by Edward Hicks, a Quaker. Samuel F. B. Morse, George Inness, Winslow Homer, Mary Cassatt, John Singer Sargent, and James Abbott McNeill Whistler are also represented, and there is also a gallery devoted to American decorative arts.

LOCATION: 55 Salisbury Street. HOURS: 9–4 Tuesday–Friday, 12–5 Saturday, 1–5 Sunday. FEE: Yes. TELEPHONE: 508–799–4406.

HARTFORD
AND
CENTRAL
CONNECTICUT

OPPOSITE: Gilded dome of the Connecticut State Capitol in Hartford.

Hartford, Wethersfield, and Windsor comprise the heartland of English settlement in Connecticut. These were the first three towns the English established in the state to compete with the Dutch. The first European to explore the Connecticut River had been a Dutchman, Adriaen Block, who voyaged up the river as far as the Enfield Falls in 1614. The Dutch set up a post at Hartford, but gave it up when the English arrived.

In the 1630s furs, farm land, and freedom brought settlers to this region from Massachusetts, where beaver and land were growing scarce and the government restrictive. Thomas Hooker arrived in Hartford, with his congregation from Cambridge, in 1636. His views of government had been broader than those of the rulers of Boston, though not democratic. He believed a governing body should be elected by "the people" (male Congregationalists).

It was difficult for a farmer to prosper in the 1600s unless he had ample pasture land for cattle. If a farmer could sell a few cattle every year, it yielded the necessary cash to buy farm equipment, clothing, and perhaps a few luxury items from England. Timber was another resource that lured the farmers: The West Indian plantation owners needed barrels in which to ship their rum and molasses, and Connecticut provided the staves, which were sometimes coopered into barrels on the voyage south. Other central Connecticut products included cattle, horses, beef, pork, and wheat. The Connecticut River offered easy access to the sea, and the treeless flood plains bordering the river were fertile, lush with grass for grazing, and free of the glacial boulders that made tilling so difficult in Massachusetts.

Central Connecticut was home to Yankee ingenuity and the Yankee Peddler. In the eighteenth and nineteenth centuries, peddlers from Berlin and other towns ranged all over the country to sell Connecticut's tinware, locks, clocks, and other household items, and they may have been the inventors of the installment plan. Yankee thrift had its cruel side too: Instead of building a proper prison, Connecticut confined its criminals in an abandoned mine in East Granby until 1827.

Wethersfield and Windsor preserve many signs of early settlement. Hartford is no longer "Colonial" in style, but has two state capitols, as well as the Wadsworth Atheneum and the Mark Twain House, both important in American literary history.

OPPOSITE: Detail from Frederic E. Church's Thomas Hooker and Company Journeying through the Wilderness from Plymouth to Hartford in 1636, *painted in 1846.*

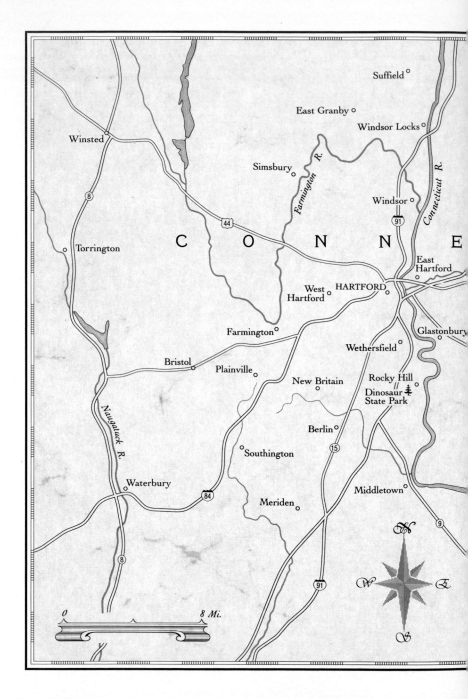

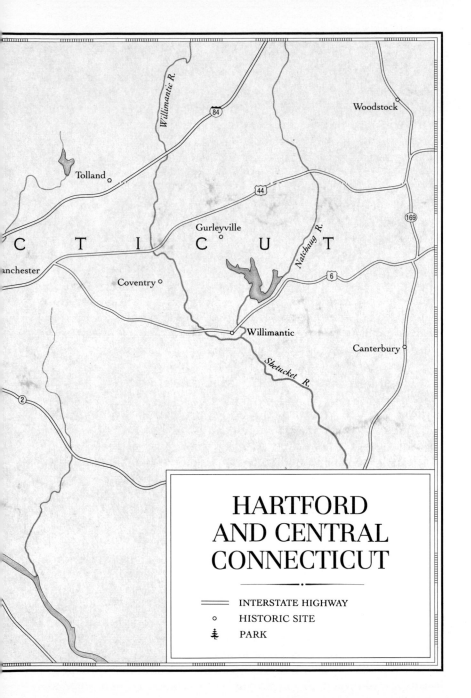

HARTFORD
AND CENTRAL
CONNECTICUT

INTERSTATE HIGHWAY
○   HISTORIC SITE
🌲   PARK

HARTFORD

The capital of the state only since 1875, Hartford was one of the earliest English settlements in Connecticut. The Dutch had arrived first, in 1633, when they built a trading post and a fort on the Connecticut River, but the English at Hartford, Windsor, and Wethersfield came to dominate commerce with the Indians, so the Dutch left in 1654. The English settlement was founded in 1635 by John Steele and sixty or so companions, who were followed in 1636 by the Reverend Thomas Hooker and his band of one hundred Puritans (most of them women and children). Restive under the stern theological rule of the Massachusetts Bay Colony, they made a two-week trek to the site from Cambridge, Massachusetts. Hartford and the neighboring settlements prospered from trade in furs, timber, fish, and tobacco, but one issue provoked uneasiness: The colony had no legal right to exist. In 1662 Governor John Winthrop, Jr., traveled to England and, by unknown means, persuaded King Charles II to grant a generous royal charter that legally established the Connecticut Colony, recognized its self-government, and set boundaries from Narragansett Bay to the Pacific. The colony of New Haven was swallowed up, against its will.

The charter was the object of one of the most famous, and most curious incidents in Colonial lore. In 1686 King James II decided to take New England under his personal control and appointed the authoritarian Edmund Andros governor. The story goes that Andros appeared in Hartford to collect the charter, which was placed before him one October afternoon amidst a long discussion about the legalities of his tenure. As the sun set, candles were brought, and were suddenly extinguished. In the darkness, the tradition maintains, the charter was whisked from under the nose of Andros and spirited away to be hidden in the hollow of a great oak tree, known thereafter as the Charter Oak. In 1689, when William and Mary came to the throne, the colony's rights were restored, and the charter was brought out of hiding in 1715.

Hartford's prosperity as a shipping center grew through the 1700s. In 1794 a partnership of wealthy citizens organized by Jeremiah Wadsworth began to offer fire and shipping insurance. The Hartford Fire Insurance Company was founded in 1810, and the city's firms developed a reputation for reliability in the face of catastrophes that wiped out less stable firms. Shipping and manufacturing continued to enrich the city, thanks to men such as

The Senate Chamber of the Old State House.

Samuel Colt, the inventor of the revolver. The blue-onion dome of the **Colt Armory** (not open to the public) is a landmark easily visible from the highway. His mansion, **Armswear** (80 Wethersfield Avenue, 203–246–4025), has been converted to a private rest home, but the public may view the small collection of Coltiana in the drawing room. In **Colt Park,** a monument to the inventor depicts him whittling his gun out of wood at the age of sixteen. Colt could not convince government bureaucrats of the usefulness of his revolver, but General Zachary Taylor demanded them for his soldiers during the Mexican-American War, and the ensuing onrush of orders made Colt enormously wealthy.

Old State House

The first building built as a state house after the ratification of the Constitution, the Old State House was designed by Charles Bulfinch and erected between 1792 and 1796. It is a graceful work of the Federal style, quite similar to Bulfinch's state house in Boston.

In 1879 it became the city hall, and then fell into disuse in 1915, but the building has since been carefully restored. The Senate Chamber displays a portrait of George Washington by Gilbert Stuart. The city's visitor center is located here.

LOCATION: 800 Main Street. HOURS: 10–5 Monday–Saturday, 12–5 Sunday. FEE: None. TELEPHONE: 203–522–6766.

Wadsworth Atheneum

The nation's oldest public art museum, the Atheneum opened in 1844 in a Gothic Revival building designed by Ithiel Town and Alexander Jackson Davis. Named for Daniel Wadsworth, the force behind its founding and early financing (the civic-minded Wadsworth moved his own house to clear space for the original art gallery), the Atheneum has a superb collection of European and American art, including Colonial furniture. Also included in the museum's holdings are important Hudson River School paintings (the artist Frederic E. Church, born in Hartford in 1826, was a close friend of Daniel Wadsworth). John Trumbull, who married Wadsworth's niece, bequeathed some of his paintings to the museum. A collection of Colt firearms is also on display.

LOCATION: 600 Main Street. HOURS: 11–5 Tuesday–Sunday. FEE: Yes. TELEPHONE: 203–278–2670.

State Capitol

Richard Upjohn designed this exuberant building, a marble and granite monument to the state's rousing success in business. It was completed in 1879 at a cost of two and a half million dollars. The restraint of the old Bulfinch State House was overwhelmed by the new building's massive facade and lofty towers. The capitol is topped by a gilded dome, added by Upjohn, it is said, at the insistence of Hartford's citizens, who thought that a capitol should have a dome whether or not it was appropriate to the design. Within, the humble citizen is awed by echoing marble floors, brass appointments, painted columns, and stained glass. The capitol provokes various architectural opinions: Frank Lloyd Wright called it, "the most ridiculous building I know of." On permanent exhibit are figureheads from the flagship *Hartford* and the U.S.S. *Connecticut*, a wagonwheel from the Civil War inscribed with the dates of various battles, and the original plaster of Paris model of the statue *Genius*, which stood on the capitol dome. Blown off in a hurricane, it was melted down for bullets in World War I. There is also a Hall of Flags, lined with banners from the Civil, Spanish-American, and two World Wars.

LOCATION: Capitol Avenue and Trinity Street. HOURS: 9–3 Monday–Friday. FEE: None. TELEPHONE: 203–240–0222.

Butler-McCook Homestead

This homestead is an eighteenth-century house that was occupied by the Butler and McCook families until 1971. The oldest portion of the house, the kitchen area, was built in 1782 as a blacksmithy and butcher shop. The house displays furniture from the eighteenth to early twentieth centuries and a family collection of silver, china, bronzes, and Oriental armor. Also on exhibit are children's toys and books.

LOCATION: 396 Main Street. HOURS: Mid-May through mid-October: 12–4 Tuesday, Thursday, Saturday, Sunday. FEE: Yes. TELEPHONE: 203–522–1806.

The **First Church of Christ** (Main and Gold streets) was built in 1807, possibly from a design by Daniel Wadsworth. The one-and-a-half-ton bell in the steeple contains portions of the bell carried to Hartford by Thomas Hooker and his congregation from Cambridge, Massachusetts, in 1636. The adjacent **Ancient Burying Ground** was begun in 1640 and is the site of the graves of the city's early leaders and citizens.

The **Charter Oak Memorial** (corner of Charter Oak Avenue and Charter Oak Place), a granite column erected in 1906, stands on the approximate site of the Charter Oak where, according to tradition, the charter was hidden in 1687. Even before the oak attained its place in Hartford's history, it had been a sacred tree to the local Indians, who held councils in its shade and made their spring plantings when the oak's leaves had grown to the size of a mouse's ear. When a windstorm toppled the oak on August 21, 1856, its fall provoked an outpouring of civic grief. Samuel Colt dispatched his company band to play funeral music by the side of the tree. The local poet Lydia Sigourney composed an elegy. Botanists measured its girth (thirty-three feet), counted the oak's rings, and pronounced its age to be nearly a millennium. Mementoes of all sorts were made from the oak—a frame for the charter, a chair for the lieutenant governor, a cradle for Samuel Colt's son.

Samuel Clemens, his wife, Olivia, and three of their children.

Connecticut Historical Society Museum

The museum displays a collection of seventeenth- and eighteenth-century furniture and portraits, and a wide-ranging collection of Connecticut's manufactures, including silver, pewter, glass, and clocks, and items such as a sword owned by General Israel Putnam and Nathan Hale's powder horn.

LOCATION: 1 Elizabeth Street. HOURS: 12–5 Tuesday–Sunday; Closed Saturday June through August. FEE: None. TELEPHONE: 203–236–5621.

Raymond E. Baldwin Museum of Connecticut History

The museum has a permanent exhibition, "To Shape a State," that surveys the development of manufacturing in the state from the 1790s to the present. The exhibit focuses on the manufacture of firearms, machine tools, fabricated metals, and textiles, displaying a musket made by Eli Whitney's armory, Colt firearms, Terryville clocks, household appliances, a Pratt and Whitney engine, and photographs that document manufacturing processes. The museum also exhibits portraits of Connecticut's governors and the Royal Charter issued to the colony in 1662 by King Charles II.

LOCATION: 231 Capitol Avenue. HOURS: 9–4:45 Monday–Friday, 9–12:45 Saturday. FEE: None. TELEPHONE: 203–566–3056.

Mark Twain House

After a childhood in Hannibal, Missouri, and a young-manhood in rough-and-tumble California and Nevada, the author of *The Adventures of Huckleberry Finn, Life on the Mississippi,* and *Roughing It* lived for seventeen years among Connecticut Yankees in a house of Victorian splendor. Samuel Clemens visited his publisher in Hartford in 1868 and found the city to be one of the most beautiful places he had ever seen: "A vision of refreshing green," where the houses were more like "massive private hotels."

The section of Hartford he chose was called Nook Farm, a 140-acre neighborhood favored by writers, among them Harriet Beecher Stowe, Charles Dudley Warner, and William Gillette. He hired the architect Edward Tuckerman Potter to design this house, one with enough dash and daring to satisfy the author and his wife, at a cost of more than $100,000. A reporter for the *Hartford Daily Times* took one look at this architectural extravaganza and wrote that it was one of the "oddest looking buildings in the state ever designed for a dwelling." The exterior walls are decorated with stripes of vermillion and black, and the steep slate roof is adorned with diamond-shaped patterns in three colors. There are five balconies and three turrets (one of them octagonal and fifty feet high). In every one of the nineteen rooms can be seen Clemens's love of color, ornament, and lavish expenditure. He had a window set directly over a fireplace so that he could see flames and snowflakes

OVERLEAF: Library of the Mark Twain House, Hartford.

at the same time. Clemens redecorated the house in 1881, retaining the firm of Associated Artists, led by Louis Comfort Tiffany, who designed a large and comfortable library for Clemens. But the children took over the room and the author ended up working in his third-floor billiard room.

The **Harriet Beecher Stowe House,** adjacent to the Twain house, was Stowe's home from 1873 to 1896. Although she is best remembered as the author of *Uncle Tom's Cabin,* which brought her worldwide fame when it was published in 1852, she wrote thirty books in her long literary career. The house is furnished with many items belonging to the author.

LOCATION: 77 Forest Street. HOURS: June through October: 9:30–4:30 Daily; November through May: 9:30–4 Tuesday–Saturday, 1–4 Sunday. FEE: Yes. TELEPHONE: 203–525–9317.

EAST HARTFORD

East Hartford has been a manufacturing center since the 1780s. The town's main industries entailed the manufacture of paper, cotton, watches, and hats. General Rochambeau's French troops camped here during the Revolution. The site of the encampment is marked with a plaque on the corner of Lawrence Street and Silver Lane, so named because the troops were paid in silver—such an exceedingly rare commodity at the time that the townspeople never forgot where they had seen it. The Rochambeau plaque shows a bag of silver coins. The restored **Huguenot House** (307 Burnside Avenue, 203–528–0716) was built by a saddlemaker in 1761. A one-room schoolhouse and blacksmith shop are on the grounds.

WEST HARTFORD

Noah Webster, the compiler of the first American dictionary, was born in a farmhouse here in 1758. Now the **Noah Webster House & Museum** (227 South Main Street, 203–521–5362), it displays some of Webster's books, papers, household items, and his desk. The adjacent museum has changing exhibits about Webster and other historical subjects. The **Sarah Whitman Hooker House** (1237 New Britain Avenue, 203–523–5887) has been restored with period furnishings. During the Revolution, British officers who had been captured in Ethan Allen's raid on Fort Ticonderoga were held at this house.

OPPOSITE: Stairway of the Twain House, Hartford.

WETHERSFIELD

Wethersfield and Windsor both claim to be the first permanent English settlement in the state. Wethersfield is an exceptionally well-preserved eighteenth-century town because, like Litchfield, it neither endured nor enjoyed a nineteenth-century manufacturing boom that would have wiped out the early buildings. Thus, Wethersfield is one of the best places in New England to see old Colonial homes. The **Wethersfield Historical Society** (150 Main Street, 203–529–7656), housed in the 1804 Old Academy Museum, displays a collection of local historical artifacts. The 1793 **Captain James Francis House** (120 Hartford Avenue, 203–529–7656) features nine rooms of furnishings from the eighteenth and nineteenth centuries.

The town was settled in 1634 by men from Watertown, Massachusetts. The **Ancient Burying Ground** behind the Congregational Church has some of the oldest graves of Connecticut settlers. The April 1637 "Wethersfield Massacre," in which Pequot Indians killed nine people and kidnapped two girls, touched off the bloody and brutal Pequot War.

Its site on the Connecticut River made Wethersfield an early center of shipbuilding and trade with the West Indies. As early as the 1640s, the town was exporting barrel staves, fish, salt beef, corn, and pork. After 1700 the lucrative exports included horses, lumber, beaver skins, bricks, and onions, for which Wethersfield was particularly famous. In return, the town received rum, molasses, sugar, and wool. **Cove Warehouse** (Cove Park, 203–529–7656), where seagoing ships loaded and unloaded their goods, is America's only remaining warehouse from the seventeenth century. In the late 1600s floods changed the course of the Connecticut River, transforming Wethersfield's harbor into a cove and causing the town to move its shipping operations to nearby Rocky Hill. Many Colonial houses can be seen in the **historic district** along Main, Broad, State, Garden, Elm, Marsh, and Hart streets, Middletown Avenue, and Hartford Avenue. Most were built by sea captains, and today are privately owned and not open to the public.

Buttolph-Williams House

With its overhanging second story and small casement windows, the Buttolph-Williams House, like the Stanley-Whitman House in

Farmington, evokes the medieval character of the 1600s. In fact, the house was probably built between 1715 and 1725 for an affluent family. The interior has been accurately restored with antiques from Wethersfield and other parts of Connecticut.

LOCATION: 249 Broad Street. HOURS: May through October: 12–4 Tuesday–Sunday. FEE: Yes. TELEPHONE: 203–247–8996.

Webb-Deane-Stevens Museum

This complex of three houses illustrates aspects of daily life in Wethersfield from the middle of the eighteenth century to the early nineteenth. The **Webb House** was built in 1752 by a prosperous West Indies merchant, Joseph Webb. He died in 1761 and his widow married a lawyer, Silas Deane, who built the **Deane House**

The Deane (left) *and Webb* (right) *houses, Wethersfield.*

next door. Deane was the nation's first diplomat abroad. He served in France during the Revolution, and recruited Lafayette, Steuben, de Kalb, and Pulaski to the American cause. Deane came under a cloud of suspicion, charged with profiteering and treason, but the allegations were later said to be "a gross injustice" and Congress voted $37,000 to his heirs in 1842 as restitution.

In May 1781 the Webb House was the meeting site for an important conference between George Washington and the Comte de Rochambeau, commander of French forces in America. It has often been written that they laid plans for the decisive Yorktown campaign here. They did discuss plans for a joint operation at Yorktown, but they actually agreed to attack at New York City. It was not until August that Washington gave up on the New York plan (because the states had not sent him enough troops) and shifted his attention to Virginia. The restoration of the house has been very accurate. Especially noteworthy are the room where Washington and Rochambeau met, and the room where Washington slept, which is still decorated with the original wallpaper purchased for his visit.

The Webb and Deane houses were the homes of pre-Revolutionary merchants and professionals. Isaac Stevens was a leatherworker who built his more modest Georgian house after the Revolution. The **Stevens House,** still furnished with many items owned by its builder's family and his descendants, reveals a middle-class lifestyle of the early decades of the nineteenth century. The broad collection of items on display reflects the increasing availability of consumer goods—ceramics from England, furniture, clocks, and stoves made in Connecticut—in the early nineteenth century.

LOCATION: 211 Main Street. HOURS: Mid–May through mid–October: 10–4 Tuesday–Saturday, 1–4 Sunday. FEE: Yes. TELEPHONE: 203–529–0612.

GLASTONBURY

Settled around 1650, Glastonbury possesses many fine old houses, but only one, the **Welles-Shipman-Ward House** (972 Main Street, 203–633–6890) has been restored and opened to the public. Built in 1755 by Captain Thomas Welles as a wedding present for his son, the two-story clapboard house has been restored to its mid-eighteenth-century appearance with period furnishings. The main parlor features ornate woodwork. The **Museum-on-the-Green,** the headquarters of the Historical Society of Glastonbury, has exhibits of local historical artifacts. The museum is adjacent to the **Green Cemetery,** which was started in 1692. The headstone of Marcy Halle, who died in 1719, gives the cause of death thus:

> *Here lies one wh*
> *os lifes thrads*
> *cut asunder she*
> *was strucke dead*
> *by a clap of thundr.*

In 1873, Julia and Abby Smith, then in their seventies, refused to pay taxes to Glastonbury on the grounds that the law forbade them to vote, and that taxation without representation was tyranny. The town confiscated their cows, the press picked up the story, and the Smiths found themselves national heroines. Sympathizers sent money, which the sisters used to start an equal-suffrage fund.

An itinerant Yankee peddler offering his wares in an 1853 painting by J. W. Ehninger.

ROCKY HILL

Rocky Hill became the chief port of Wethersfield when the Connecticut River changed course. The most notable historic site is **Dinosaur State Park** (West Street, 203–529–8423) in which a geodesic dome encloses five hundred dinosaur tracks, discovered in 1967. Eight-foot-tall, twenty-foot-long reptiles made the tracks about 185 million years ago as they prowled the mudflats at the edge of a lake. Nature trails run through the museum's forty acres.

BERLIN

Berlin was the home of the famed Yankee Peddlers, the Connecticut salesmen who roamed all over the country in the eighteenth and nineteenth centuries selling goods from carts. This mode of business was begun by Edward and William Pattison, who in 1740 made the first tinware in America and sold it door to door. As they expanded they hired more salesmen, who traveled as much as fifteen hundred miles to sell the tinware and other Connecticut goods. Berlin's products included guns, hats, carriages, silk, carpets, and bricks. Simeon North, the first pistolmaker to receive a government contract (in 1799) had his shop here. He later moved to Middletown, where he developed the techniques of manufacturing with interchangeable parts at a time when Eli Whitney was working along similar lines. The **Berlin Historic District** encompasses some fifty eighteenth- and nineteenth-century houses.

NEW BRITAIN

New Britain got its start in industry on a small scale—making sleigh bells—but, by the middle of the nineteenth century, the town was a vigorous manufacturing center for all manner of hardware: Screws, nuts, bolts, ball bearings, locks, and tools are just a few of the products that earned New Britain the nickname "Hardware City." To soften the city's hard industrial edge, the town fathers purchased ninety acres of land in 1869 and hired the eminent landscape designer Frederick Law Olmsted to lay out **Walnut Hill Park**. The **New Britain Museum of American Art** (56 Lexington Street, 203–229–0257), founded in 1903, houses a superb collection of American paintings by such artists as John Trumbull, Gilbert Stuart, John Singer Sargent, Thomas Hart Benton, Winslow

Homer, and Mary Cassatt, as well as works by members of the Hudson River School.

PLAINVILLE

Plainville was on the route of the ill-fated **Farmington Canal,** a section of which is preserved in Norton Park. The **Plainville Historic Center,** housed in the former town hall (29 Pierce Street, 203–747–6577), is a small museum of local history.

FARMINGTON

This picturesque town was a bustling manufacturing center in the 1800s for linen, hats (from Hatter's Lane), candles, carriages, silver, and clocks. The short-lived Farmington Canal brought even more prosperity.

Stanley-Whitman House

The Stanley-Whitman House was built about 1720 with an eighteen-inch, projecting overhang and diamond-paned windows. These are marks of medieval building techniques, which survived even into the eighteenth century in Connecticut. The purpose of the overhang, which creates a second floor that is slightly larger than the first floor, is debatable. It may have been traditional, or the result of English property taxes that imposed a levy based on the size of the ground floor; or, it may have been purely decorative. Half of the house has been furnished to the 1720s, the other half to the period of the Revolution.

LOCATION: 37 High Street. HOURS: March through December: 12–4 Wednesday–Sunday. FEE: Yes. TELEPHONE: 203–677–9222.

Hill-Stead Museum

Theodate Pope Riddle, one of America's first important woman architects, worked with Stanford White to design this country estate in 1898 for her father, Alfred Atmore Pope. He had made his fortune in iron in Ohio, and was one of the earliest American collectors of paintings by the French Impressionists. On view in the house are exceptionally fine examples of works by Monet, Manet, Degas, Cassatt, and Whistler, among others; on the grounds is a

The Guitar Player *by Edouard Manet, in the Hill-Stead Museum.* OPPOSITE: *Farmington.*

sunken garden planted by Beatrix Farrand. Henry James, Theodore Roosevelt, and Mary Cassatt were among the home's visitors during the Popes' and Riddles' residency, from 1901 until 1946, at which time Mrs. Riddle died and left the estate as a museum in her father's memory.

LOCATION: 35 Mountain Road. HOURS: 2–5 Wednesday–Friday, 1–5 Saturday–Sunday. FEE: Yes. TELEPHONE: 203–677–9064.

SOUTHINGTON

Shops here manufactured tin items beginning in the late eighteenth century, after Southington's Seth Peck patented machinery for this purpose, in 1819. The **Barnes Museum** (85 North Main Street, 203–628–5426), a house built in 1836, displays the furnishings and decorative items owned by the Barnes family. Facing the town green is the **Congregational Church,** built in 1828 in the Greek Revival style.

BRISTOL

Bristol was a major producer of clocks, first with wooden gears and, since 1800, with brass. After 1913 Bristol shops manufactured nonjeweled, or "Dollar," watches, as they were often called. The **American Clock & Watch Museum** (100 Maple Street, 203–583–6070) displays 1,800 watches and clocks. A true example of Yankee ingenuity came out of Bristol. Everett Horton's wife did not like having him go fishing, and the law forbade it on Sunday, so Horton fooled all of his tormentors by inventing the collapsible (thus concealable) steel fishing rod.

WINDSOR

Windsor claims, though Wethersfield disputes it, that it is the oldest permanent English settlement in Connecticut. In September 1633, a group of Pilgrims from Plymouth Colony sailed up the Connecticut River, past the guns of the Dutch fort at Hartford (where they defied an order to stop), and landed at the mouth of the Farmington River. They had the foresight to bring a "prefab" frame house with them, which they quickly erected, along with a palisade that was strong enough to discourage a war party of seventy Dutchmen. Windsor's **Palisado Avenue** and **Palisado Green** are named for this stockade. The settlers barely survived the first winter, an extremely bitter one during which the Connecticut River froze in mid-November. The original settlers were soon followed by two groups from Dorchester (now Boston), Massachusetts, and from England.

In 1637, during the Pequot War, the Indians attacked Wethersfield and a Windsor man, Captain John Mason, led the English against the Indians' settlement in Mystic, the inhabitants of which were put to death brutally. Peace descended, and as early as 1640 Windsor farmers were planting tobacco, for which the region's soil was ideally suited, and exporting it to England and the West Indies. In the nineteenth century the region specialized in raising the broad-leafed tobacco needed for making cigar wrappers. In order to create the necessary tropical climate for the weed, Windsor's farmers spread tents of cheesecloth over the fields, producing a thin leaf ideal for wrappers. Some of the colonial houses on Broad Street are of brick, another early product of the town.

Fyler House/Wilson Museum

One of the oldest buildings in the state, the Fyler House dates to
1640. It was built upon land deeded to Lieutenant Walter Fyler in
appreciation for his service against the Pequots. The house has
been restored and displays furnishings of the seventeenth and
eighteenth centuries. On the grounds is the Wilson Museum, which
displays artifacts from the colonial period.

LOCATION: 96 Palisado Avenue. HOURS: April through November:
10–12, 1–4 Tuesday–Saturday. FEE: Yes. TELEPHONE: 203–688–
3813.

Oliver Ellsworth Homestead

Oliver Ellsworth was born here in 1745, five years after his father
had built the house. In 1777 he attended the Continental Congress
and he was the state's senator from 1789 to 1796. He was on the

Oliver Ellsworth and his wife Abigail in a 1792 portrait, with their house in the background.

committee that prepared the first draft of the Constitution, helped organize the federal judiciary system, and served as the third chief justice of the Supreme Court. It is said that, as U.S. envoy to France, Ellsworth greatly impressed Napoleon, who gave him the Gobelin tapestry which, along with a fine collection of furniture, silver, pewter, and china, is now displayed in the house. The large parlor has superb panelling.

LOCATION: 778 Palisado Avenue. HOURS: April through October: 1–5 Tuesday–Saturday. FEE: Yes. TELEPHONE: 203–688–8717.

SIMSBURY

Scouts from the British navy, looking for pine trees for pitch and turpentine, reconnoitered Simsbury in 1643 and reported fine timber growths and pastures, which soon attracted settlers from Hartford and Windsor. Simsbury boomed with the discovery of copper in East Granby in the early 1700s. German workers came in to run the mining and smelting which, in defiance of British laws restricting manufacturing, had to be done in secret. The first copper coins in the colonies—Higley pennies—were made here in 1737 by John Higley and stamped "I am good Copper."

Schoolroom at Massacoh Plantation, Simsbury.

Historic Simsbury has been preserved and restored at **Massacoh Plantation** (800 Hopmeadow Street, 203–658–2500), a complex of eighteenth- and nineteenth-century buildings. The grounds include **Phelps Tavern,** built in 1771, a replica of Simsbury's 1683 **meeting house,** the 1795 **Hendrick's Cottage,** a **fusemanufacturing shop,** a 1740 **schoolhouse,** and a collection of peddler's items donated by the widow of a peddler in 1925.

OLD NEW GATE PRISON AND COPPER MINE

Copper was discovered on this site in East Granby in 1707, and was mined until 1773, after which the thrifty Yankees were even able to find a use for this hole in the ground. They converted the aban-

A ca. 1800 engraving of the above-ground buildings at Old New Gate Prison, where prisoners were confined in "Gloomy Caverns" under ground.

Ruins at New Gate Prison, East Granby.

doned mine into a prison, named after London's Newgate Prison,
for horse thieves, burglars, adulterers (a certain Clark Payne
served four years underground for illegal modes of amorousness)
and counterfeiters—an appropriate punishment for the latter since
the mine's copper had been used to make coins. During the Revolution, Tories were pent up here. It was not a pleasant place:
Contemporary accounts described the "miserable existence" with
its "foul vermin, reeking filth and horrible stench." In the cramped
living quarters, constantly wet from seepage, "the clothing of the
prisoners grows mouldy and rotten, and falls away from their
bodies, while their limbs grow stiff with rheumatism." Prisoners did
not spend all their time below ground: During the day they worked
in the prison yard, and at night they slept below. One bar in a
prison wall shows signs of sawing, reputedly with a watch spring.
The prison went out of use in 1827, and it has been restored.

LOCATION: Newgate Road, East Granby. HOURS: Mid–May through
October: 10–4:30 Wednesday–Sunday. FEE: Yes. TELEPHONE: 203–
653–3563.

WINDSOR LOCKS

The town was named Windsor Locks in 1833 after the locks of a canal built to bypass falls in the Connecticut River. The canal opened in 1829 and closed in 1844 with the coming of a railroad line. A portion of the canal and its locks can be seen from Route 159 in the center of the town. The **New England Air Museum** (Bradley International Airport, 203–623–3305) displays aircraft from a 1909 Bleriot to jet fighters.

SUFFIELD

Hatheway House (55 South Main Street, 203–668–0055) was built in 1760 and has been restored with eighteenth-century items. The house's original furnishings include unusual, hand-blocked French wallpaper and delicately detailed plasterwork.

The **King House Museum** (232 Main Street, 203–668–5256) was built in 1764 for Dr. Alexander King. It has been restored and furnished with period items, and displays Bennington pottery, Connecticut glassware, and a tobacco and cigar collection.

TOLLAND

Tolland is a farming town that was founded in 1715 by settlers from Windsor. Noah Grant III, the grandfather of Ulysses S. Grant, was born in Tolland. During the Revolution, Hessian prisoners were held at the **Benton Homestead** (Metcalf Road, 203–871–7390), a 1720 house that has been restored. The **Hicks/Stearns Museum** (63 Tolland Green, 203–875–7552) displays furniture and other artifacts from the Colonial to Victorian periods. The **Old Tolland Jail Museum** (Tolland Green, 203–871–7390) houses the historical society's collection of furniture, tools, and Indian artifacts. The jail cells, built sturdily of stone and iron in 1856, are open to visitors.

GURLEYVILLE

The **Gurleyville Gristmill** (Stonemill Road, 203–429–5067), a stone mill built in the 1830s, is one of the last survivors of its type in New England. The mill preserves a complete system of nineteenth-century saw and grist milling equipment. In addition to the usual agricultural pursuits, this region was the center of Connecticut's silk industry in the late 1700s and early 1800s.

COVENTRY

The **Nathan Hale Homestead** (South Street off Route 44, 203–742–6917) was the home of Hale's family, but the famed spy never lived there. The house was not finished until a month after he had been executed on September 22, 1776. The homestead has been restored and furnished with items of the period. The **Nathan Hale Cemetery** by Coventry Lake has an obelisk memorializing the Patriot, whose body was buried by the British at an unknown place in Manhattan, where he had been hanged.

PRUDENCE CRANDALL MUSEUM

At her house in Canterbury, Prudence Crandall opened a private school in 1832 and admitted a black girl, which led the white parents in the town to threaten a boycott. In 1833 Crandall reopened the school with the purpose of educating "young ladies and little misses of color," drawing students from all over southern New England and New York. The state assembly hastily passed the "Black Law," forbidding private schools from instructing blacks who were not state residents. Crandall was arrested, jailed overnight, and had to endure three court trials. One night in 1834 the school was attacked by a mob. She reluctantly closed the school. The state and Canterbury's citizens tried to make amends fifty years later, when the legislature voted Crandall a $400 annual pension, augmented by the townspeople and by Samuel Clemens. Today the museum features exhibits on local and black history.

LOCATION: Canterbury Green, Routes 14 and 169. HOURS: 10–4 Wednesday–Sunday. FEE: Yes. TELEPHONE: 203–546–9916.

WOODSTOCK

This quiet town in the rural, northeastern part of the state boasts a fine Gothic Revival building, **Roseland Cottage** (Woodstock Common, 203–928–4074), a summer retreat built in 1846 for Henry Bowen. He hired the English architect Joseph Wells, whose design called for steep gables, and profuse Gothic tracery, and painted the house purple (later replaced with an equally eye-catching pink). The interior is opulent, in keeping with Bowen's wealth and love of entertaining—Bowen's lavish Fourth of July parties were attended by four presidents (Grant, Hayes, Harrison, and McKinley).

OPPOSITE: Trompe l'oeil panelled archway between the double parlor, Roseland Cottage.

WESTERN CONNECTICUT

OPPOSITE: Garden at the Stamford Museum & Nature Center.

Western Connecticut has some of the state's most highly industrialized cities and some of its most beautiful rural towns. Paradoxically, the region of the state that today would be called "unspoiled"—the northwestern corner—was one of the most industrialized sections of eighteenth-century New England. Salisbury, Lakeville, Kent, and other towns of that area were located near rich iron ore deposits which helped make them important producers of nails, cooking pots, and arms as early as the 1730s. The hillsides, now green and attractive enough to inspire artists colonies, were stripped bare of trees two hundred years ago. The smoke and roar of forges and blast furnaces fouled the country air, and ironworkers brawled in streets now regarded as among the quaintest in the East. Although the iron industry shifted to New York and Pennsylvania, other factories in western Connecticut produced a myriad of items: Yale Locks in Stamford, Hotchkiss machine guns and Howe sewing machines in Bridgeport, and hats in Danbury, to name a few.

The state's earliest European settlements were on the Connecticut River, but the western, coastal region did not lag far behind. Fairfield and Bridgeport were settled in the late 1630s; Greenwich, Stamford, and Norwalk in the next decade. Several Colonial houses are preserved in the shore towns, but British terror raids during the Revolution, followed by residential development in the last two centuries, have wiped out most of the colonial past.

Connecticut was in the forefront of the fight for independence. Most Connecticut men of fighting age marched off to Boston at the outbreak of the rebellion, and subsequently enlisted in the Continental Army. From this part of the state came David Humphreys of Ansonia and Benjamin Tallmadge of Litchfield, who were among George Washington's closest advisors and friends. The fiery Ethan Allen, who captured Fort Ticonderoga, was born in Litchfield and operated a forge in Lakeville. The region's farmers and manufacturers provided crucial food and weapons to the Continental Army, earning Connecticut the nickname, "the Provisions State." Only three men won the Revolutionary medal of heroism, the Purple Heart (a decoration revived in the twentieth century for soldiers wounded in battle), and all three were from Connecticut. Most Loyalists were either driven out (Patriots had little regard for the rights and liberties of Loyalists) or

OPPOSITE: Detail of Jurgan F. Huge's watercolor of downtown Bridgeport (1876).

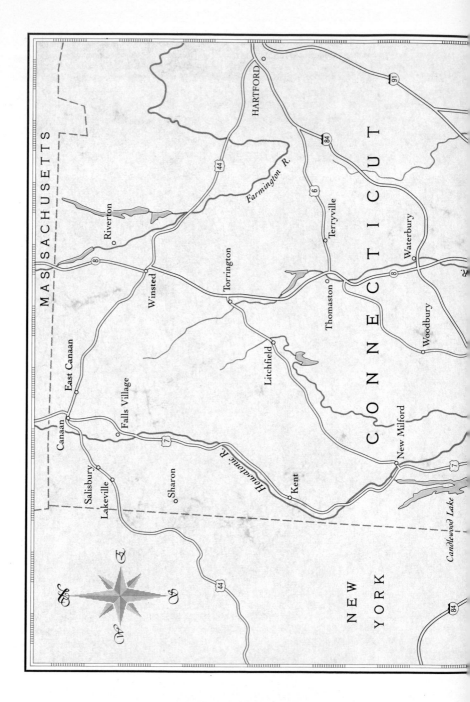

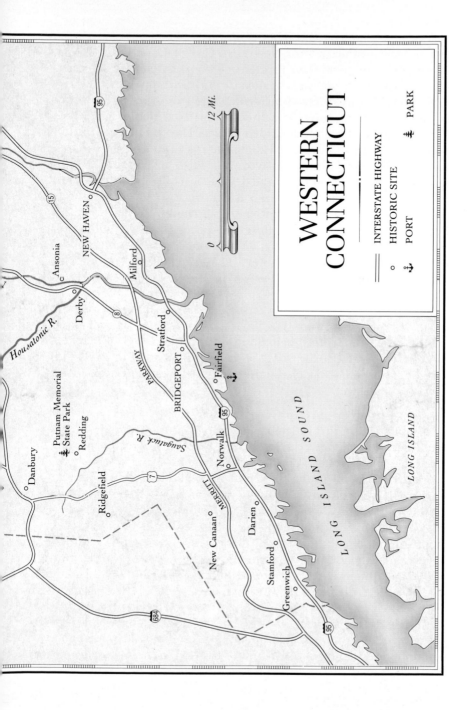

WESTERN
CONNECTICUT

—— INTERSTATE HIGHWAY
o   HISTORIC SITE
⚓ PORT   ⚱ PARK

0   12 Mi.

left of their own accord for New York City or Long Island. Some took their revenge on their former neighbors when they accompanied British troops on raids against Connecticut towns.

Several towns suffered heavy damage from the six-day series of British raids in July 1779 under New York's Tory governor, William Tryon. Tryon first landed at New Haven on July 5th, and then worked his way westward along the coast, putting the torch to Fairfield, Greens Farms, and Norwalk. His earlier raid on Danbury, in 1777, had resulted in the destruction of some forty homes, barns, and storehouses. Property losses were so severe that after the Revolution the state granted the burned-out citizens half a million acres in the Western Reserve—part of modern Ohio that had been included in Connecticut's Colonial grant. Some important Revolutionary sites in western Connecticut are Putnam Cottage in Greenwich, Keeler Tavern in Ridgefield, Putnam State Park in Redding, and the Eells-Stow House in Milford.

This chapter begins at Greenwich and proceeds east along the shore of Long Island Sound to Norwalk, digresses to Danbury, and picks up the shore route again until Milford is reached. The itinerary then proceeds north, roughly following Route 8 to Route 44. The final portion of the chapter covers northwestern Connecticut.

GREENWICH

Greenwich was settled in 1640 by two Englishmen from Massachusetts, after they bought the land from the Indians for twenty-five coats. During the Revolution, in February 1779, the British destroyed a saltworks in the town and burned a number of houses. General Israel Putnam was staying at Knapp's Tavern, now preserved as **Putnam Cottage** (243 East Putnam Avenue, 203–869–9697), when the British dragoons appeared. The general fled and, according to legend, made good his escape by spurring his horse over a cliff. A plaque near the cottage marks the site of his legendary leap. Putnam, known to the soldiers as "Ol' Put," had been a commander at the battle of Bunker Hill.

Located in the Strickland Road Historic District in Cos Cob, the **Bush-Holley House** (39 Strickland Road, 203–869–6899) is a seventeenth-century saltbox house with some Dutch elements. From the 1880s, the house was an inn run by Emma Holley and her husband, Elmer Livingston MacRae, a sculptor. The inn attracted such writers and artists as Willa Cather, Lincoln Steffens, Anya Seton, and Louis Comfort Tiffany. The house has been restored with eighteenth- and nineteenth-century furniture and paintings.

STAMFORD

Stamford was settled in the 1640s by families from Wethersfield. The oldest surviving house in the city is the **Hoyt-Barnum House** (713 Bedford Street, 203–323–1975, open by appointment only). Built in 1699, it has been restored and furnished following the 1738 inventory of the first owner.

In 1806 Stamford's citizens conducted an early protest against real estate development. The company that was then improving the Boston Post Road straightened it by running it through the Stamford cemetery. By night, the townspeople used oxen to litter the construction site with large rocks. In the morning the road-workers would remove the rocks and start all over again. Eventually the road company won out.

Stamford resident Simon Ingersoll invented the friction clutch, the spring scale and, in 1858, a steam-driven wagon which he drove around the streets. Linus Yale devised the first cylinder lock in 1848, and manufactured them here, revolutionizing lock design and launching a major American industry. Stamford boomed in the 1890s when local merchants promoted the town as an industrial center, inviting New York investors to develop businesses here. The **Stamford Historical Society Museum** (1508 High Ridge Road, 203–329–1183) exhibits furniture, tools, quilts, dolls, and other items of local historical interest.

The **Stamford Museum & Nature Center** (39 Scofieldtown Road, 203–322–1646) is a 118-acre park with a working farm that demonstrates nineteenth-century methods of farming, beekeeping, blacksmithing, and cooking. Seasonal activities include ice harvesting in January, maple sugaring in February or March, sheep shearing in May, and a September harvest festival. In the main building five galleries feature a permanent exhibit of North American Indian cultures, changing exhibits on natural history, and colonial artifacts and technology.

OVERLEAF: New Canaan Historical Society Museum, a grouping of five museums whose exhibits cover the eighteenth and ninteenth centuries.

NEW CANAAN

The **New Canaan Historical Society Museum** (13 Oenoke Ridge, 203–966–1776) is a complex of five buildings that house seven museums and a library. The **Town House** has a re-creation of a nineteenth-century drugstore, a costume museum, and a library on genealogy and history. The Society also administers the **Hanford-Silliman House,** furnished with mid-eighteenth-century furniture and artifacts. The other museums include the 1799 **Rock School;** the **New Canaan Hand Press,** re-creating a nineteenth-century printing office; the **Tool Museum;** and the **John Rogers Studio and Museum,** built in 1878. John Rogers was the creator of the sentimental "Rogers group" sculptures, vignettes of daily life that were hugely popular in American homes from the 1860s to the 1880s, when some seventy to eighty thousand of the two-foot-high plaster groups were sold. General George Armstrong Custer was known to have lugged two of these plaster scenes from camp to camp in the Dakota Territory.

DARIEN

On July 22, 1781, forty Tories who had lived in Darien returned to the town with British troops, surrounded the church during services, and rounded up the men and boys, six of whom later died in prison. The **Bates-Scofield Homestead** (45 Old Kings Highway North, 203–655–0834) is a restored 1736 farmhouse that typifies the mid-eighteenth-century Connecticut farm. The house features a kitchen and buttery, a weaving room with a spinning wheel, loom, and wool winders, and a Colonial herb garden.

NORWALK

Settled in 1649, Norwalk has been an important manufacturing center since the mid 1700s, when clocks, watches, paper, pottery, and nails were made here. In 1776 Nathan Hale, disguised as a schoolmaster, departed from Norwalk on his fatal mission of espionage. He was rowed to British-held Huntington, Long Island, from which he made his way to New York City. Governor William Tryon raided Norwalk in July 1779 and burned the town. There is a

OPPOSITE: Nineteenth-century drugstore at New Canaan Historical Society Museum.

monument (East Avenue) to the four hundred Patriot defenders who tried vainly to repel the raiders.

The **Lockwood-Mathews Mansion** (295 West Avenue, 203–838–1434) was built in 1864 by the financier and treasurer of the New York Stock Exchange, Le Grand Lockwood. The magnificent four-story, sixty-room mansion is lavishly decorated with frescoes, gilt, marble, and carved woodwork, and cost 1.2 million dollars.

RIDGEFIELD

After raiding Danbury in April 1777, a British column retreated toward Ridgefield, pursued by local militia and Continental Army troops under the command of David Wooster. At the north end of town, American troops commanded by Benedict Arnold were waiting for them, and a sharp skirmish ensued. During the battle, the British shelled the town, including **Keeler Tavern** (132 Main Street, 203–438–5485), which still has a cannonball lodged in a wall. The British forced their way through and escaped to boats on Long Island Sound. For fifty years, Keeler Tavern was a summer home of architect Cass Gilbert.

REDDING

Under the command of General Israel Putnam, three brigades of the Continental Army—about 3,100 men—camped at **Putnam Memorial State Park** (Routes 58 and 107, 203–938–2285) during the winter of 1778–1779. The site was selected for winter quarters because it was roughly equidistant from the Hudson and from Long Island Sound, thereby permitting the army to rush to either location in an emergency. The 183-acre park includes a small museum with exhibits and a reconstructed blockhouse.

DANBURY

A supply depot during the Revolution, Danbury was the target of a highly destructive raid in April 1777, during which the British burned some forty Patriots' homes, barns, and warehouses. Tory houses were clearly marked and spared. **Wooster Cemetery** on Ellsworth Avenue is named for General David Wooster, who died of wounds suffered in the subsequent fighting at Ridgefield. A hero's death in battle redeemed an otherwise lackluster record: He

OPPOSITE: Entrance hall of Lockwood-Mathews Mansion, Norwalk. OVERLEAF: Southport Harbor.

had been called "dull and uninspired," and fit to be "general of a hayfield." The Masons erected a huge monument to Wooster at the cemetery in 1854, and Congress voted one as well—but never got around to building it. Also buried in Wooster Cemetery is the composer Charles Ives, a Danbury native.

The **Danbury Scott-Fanton Museum** (43 Main Street, 203–743–5200) includes two historic buildings. The 1785 **Rider House,** home of a carpenter and cabinetmaker, displays antique tools and period furnishings. The 1790 **Dodd Hat Shop** preserves the early and modern hatting history of Danbury, where an early hat shop was opened, in 1780, that produced three hats a day.

FAIRFIELD

Fairfield was settled in 1639, shortly after the Pequot Indians were defeated in the nearby Great Swamp Fight, which ended the Pequot War. A granite monument in Southport marks the site of the battle (Route 1, near intersection with I-95). Fairfield was the home port of Captain Samuel Smedley, a teenage privateer who captured more ships during the Revolution than any other American commander. The town was almost entirely destroyed in Tryon's raid of July 1779; the four houses that survived the raid still stand on Beach Road. Fairfield's men took their revenge by raiding Tories on Long Island via whaleboats debarking from Southport and Black Rock harbors. In the **Old Burying Ground** (Beach Road), where the oldest surviving stone dates to 1687, more than one hundred Revolutionary soldiers are buried. The **Fairfield Historical Society Museum** (636 Old Post Road, 203–259–1598) displays eighteenth- to twentieth-century art, furniture, silver, china, glassware, textiles, and tools from the Fairfield area. The **Ogden House** (1520 Bronson Road, 203–259–1598) is a house museum operated by the Fairfield Historical Society to depict the lives of a farming family before the Revolution. **Bronson Windmill** (3015 Bronson Road), with its eighty-foot-high octagonal tower, is a well-preserved example of late-nineteenth-century agricultural engineering.

Southport Harbor, in the southwest part of Fairfield, was a wealthy shipping center in the nineteenth century. In 1836 a historian wrote that, "more shipping is owned in this place in proportion to its size, than in any other place between New York and Boston." There are nearly two hundred fine eighteenth- and nineteenth-century houses, all privately owned, in the historic district.

BRIDGEPORT

Bridgeport was founded on the site of a Pequonnock Indian village in 1639. The white settlers and the Indians shared the area until 1765, when the townspeople paid the Indians to leave. In the nineteenth-century, Bridgeport became a center for manufacturing, making such items as brass and cast-iron fittings, tools, heavy machinery, carriages, and ammunition. Elias Howe, the inventor of the sewing machine, opened his factory here in 1865. The first gramophones, Alexander Graham Bell's early phonographs, were made here. Bridgeport also supplied the world with corsets, including the first rustproof model, which "effected a radical improvement." The **Museum of Art, Science & Industry** (4450 Park Avenue, 203–372–3521) displays a large collection of American folk art, furniture, decorative arts, samplers, and Colonial portraits. The H.M.S. *Rose,* a replica of an eighteenth-century British frigate built for the Bicentennial celebration in 1976, is docked at Captain's Cove Marina (203–335–1433).

Showman and circus magnate, P. T. Barnum, made Bridgeport the headquarters for "The Greatest Show on Earth." The **Barnum Museum** (961 Main Street, 203–384–5381), housed in a

Detail of a frieze on the facade of the Barnum Museum, Bridgeport.

Romanesque Revival building built by the showman in 1890, displays circus items, exotica such as an Egyptian mummy, and a model of a circus with half a million figures. Barnum's most famous attraction, Charles S. Stratton (better known as General Tom Thumb), was born in Bridgeport in 1838, and stopped growing at the age of seven months, when he was twenty-five inches tall; in 1844 Barnum took him on a European tour. Barnum, one of the city's greatest boosters and benefactors, was the mayor and an assemblyman, interceding with federal bureaucrats to get the harbor dredged, and with railroad officials to get the trains running on schedule. He donated waterfront land for the public beach and park. Barnum and Tom Thumb are buried in the 140-acre **Mountain Grove Cemetery** (North Avenue at Dewey Street).

STRATFORD

Stratford was the site of a skirmish with the long-suffering Pequot as they fled west to their final battle at Fairfield. During the Revolution, some Stratford men traded with the enemy and made a practice of profiteering, causing the town to pass a law against "the wicked tribe of monopolizers . . . and stock jobbers who Inhance the prices of the necessaries of life." The **Captain David Judson House** (967 Academy Hill, 203–378–0630), built about 1723, has been restored to its mid-eighteenth-century appearance. A museum behind the house displays artifacts relating to local history.

MILFORD

Three eighteenth-century houses are preserved by the Milford Historical Society (34 High Street, 203–874–2664) at the site of the old town wharf facing Milford Harbor. **Stockade House,** built about 1780, is undergoing restoration. Interior panels have been removed, so visitors can see how a typical New England saltbox house was constructed. The **Bryan-Downes House,** built about 1785, has not been restored; it is used as an exhibit center for local historical items. The **Eells-Stow House** is the most important of the three. Believed to be the oldest surviving house in the town, it was built about 1700 by Samuel Eells, who settled in Milford in 1668. During the Revolution it was the home of Stephen Stow and his wife, Freelove. In 1777 a British prison ship put ashore two hun-

OPPOSITE: Charles S. Stratton, known as General Tom Thumb.

dred American prisoners who were dying of smallpox. Stow volunteered to nurse them, and died of the disease himself. He was buried in a common grave with forty-six other smallpox victims in the Old Burying Ground (Prospect Street).

DERBY

Derby was founded as a trading post, in the 1640s, at the junction of the Housatonic and Naugatuck rivers. Derby men traded with the West Indies and Europe, shipping lumber, livestock, and food in exchange for rum, wine, fruit, brandy, and slaves. In 1800 Derby became the site of an annual celebration by the state's blacks during which they elected a "governor" to settle disputes and levy fines for misconduct. A copper mill was built here in 1836, and two years later a pin-making factory was built by John I. Howe, an inventor who mechanized the process.

GENERAL DAVID HUMPHREYS HOUSE

Humphreys (1752–1818) had a life distinguished by many and varied accomplishments. He graduated with distinction from Yale in 1771. A colonel in the Continental Army, he was George Washington's personal aide and secretary, became one of Washington's closest friends, and was given the honor of receiving the British colors at the surrender at Yorktown. He served as a diplomat in England, France, Portugal, Algeria, and Spain, from the last of which he imported merino sheep to improve American stock, and ultimately he began a wool-making enterprise. A mill owner himself, he pressed for improvements in the education and housing of workmen and for laws requiring that factories be inspected. He was one of the Hartford Wits, a group of prominent lawyers and politicians who wrote political and satirical verses. His house has been restored with eighteenth-century furnishings. The **Old Town Burying Ground** is across the street from the Humphreys house.

LOCATION: 37 Elm Street, Ansonia. HOURS: 9–4:30 Monday–Friday. FEE: None. TELEPHONE: 203–735–1908.

WATERBURY

Waterbury, settled in 1674, was the chief brass-producing city in the country in the nineteenth and early twentieth centuries. It also gained fame as the home of Robert H. Ingersoll's one-dollar pocketwatch. The Indians called the area Mattatuck, meaning "badly wooded region," which is exactly what it was. In the early 1800s the townspeople began to make clocks, brass (with technology stolen from British manufacturers), pewter, and buttons. Intense improvisation and innovation led to the production of so much brass by the early 1840s that Waterbury didn't know what to do with it. Fortunately, they devised a method of making pins from brass wire. Waterbury's factories provided the copper and brass for Boulder Dam in Colorado. The Waterbury Clock Company made the first cheap pocketwatches but couldn't find a market for them; Robert Ingersoll then bought the factory's entire output every year and ultimately sold five million. The **Mattatuck Museum** (144 West Main Street, 203–753–0381) has exhibits concerning local history.

WOODBURY

The Reverend Dr. Samuel Seabury was elected America's first Episcopal bishop in the **Glebe House** (Hollow Road, 203–263–2855) in 1783. Built in the middle of the eighteenth century, it is named for the "glebe," or portion of land allotted to an Anglican clergyman as part of his payment. The interior displays local and regional eighteenth-century furnishings.

THOMASTON

Thomaston has been a center of clockmaking since 1803, when Eli Terry, Sr., who had invented the shelf clock, opened a factory here. He made clocks by machine, cutting the retail price from $25 to $5. His clocks were sold all over the country by itinerant salesmen, on the installment plan. Seth Thomas opened a factory here, in 1812, which was soon to be the largest in the world. To the east in **Terryville** Eli Terry, Jr. made clocks, his son James made locks, and another son, Andrew, made malleable iron. The **Lock Museum of America** (130 Main Street, 203–589–6359) displays the world's largest collection of locks and keys, some 22,000 items.

LITCHFIELD

Litchfield is many people's idea of a perfect New England village. Its broad, tree-lined streets and handsome houses were carefully restored in the nineteenth and twentieth centuries. Between 1876 and 1913, the townspeople remodeled Victorian buildings in the

Colonial style and hired the Olmsted landscape firm to redesign the common. But in the late eighteenth and early nineteenth centuries, Litchfield had all the noise and smell of a typical manufacturing town. There were forges, nail and comb factories, eighteen sawmills, saddlers, grain mills, a paper mill, and five malodorous tanneries (Litchfield was renowned for the quality of its boots and shoes). The local inventor Benjamin Hanks patented a tower clock that would wind itself—by means of a windmill—so that no one would have to climb the steeple stairs on Saturday night to wind the clock for Sunday. Litchfield was so successful, and its citizens such astute investors in farm land and shipping, that the mills and factories were no longer needed. As the industries disappeared, the town settled into an easy prosperity.

Litchfield's most prominent family was the Beechers. Pastor Lyman Beecher was the father of two of the most famous people in nineteenth-century America—Harriet Beecher Stowe, the author of *Uncle Tom's Cabin*, and the Reverend Henry Ward Beecher, the best-known preacher in the nation. His sermons at Plymouth Church in Brooklyn, New York attracted hundreds of listeners every Sunday.

Another famous Litchfield citizen was Benjamin Tallmadge, a distinguished officer in the Revolution. He led troops at several battles in New York and New Jersey, and at Valley Forge. In November 1780, he led a raiding party of dragoons that destroyed British supplies on Long Island. He also had a role in two famous episodes of espionage: He was a friend of Nathan Hale, and he identified Major John André as a British officer and spy after André's capture. Tallmadge accompanied André to the gallows and, like many American officers present at the execution, was moved by his courage.

The **Benjamin Tallmadge House** (North Street, 203–567–8498), like most of the houses in the town, is a private residence, but Litchfield's houses are open to the public on Open House Day each July. The **Litchfield Historical Society** (South and East streets, 203–567–4501) can provide information about these tours.

One historic site open on a regular basis is the **Tapping Reeve House and Law School** (South Street, 203–567–4501), the country's first school of law, founded in 1773. Its roster of students includes two vice presidents (Aaron Burr and John C. Calhoun), seventeen U.S. senators, and three justices of the Supreme Court.

OPPOSITE : Litchfield home with Palladian window and Ionic columns.

WINSTED

Winsted was a center of clockmaking in early 1800s. A 150-foot waterfall from Highland Lake provided power for a clockworks, starting in 1807, that later grew into the William L. Gilbert Clock Company. In the early twentieth century, Winsted produced scythes, furs, fishing tackle, wire, coffin fittings, electrical products, and twelve million pins a day. Many old houses (private) can be seen along Main Street. Nevertheless, for all its practicality, Winsted and the surrounding area has given rise to tall tales of witchcraft, owls that talk, and mysterious "wild men."

RIVERTON

The **John T. Kenney Hitchcock Museum** (Route 20, 203–379–1003), housed in a converted 1829 Episcopal church, displays an excellent collection of ornamented furniture—the brightly painted tables and chairs that furnished the homes of people of modest means in the eighteenth and nineteenth centuries. The museum also exhibits clocks, decorated tinware, and quilts.

FALLS VILLAGE

Lumbering and iron processing were the industries in this small town on the Housatonic River. Massive stone ruins of a failed canal (the builders did not use mortar and the canal leaked), built between 1849 and 1851 to power mills, are near Main Street.

SHARON

This exceptionally picturesque town, near the Taconic Highlands, was a flourishing eighteenth-century manufacturing center that produced stoves, tools, cigars, shoes, barrels, and wooden mousetraps. Benjamin Hotchkiss invented the Hotchkiss exploding shell here, but later moved his factory to Bridgeport. His brother Andrew, who developed the Hotchkiss repeating rifle and an air-cooled machine gun, was born almost entirely paralyzed. He invented mechanical devices that enabled him to move his limbs.

There are many beautiful stone and brick houses, including the pink-hued **Gay-Hoyt House** (Main Street, private), built during

OPPOSITE: Riverton Cascades.

the Revolution by Lieutenant Colonel Ebenezer Gay, who helped provision the Continental Army.

KENT

Settled in 1738, Kent became one of the area's iron-production centers. The **Sloane-Stanley Museum** (Route 7, 203–927–3849) has a fine collection of wooden and iron tools; an 1826 iron furnace is also on the grounds.

The region's great natural beauty attracted artists in the nineteenth century, including the landscape painter George Inness; from **Flanders Cemetery** (Route 7, north of the village) the visitor can see such a vista of the Housatonic Valley. Here, the gravestone of Captain Jirah Swift, killed in the Revolution at age thirty-nine, laments that, "I in the Prime of Life must quit the Stage/Nor see the End of all the Britains Rage."

Southeast of Kent, in Washington, the **American Indian Archaeological Institute** (Curtis Road off Route 199, 203–868–0518) displays Indian tools, clothing, crafts, re-created bark houses, a garden, and a simulated archaeological site.

CANAAN

The remains of eighteenth-century iron forges can be seen on Lower Road. The **Mountain View Cemetery** (Sand Road) contains the grave of Captain Gershom Hewitt, whose marker notes that he, "through a ruse, secured the plans of Fort Ticonderoga for Col. Ethan Allen." Pretending to be the village idiot, Hewitt wandered about the fort unchallenged and reported on the defenses to Allen.

LAKEVILLE

Lakeville and nearby Salisbury were the sites of the country's most important iron mines and forges in the eighteenth century. Ethan Allen (later of Fort Ticonderoga fame) was part-owner of the Lakeville iron forge from 1762 to 1765. Even in a town used to tough ironworkers, Allen was a walking scandal, thanks to his cursing, brawling, and odd religious beliefs. His forge produced two tons of iron and consumed ten cords of wood each day. The ore here was especially pure, which made it valuable for the forg-

OPPOSITE: Canaan train station.

ing of artillery. The Lakeville forge supplied cannon to the Continental Army during the Revolution. In one seven-month period, the forge shipped one hundred sixteen tons of cannon and thirty-eight tons of shot and balls to Washington's armies. The forge was so crucial to the fate of the rebellion that the ironworkers were provided with all the meat and rum they wanted—at a time of acute food shortages—and forty armed guards patrolled the area.

In 1808 one of the local iron barons, John Milton Holley, built an addition to the 1768 **Holley-Williams House** (Upper Main Street, 203–435–2878). His descendants lived there until 1971 when it was willed to the town as a museum. The house has undergone few changes and offers a glimpse of nineteenth-century life. In the mid-1800s, the Lakeville forge was replaced by a cutlery factory, the most important in the country. **Pocketknife Square** was named for the product that made the town rich again. A score of eighteenth- and nineteenth-century buildings line Main Street.

Mount Riga Blast Furnace

The Mount Riga furnace was built around 1810 (the date "1845" chiselled into a stone refers to a repair). It stands on a 1,000-foot-high plateau, near a lake that supplied waterpower to operate bellows and amid a forest that provided timber for charcoal. It reached its peak of production during the War of 1812, when it manufactured anchors for the navy. "Old Ironsides" and the USS *Constellation* were both equipped with Salisbury anchors. Before the navy would take delivery, the anchor had to be tested. The entire town would gather to watch as a twenty-ton anchor was raised atop a one-hundred-foot tower and dropped. If it didn't break, it was accepted. In 1847 the bellows failed and the molten iron in the furnace abruptly cooled—the opposite of a nuclear "meltdown"—into a solid "salamander." This was every ironmaster's nightmare: The only way to dislodge the salamander would have been to fire a cannon at it point blank; the owners decided to abandon the furnace instead. The furnace, which has not been restored, is on private property but it may be viewed from the road.

LOCATION: A 3.5 mile road off Route 44 in Salisbury winds up to the furnace.

OPPOSITE: Mount Riga Furnace.

CONNECTICUT'S EASTERN SHORE

OPPOSITE: *The whaler* Charles W. Morgan *at Mystic Seaport.*

The eastern shore of Connecticut, from New Haven to Stonington, remains a string of pleasant seaside villages. With the exceptions of New Haven, with its railyards and gun factories, and New London, with its modern submarine and boatyards, the shoreline escaped the cycle of industrialization and decline in the nineteenth and twentieth centuries. Long Island Sound is still fringed with the marsh grass that was highly prized by the early colonists. The "sea meadows," as they called them, provided, without cultivation, abundant hay for their cattle, although harvesting it was a messy, muddy chore, made all the more annoying by tick bites and the Englishman's horror of snakes.

The oldest stone house in New England is the Henry Whitfield House at Guilford, a town that boasts some four hundred eighteenth- and nineteenth-century buildings. Tucked under a highway overpass in New London is the gristmill built by one of the earliest colonists, John Winthrop, Jr.

While central and western Connecticut were the homes of the state's inventors and industrialists, the eastern shore was the domain of the seafarer. Although Nantucket and New Bedford are more famous, New London was one of the country's prime whaling ports in the nineteenth century. Whale Oil Row and the Deshon-Allyn House are evidence of the fortunes whaling brought to New London. Stonington also remains an active fishing village, but the greatest monument to Connecticut's maritime past is undoubtedly Mystic Seaport. This authentic recreation of a seaport features the *Charles W. Morgan,* a mid-nineteenth-century whaling ship, many other historic vessels, and a whole village of functioning workshops where the old crafts of the sea are demonstrated. On a much smaller scale Norwich, on the Thames River above New London, still has remnants of its past as an important center of trade between Connecticut and the West Indies. Essex, about twenty miles up the Connecticut River, a bustling shipbuilding center in the nineteenth century, is today a favorite port for pleasure craft. Also on the Connecticut River is the Goodspeed Opera House at East Haddam, a vestige of the days when steamboats carried commerce and vacationers between Hartford and New York.

Eastern Connecticut was the site of the state's only major battle during the Revolutionary War—Benedict Arnold's traitorous attack on New London and Groton in 1781. At Fort Griswold in Groton some eighty-five Patriots were massacred after they had surrendered. The inland town of Lebanon was the home of a

Tobacco field and barns in Middletown in the eighteenth century.

Revolutionary hero who never fired a shot: Governor Jonathan Trumbull, who managed the flow of supplies from the "Provisions State" to George Washington's armies.

New England has been efficient in obliterating traces of the Indian culture that flourished before colonization. This region has one of the few sites set aside to commemorate the Indian past—Fort Shantok State Park in Uncasville, a town named for "the Last of the Mohicans." Descendants of Uncas's tribe still live in the area.

This chapter begins at New Haven and proceeds east along the shore of Long Island Sound to Stonington, with a detour north, along the Connecticut River, to Middletown.

NEW HAVEN

New Haven was founded by John Davenport, a charismatic Puritan minister, and Theophilus Eaton, a wealthy Puritan merchant, soldier, and diplomat, who led about five hundred followers to New Haven in 1638. Probably the wealthiest group yet to settle in New England, they came from London by way of Boston, where they were informed about the good harbor by men returning from the Pequot Wars. In the words of one historian, they "had decided to found a colony with the minimum of pioneering discomfort, by

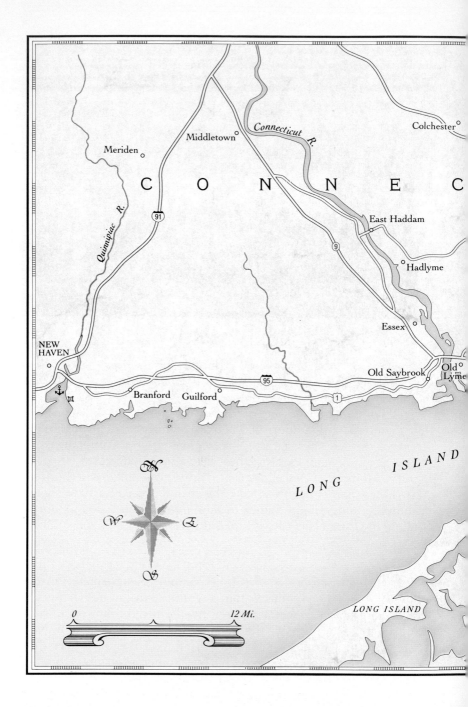

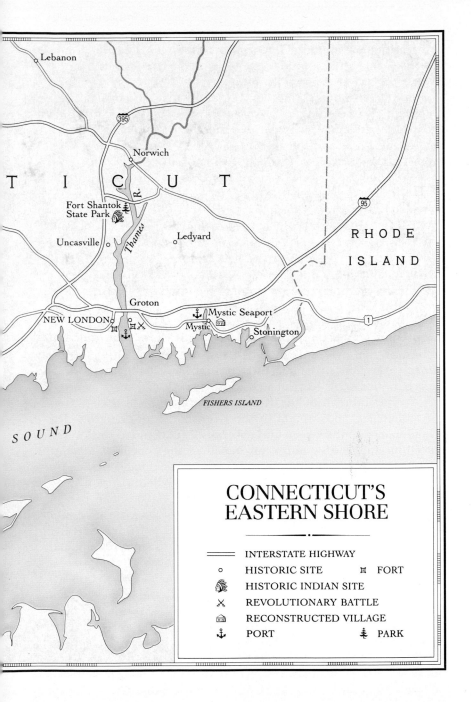

Lebanon

395

Norwich

T I C U T

Fort Shantok
State Park

Uncasville

Ledyard

95

R H O D E

I S L A N D

Groton

NEW LONDON

Mystic Seaport

Mystic

Stonington

1

FISHERS ISLAND

S O U N D

CONNECTICUT'S
EASTERN SHORE

══════ INTERSTATE HIGHWAY

○ HISTORIC SITE   ⊞ FORT

⚜ HISTORIC INDIAN SITE

✕ REVOLUTIONARY BATTLE

⌂ RECONSTRUCTED VILLAGE

⚓ PORT   ⚘ PARK

virtue of the maximum of financial preparation." They laid out a town in a grid pattern of nine squares, with the Green at the center. At first they lived in dugouts in the ground, but soon they built "fair and stately houses, wherein they at the first outdid the rest of the country," according to a disapproving Dutchman in 1639. Their earliest commercial ventures failed but New Haven's shipping in the 1700s and industry in the 1800s kept the city secure. From 1701 to 1875 New Haven and Hartford together formed the joint capital of the state. This town won a victory over Hartford in 1716 when it became the seat of Yale College but, of course, Hartford later became sole capital.

The only remnant of the original colony is the city's grid plan. The **New Haven Green** is bounded on three sides by commercial buildings, and on the other by the Yale campus. On the Green itself are three churches, built between 1812 and 1815, that are exceptionally fine examples of New England's church architecture. **Center Church,** the United Church of Christ, was built in 1812 by Ithiel Town. The congregation was descended from that of the town-founder John Davenport. To its right is **United Church,** also in the Georgian style, built by David Hoadley. On the left is **Trinity Church.** Also built by Ithiel Town, it is perhaps the first American church in the Gothic Revival style.

At the outbreak of the Revolution, Benedict Arnold—druggist, bookseller, and captain in the Governor's Foot Guards—led his militiamen to the Green and successfully demanded the keys to the municipal powder house on behalf of the rebellion. Powder House Day is celebrated today with an annual drill and parade on the Green. On July 5, 1779, Major General William Tryon, with three thousand British troops, invaded New Haven. The British hoped to draw General Washington out of New York so they could attack him on the roads to Connecticut. It did not work, and the British retreated on July 6 when confronted by a superior colonial army. A few dozen colonists resisted fiercely, losing twenty-seven of their own while inflicting seventy-three casualties on the invaders. In the initial assault, the British captured and burned **Black Rock Fort** (Woodward Avenue, 203–787–8790), which was later rebuilt. The fort is being restored along with the adjacent **Fort Nathan Hale,** of the Civil War era. The British also burned the **Pardee-Morris House** (325 Lighthouse Road, 203–562–4183). The house was rebuilt by the owner, Amos Morris and his son Amos II, between 1780 and 1820. It is now a house museum.

In the early nineteenth century, New Haven became an important commercial port, importing tea and silk and commissioning porcelain from China. It traded regularly with coastal ports from Boston to the Carolinas and with Newfoundland and the West Indies. In the early 1820s New Haven's businessmen conceived of building a canal from New Haven to Northampton, Massachusetts, where it would join the Connecticut River. The Farmington Canal, it was hoped, would bypass entrenched shipping interests at Hartford and make New Haven one of the major East Coast ports. In 1835 the canal was completed and the first boat made the trip from New Haven to Northampton. The canal was a financial failure and in 1846 it was drained and turned into a railroad line which operated until 1902. A portion of the old canal bed, with a rail line running in it, can still be seen in several locations.

Manufacturing boomed in the mid- and late-nineteenth century: Most notably, New Haven concerns produced Winchester repeating rifles, carriages, hardware, pianos, corsets, bicycles, and cigars. New Haven's importance in arms manufacturing was a result of the inventions of Eli Whitney (1765–1825). Born in Westboro, Massachusetts, he put himself through Yale (Class of 1792) and then moved to Georgia to practice law. While in the South, he invented his cotton gin (short for "engine"), which speedily and efficiently separated cotton fibers from the seeds. He established a factory in New Haven to produce cotton gins, but the machine was so simple to make that Whitney's design was universally copied, despite his patent. In New Haven he devised the technique of manufacturing objects with interchangeable parts. (Pistolmaker Simeon North was working along similar lines in nearby Middletown.) It was an enormous leap forward in the history of manufacturing: Items that had previously been made and assembled by skilled craftsmen, who devoted long periods of time to their construction, could be mass-produced and assembled by unskilled labor at a fraction of the cost. To put his idea into practice, Whitney invented a milling machine that could manufacture small parts with precision, and he built an armory where he mass-produced muskets for the government. At the site is the **Eli Whitney Museum** (Whitney Avenue at Armory Street in Hamden, 203–777–1833) which has exhibits about New England industry.

OVERLEAF: *Interior of New Haven's beautifully proportioned Center Church with its Tiffany window.*

New Haven was also home to important artists in the nineteenth and twentieth centuries. Among them was the painter Nathaniel Jocelyn, best known for his portrait of Cinque, the black leader of the 1839 slave rebellion. The inventor of the telegraph, Samuel Morse, taught painting at Yale, and George Henry Durrie, famous as the Currier & Ives winter-scene artist, also lived and worked in New Haven.

The **Grove Street Cemetery** (Grove and Prospect streets), the first incorporated cemetery in the United States and the first to be laid out in family plots, dates to 1797. The imposing—and somewhat eerie—Egyptian Revival gateway with the inscription "The dead shall Rise," was built in 1848. A chart posted inside the gate provides the locations of graves. Eli Whitney, Harriet Beecher Stowe, Charles Goodyear (the inventor of vulcanized rubber), and General Alfred Terry, who was Custer's superior officer in the campaign that led to the Battle of Little Big Horn, are all buried here. The **New Haven Colony Historical Society** (114 Whitney Avenue, 203–562–4183) has eleven galleries that display works by the artists mentioned above as well as silver, Chinese porcelain, and other decorative arts; photographs and maps of old New Haven; and an original cotton gin.

Yale University

Yale was founded at Branford in 1701, and located in Saybrook from 1701 to 1716 when it came to its permanent home in New Haven. It was named after Elihu Yale, a merchant born in Massachusetts who, in 1718, donated a collection of books to be sold for the school's benefit. The college officially became a university in 1887. Among Yale's well-known graduates were the theologian Jonathan Edwards (Class of 1720); Noah Webster (1778); John C. Calhoun (1804), vice president under John Quincy Adams; novelist James Fenimore Cooper (who was expelled); Samuel F. B. Morse (1810); and President William Howard Taft (1878).

The gateway to the campus is Phelps Gate, which faces the New Haven Green and leads to the **Old Campus,** a quadrangle of dormitories built between 1842 and 1928. **Connecticut Hall,** a Georgian-style brick building erected in 1717, is the oldest on campus. Nathan Hale (Class of 1773) had his room in this building, and a statue of him stands in front of it.

OPPOSITE ABOVE: Towers of the three churches on the New Haven Green. BELOW: Connecticut Hall on the Old Campus at Yale University.

Across High Street from the Old Campus is **Harkness Tower,** a 221-foot-tall bell tower that is a Connecticut landmark. The campus is organized into twelve colleges, each with its own rooms, library, administrative offices, and dining halls. Yale's neo-Gothic and neo-Georgian buildings, with their quiet, shady courtyards and ivy-covered walls, were constructed between 1919 and 1941 to designs by James Gamble Rogers, with funds provided by the Harkness family. Pierson, Silliman, and Timothy Dwight colleges were built in the red-brick Georgian style. Davenport is a hybrid—a Gothic facade faces York Street, but the interior is Georgian.

The **Yale Center for British Art** (1080 Chapel Street, 203–432–4594) displays British paintings, drawings, prints, and sculpture, including works by Anthony van Dyck, Thomas Gainsborough, J. M. W. Turner, William Blake, and Joshua Reynolds.

The **Yale Peabody Museum** (170 Whitney Avenue, 203–432–3740) is the largest museum of natural history in New England, with a renowned collection of dinosaur fossils, birds, Indian artifacts, and minerals. The **Yale University Art Gallery** (1111 Chapel Street, 203–432–0600) is the oldest university art gallery in the country. Its broad collections include an excellent sampling of American paintings and decorative arts, and superlative collections of American furniture and silver.

Detail of Winslow Homer's The Morning Bell *(1872) in the Yale University Art Gallery.*

BRANFORD

Branford was founded in 1638 when the New Haven Colony "purchased" land from the Indians. During the Revolution a salt works here provided salt to preserve food for the Continental Army. There are several buildings of interest on or near the town Green: the Gothic-style **Trinity Episcopal Church,** the **Branford Academy** (1820), and the **James Blackstone Memorial Library** (1896). The only house open to the public is the **Nathaniel Harrison House** (124 Main Street, 203–488–4828 and 488–8835), built in 1720. The **Stony Creek District,** once a fishing village, affords views of the **Thimble Islands,** another archipelago upon which Captain Kidd is said to have buried treasure, in 1699. East of Branford on Route 146 are **Leete's Island** where, in June 1777, Guilford militiamen repulsed a British raiding party, and **Sachem's Head,** the site of a bloody battle during the Pequot War in 1637. The area was so named because the Mohegan chief, Uncas, displayed the head of a slain Pequot in a tree.

GUILFORD

Thanks in part to the successful stand of the militiamen at Leete's Island, Guilford escaped destruction by the British during the Revolution. Thus several early Colonial houses survive today and, in addition, some four hundred houses from the eighteenth and nineteenth centuries, nearly all privately owned, are also found in this town.

For its first hundred years Guilford was a farming town, but in the eighteenth century, mills and a shipyard opened. Guilford seamen fished and transported goods to New York and Boston. The strong backs and skillful seamanship of the townsmen stood them in good stead during the Revolution. In the month before the Leete's Island skirmish, Colonel Return Jonathan Meigs led Guilford men in a raid on the British stronghold at Sag Harbor, Long Island. In 13 whaleboats escorted by 2 sloops, 170 Patriots rowed 50 miles, at night, to Long Island, where they burned 10 British transports, wharves, and 100 tons of hay. With not a man lost, they rowed back in time for lunch.

Harriet Beecher Stowe lived for a year on her grandmother's farm when she was four years old, and it was here that she met blacks for the first time—the indentured servants of her grandmother. A Guilford quarry yielded the granite for portions of the Brooklyn Bridge and the base of the Statue of Liberty.

Henry Whitfield House

Built in 1639, the year the town was settled, the Whitfield House is the oldest stone house in New England. The Guilford Puritans, according to local legend, hired Mennuncatuck Indians to haul the stones from a nearby outcropping. In addition to being Whitfield's home, the house was to serve as the colony's gathering place and fortress (as it turned out, no Indians ever attacked). The house has undergone many changes over three centuries, and Whitfield might not recognize the building if he saw it today. Nonetheless, the restoration, carried out in the 1930s, conveys the atmosphere of the early settlement. The first floor consists of a large hall for daily living activities and a hall chamber, the private quarters for the master of the house. On the second floor are three chambers which might have been space used for sleeping in the seventeenth century. The museum is furnished throughout with rare seventeenth- and eighteenth-century pieces. The third floor garret houses exhibits of local historical artifacts.

LOCATION: Stone House Lane. HOURS: April–November: 10–5 Wednesday–Sunday; November–March: 10–4 Wednesday–Sunday. Closed December 15–January 14. FEE: Yes. TELEPHONE: 203–453–2457.

The **Hyland House** (84 Boston Street, 203–453–9477) is an early New England salt-box house, with an overhanging second floor, built in 1660 by George Hyland. It was saved from demolition early in this century, restored to its seventeenth-century state, and furnished with period items. An original exterior wall with hand-split clapboards and an original casement window were found during the restoration.

The **Thomas Griswold House** (171 Boston Street, 203–453–3176) is another salt-box, built in 1735. Occupied by descendants of the builder until 1958, the Griswold House today displays clothing, tools, books, and other items of local history. A restored blacksmith shop and a colonial garden are on the grounds.

OPPOSITE: The 1639 Henry Whitfield House, the oldest stone house in New England, was intended to serve, in part, as a fortress.

OLD SAYBROOK

Saybrook was the home of David Bushnell, a poor farmboy who finally saved enough money to put himself into Yale at the age of thirty-one. At Yale he experimented with exploding gunpowder charges underwater, and designed a clockwork timing device to trigger the explosion. After his graduation in 1775 he put his "great mechanical powers" (in George Washington's words) to work for the Revolution. He designed and built a craft he called a "sub-marine," in which a man could submerge for thirty minutes, maneuver to the hull of a ship, and attach a 150-pound Bushnell mine to the hull. He dubbed his craft the *American Turtle,* and it was tested in Saybrook's Otter Cove by his brother Ezra, before the gaze of Benjamin Franklin. Although the *Turtle* failed three times to sink British ships (the pilot could never get the mine attached to a hull), Bushnell's craft was a truly remarkable mechanical achievement. He anticipated the modern submarine in his design of a ballast tank, conning tower, and a depth gauge with a luminous dial.

General William Hart House (350 Main Street, 203–388–2622), built in 1767, is an example of the type of house built by affluent colonials just before the Revolution. The first floor rooms have fine wood panelling, and the library fireplace is decorated with Staffordshire tiles depicting scenes from Aesop's Fables. The restoration of the house extended to the gardens—fruit trees, lilacs, roses, and 125 herbs used for cooking and healing have been planted.

ESSEX

Essex was one of the Connecticut River's important shipbuilding sites from the mid-1700s to the 1840s. At one time the town had eight shipyards, and during the War of 1812 the British raided and burned some twenty-eight ships. Essex imported molasses, rum, sugar, and from Zanzibar, ivory, which was made into piano keys at a nearby factory. In 1799 an Essex man invented the first machine for making ivory combs.

Steamboats made commercial runs on the Connecticut River as early as 1823, and Essex was one of their stopping points. In 1833 the boilers of the *New England* exploded off Essex, killing fifteen passengers. The **Connecticut River Museum,** located by the river at Steamboat Dock (203–767–8269), exhibits ship models,

David Bushnell's Revolutionary War submarine, The American Turtle. OVERLEAF: *Lighthouse and docks at Essex on the Connecticut River.*

paintings, a full-size, working reproduction of David Bushnell's 1775 submarine, *American Turtle,* and other items of river history. The **Griswold Inn** (48 Main Street, 203–767–1812), built in 1776, remains an inn and tavern today. The **Valley Railroad** (Railroad Avenue, 203–767–0103), which originally ran from Old Saybrook to Hartford, now travels nine scenic miles from Essex through the hills above the Connecticut River. Items relating to the history of Essex are displayed at **Hill's Academy Museum** (22 Prospect Avenue, 203–767–0681), a Greek Revival schoolhouse built in 1832 on land donated by Joseph Hill. To support the school, Hill donated the proceeds from a shad fishery, amounting to some $600 a year. The academy is the headquarters of the Essex Historical Society, with displays of nineteenth-century art, tools, and Civil War items.

Gillette Castle, the idiosyncratic home of actor William Gillette, overlooking the Connecticut River at Hadlyme. OPPOSITE: The castle's main hall.

Pratt House (20 West Avenue, 203–767–8987 and 767–0681) has been home to several generations of the Pratt family; the main portion of it was erected in 1732. The ell at the rear may have been part of the original structure built in 1648 by William Pratt, who fought the Pequot at Mystic and was among the first settlers of Essex (then known as the "Outlands" of Saybrook). The house has been restored and furnished with items from the seventeenth, eighteenth, and nineteenth centuries.

GILLETTE CASTLE

The playwright and actor William Gillette (1853–1937), who made a fortune playing the role of Sherlock Holmes on the stage, erected this eccentric, battlemented "castle" on a hilltop overlooking the Connecticut River. Five years of work (from 1914 to 1919) and a million dollars went into the project, designed by Gillette himself to resemble medieval castles on the Rhine. It has twenty-four rooms, with a fifteen-hundred-square-foot living room and a Sherlock Holmes chamber. Gillette enjoyed tinkering with locks and made most of the ones in the house himself. He also installed mirrors in his bedroom allowing him to see who was downstairs, enabling him to say he was indisposed without personally confronting his com-

pany. His amusements included a three-mile private railroad along the cliff below the castle, a small portion of which can still be seen from the river. The state now operates the castle as a museum.

LOCATION: 67 River Road, off Route 82, Hadlyme. HOURS: Late April through mid-October: 10–5 Daily. FEE: Yes. TELEPHONE: 203–526–2336.

EAST HADDAM

In the decades after the Civil War when luxurious steamboats plied the Connecticut River, East Haddam was a resort with hotels and the **Goodspeed Opera House** (203–873–8668), a grand, six-story Victorian playhouse that has been restored to its original luster and function. The opera house, the tallest wooden structure on the river, was built in 1877 by William H. Goodspeed, who built steamboats at a yard in East Haddam and operated a lucrative cruise line on the river. A local newspaper reporter attended the opening of the opera house and had some fun describing Goodspeed's extravagance: "It is simply PERFECT, from the black-walnut banister on the stairway to the ventilator, it is just perfect. The stage curtains [depicting one of Goodspeed's boats] and scenery, the floor, the seats, everything we would have had if we were going to build an opera house and Mr. Goodspeed was going to pay the bills."

In the school year of 1773–1774, after his graduation from Yale, Nathan Hale taught local children at the **Nathan Hale Schoolhouse** (Main Street). The building was moved from its original location in 1799, and for a century it was a private home. It has now been restored.

MIDDLETOWN

Settled in 1650, Middletown was so named because it is midway between Old Saybrook and Hartford. The town developed slowly at first—in 1730 there were only two merchants—but a boom in shipbuilding and West Indies trade made Middletown the colony's wealthiest town in the second half of the eighteenth century. Middletown was the home of the naval hero Thomas Macdonough who defeated a British fleet on Lake Champlain, a victory that hastened the end of the War of 1812.

OPPOSITE: Goodspeed Opera House, East Haddam. OVERLEAF: A Middletown home.

In 1831 **Wesleyan University** was founded here. It was established by Methodists, but has always been nonsectarian. **Honors College** (Main Street) is housed in an imposing, Greek Revival mansion built in 1830 by the China trader Samuel Russell, and designed by Ithiel Town. When the famous orator Edward Everett stayed at Russell's house in 1859 he wrote to his wife that "nothing could exceed the luxury of my quarters." The **General Mansfield House** (151 Main Street, 203–346–0746), built in 1810 in the Federal style, displays eighteenth- and nineteenth-century furnishings and Civil War memorabilia.

OLD LYME

Once a shipbuilding and trading center, Old Lyme is now a quiet summer retreat with fine eighteenth- and nineteenth-century, privately owned houses on Lyme Street. The **First Congregational Church,** built in 1817 and rebuilt in 1907 after a fire, may be the quintessential New England church, with its slender Ionic columns and graceful steeple and spire. It was designed by Samuel Belcher, who was also the architect of the **Florence Griswold House** (96 Lyme Street, 203–434–5542). The daughter of a sea captain, Flor-

Hamburg Cove on the Connecticut River.

A sketching class on the river near Old Lyme, ca. 1910.

ence Griswold turned her home into an artist's colony at the turn of the century. It is now maintained as a museum of painting, decorative arts, and furniture.

NEW LONDON

One of Connecticut's great seafaring towns, New London was founded in 1646 by John Winthrop, Jr. with a group of Massachusetts Puritans. Here the Thames River formed the largest and deepest harbor on the Connecticut shore. Now restored, **Ye Olde Towne Mill** (8 Mill Street, 203–444–2206) was built in 1650 for Winthrop. The gristmill on the site dates to 1800. Another relic of New London's earliest days is the **Joshua Hempsted House** (11 Hempstead Street, 203–247–8996), built by the son of a town founder. It is the oldest surviving house in New London, and its low ceilings, small casement windows, and simple furnishings convey the atmosphere of life in the early settlement; also on the grounds is the stone **Nathaniel Hempsted House,** built in 1758.

In the eighteenth century New Londoners carried on a brisk trade with the colony's other coastal settlements and with the West

Indies. At the outbreak of the Revolution, Nathan Hale was a schoolmaster here. The school where he taught, the **Nathan Hale Schoolhouse** (Captain's Walk, 203–269–5752), has been restored. When news of the fighting came from Lexington, Hale made a public speech in favor of the rebellion, then left to join the army. During the Revolution the town was an important base for privateers, who took over three hundred enemy ships. The restored **Shaw Mansion** (11 Blinman Street, 203–443–1209), built in 1756, was the state's naval headquarters, where Washington and Lafayette visited. The restoration of the stone mansion includes Shaw family furniture and decorative items.

On September 6, 1781, Benedict Arnold, leading 1,700 British troops in 32 ships, raided New London. It was a homecoming of sorts for Arnold, who grew up in nearby Norwich and knew the lay of the land, the weaknesses of the fortifications, and the militia's signal system—two cannon shots meant an attack, three all clear. After the Patriot sentries fired two shots in warning, Arnold ordered a ship to fire a third, which lulled the town into complacency. New London was assaulted because its ships carried crucial supplies and had attacked British shipping. Strategically, the raid was intended to force George Washington to divert troops from his march from New York to join the French in closing in upon the British under Lord Cornwallis. Arnold's first assault was at **Fort Trumbull** (not open to the public), but the fort was undermanned because of his trick with the signals, and the garrison fled almost immediately. The main action then shifted across the river to Groton at Fort Griswold, where the British were not under Arnold's direct command. Arnold's men burned 150 buildings. He later said the fires started accidentally and that his troops tried to put them out. (After the Revolution many New Londoners joined other Connecticut property losers in emigrating to Ohio, where they had been given lands in compensation by the government.) It was the last major battle of the Revolution in the North, and the only one in Connecticut.

Whaling began in 1784 with a single ship, and New Londoners made large profits, except during the War of 1812, when the town was blockaded by the British. After the war, the city reached the zenith of its maritime glory, with some eighty whaling ships registered, fewer only than the fleets at New Bedford and Nantucket. In 1865 one ship returned, after a fourteen-month journey, with a cargo that brought $150,000 in profit. The last whaling ship

Eugene O'Neill's Monte Cristo Cottage, New London.

docked in 1909. The prosperity brought by whaling can be seen at **Whale Oil Row** (Huntington Street)—an impressive row of four Greek Revival mansions, all designed by Ezra Chappell in 1830. The **Deshon-Allyn House** (613 Williams Street, 203–443–2545), a restored mansion, was built by Daniel Deshon in 1829 and sold to a whaling captain, Lyman Allyn, in 1851. The house's collection includes porcelain, portraits, and musical instruments. The house is near the **Lyman Allyn Museum** (625 Williams Street, 203–443–2545), which has a collection of paintings by Connecticut artists.

Another monument to New London's days as a great shipping center is the **Custom House** (150 Bank Street), built in 1833 of granite from quarries near the city. The front door was made from wood taken from the USS *Constitution*. It was designed by Robert Mills, who also designed the Washington Monument. The nearby **Union Station** (State Street) was designed by Henry Hobson Richardson, and built in 1887. During his boyhood the playwright Eugene O'Neill lived at the **Monte Cristo Cottage** (325 Pequot Avenue, 203–443–0051). His plays *Long Day's Journey into Night* and *Ah, Wilderness* were based on his experiences here.

The **U.S. Coast Guard Academy** (Mohegan Avenue, 203–444–8270) has a museum of Coast Guard history. The academy's training ship, the *Eagle,* can be visited when in port.

GROTON

Groton, settled soon after New London, also turned to the sea for its livelihood. Some of Connecticut's most adventurous mariners of the eighteenth and nineteenth centuries were Groton men.

Fort Griswold

Groton was the site of one of the most heroic, and tragic, incidents of the Revolution. When Benedict Arnold raided New London and Groton, about 140 militiamen, some of them boys, rallied to Fort Griswold, a square fort with 12-foot-high stone walls, surrounded by ditches, and situated on the heights overlooking the Thames River. Under the command of Colonel William Ledyard, the Patriots refused a demand to surrender, and the 800 British regulars, New Jersey Tories, and Hessian troops began a methodical attack. In the heated 40-minute battle, the militia repulsed several assaults before the British finally broke through, having suffered 50 killed and 150 wounded—very high casualties. Only three of the Patriots had been killed. Ledyard surrendered, handing his sword to a Tory officer, who immediately ran him through. An indiscriminate slaughter ensued. The victors shot or bayoneted 75 to 85 of the defenders, who had thrown down their weapons, and mutilated their bodies.

The fort's ramparts still stand, preserved as a state park, and a plaque marks the spot where Ledyard was murdered. A bas-relief indicates where Jordan Freeman, one of two blacks who died at the fort, killed a British officer during the assault. In 1830 a 134-foot-high granite obelisk was built as a memorial to the defenders. The museum on the grounds has a diorama of the battle.

LOCATION: Monument and Park avenues. HOURS: *Museum:* Late May through Labor Day: 9–5; *Park:* 8–sunset Daily. FEE: None. TELEPHONE: 203–445–1729.

USS Nautilus *Memorial*

The world's first nuclear-powered ship, the submarine *Nautilus,* was built in Groton and launched in 1954. In 1958 she sailed under the polar icecap from the Pacific to the Atlantic. Now decommissioned, the submarine is open to visitors, who may see her operations deck, torpedo room, living quarters, and dining quarters. The adjacent **Submarine Force Library and Museum** covers the history of submarines from the Revolutionary War to the present. Ship models, working periscopes, and a control room are exhibited. Midget submarines and an early U.S. research submarine, the *Explorer,* are also displayed on the grounds.

LOCATION: Off Route 12 outside the Naval Submarine Base. HOURS: Mid-April through mid-October: 9–5 Wednesday–Monday; mid-October through mid-April: 9–3:30 Wednesday–Monday. FEE: None. TELEPHONE: 203–449–3558.

The USS *Croaker* (359 Thames Street, 203–445–1616), a World War II submarine, saw fifteen months of duty in the Pacific, where she sank eleven Japanese ships.

LEBANON

Located on one of the main routes between Boston and New York, Lebanon was an important town during the Revolution. The French encamped here in the winter of 1780–1781. William Franklin, Benjamin's son, was imprisoned here for his Tory sympathies.

Governor Jonathan Trumbull House (West Town Street, 203–642–7558), built in 1735 and now restored, was the home of the state's first governor, Jonathan Trumbull, Sr. An ardent Patriot (in fact, the only colonial governor who favored independence at the outbreak of the Revolution), Trumbull was instrumental in managing the flow of supplies from Connecticut to Washington's armies. He held over one thousand meetings of the Connecticut Council of Safety at his store facing the Green. The phrase "Brother Jonathan," by which the British referred to the Americans, may have had its origin in George Washington's nickname for Trumbull: While wrestling with a difficult decision, the commander-in-chief once said, "We must consult Brother Jonathan."

His son John Trumbull (1756–1843) was a noted painter whose widely reproduced works chronicled the struggle for independence, in which he briefly served—as a chaplain. Jefferson said of him that he "pined for the arts," and, abandoning his military career in 1780, he went to London to study under Benjamin West.

OVERLEAF: Reenactment of the Revolutionary War battle at Fort Griswold, Groton.

In 1816 Congress commissioned him to paint the famous historical scenes that decorate the Capitol rotunda. Among Trumbull's best-known paintings are *The Signing of the Declaration of Independence, Surrender of General Burgoyne,* and *Surrender of Lord Cornwallis.* He also designed the **First Congregational Church** on Lebanon's Green. In 1875 the church's interior was divided into two floors and redesigned in Victorian style; but the hurricane of 1938 undid all that by lifting the steeple and dropping it through the roof, virtually demolishing the interior. It has now been restored to Trumbull's design.

NORWICH

Norwich, a stronghold of the Revolution, also has the dubious honor of being the birthplace of Benedict Arnold. Born here in 1741, he lived in Norwich until he was twenty-one, when he moved to New Haven. His house was torn down in 1853. More durable Patriots were the Huntingtons of Norwich: They provided the cause with soldiers, two Continental Congressmen, and a signer of

John Trumbull's 1806 painting, Norwich Falls.

the Declaration of Independence. The **Leffingwell Inn** (348 Washington Street, 203–889–9440) was frequently the meeting place for Patriots, and Washington visited it. The owner of the inn, Christopher Leffingwell, was a remarkable Connecticut Yankee. His many commercial undertakings in Norwich included a shipping brokerage, stoneware kiln, stocking factory, potash works, a store, dye house, the first papermill in Connecticut, and a chocolate factory that produced five thousand pounds of chocolate a year—with only one workman to run the milling machinery. Leffingwell was in and out of financial trouble, some caused by restrictive British trade laws, but his final ruin was brought on by his enthusiastic support of the Revolution: He helped finance Ethan Allen's attack on Fort Ticonderoga, and provided bread, flour, salt pork, and other items to the Army, paying his suppliers out of his own pocket. He was never repaid by the Congress and by the end of the war he was impoverished. Leffingwell's efforts to industrialize the town bore fruit in the next century. By the 1850s Norwich had the largest papermill in the world, and the country's largest cotton mills. The Mohcgan leader Uncas is buried at the **Royal Burial Ground.**

UNCASVILLE

The town is named for the Mohegan leader Uncas (died 1683), who was friendly toward the white settlers, with whom he sided during the Pequot War. James Fenimore Cooper used him as the model for his novel, *The Last of the Mohicans.*

The Mohegan are related to the Mohican Indians of northern New York, and it was from that region that the Mohegan came to what is now Connecticut in the early 1600s, according to their traditions. When they arrived, they disrupted the indigenous tribes, who named the newcomers Pequataug ("invaders" or "destroyers"), and they eventually came to be known as the Pequot. **Fort Shantok State Park** was the site of a battle between Uncas's Mohegan and the Narragansett, in which Uncas was aided by the settlers at Saybrook; today a burial ground is found there. Eighteen Mohegan were killed during the Revolution while fighting on the American side. Thirty-five Mohegan still live in the area, and the **Tantaquidgeon Indian Museum** (1819 Norwich–New London Turnpike, 203–848–9145), which was founded by direct descendants of Uncas, displays traditional Indian crafts, ceremonial objects, and historical items.

LEDYARD

Until the railroad finally came through in 1900, Ledyard, named for the slain commander of Fort Griswold, was a bustling river port. Merchants and sea captains from New London built homes here. The restored **Nathan Lester House** (Vinegar Hill Road and Long Cove, 203–464–2655) is a substantial farmhouse built by the relatively well-to-do Nathan Lester in 1793. When Nathan carried his bride over the threshold three years later he was fifty-four years old. There is also a museum of farming on the grounds.

Sawmill Park (Iron Street, 203–464–8740) is an eleven-acre park with a restored 1869 sawmill. The rare up-and-down saw in the mill is about 200 years old and was in use until the 1930s.

MYSTIC

Mystic was the site of the 1637 battle between Connecticut settlers and the Pequot Indians. The battleground, on Pequot Hill in West Mystic, is marked by the **John Mason Monument** (Pequot Avenue).

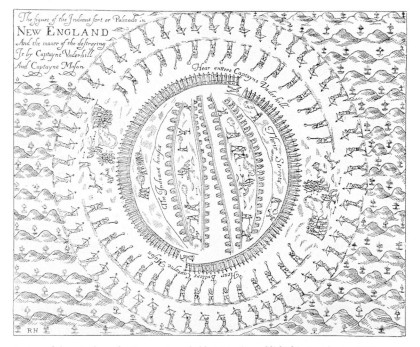

A view of the attack on the Pequot stronghold at Mystic, published in London in 1638.

Carving shop at Mystic Seaport. OVERLEAF: *Nineteenth-century figureheads, Mystic Seaport.*

Mason, from Windsor, was the leader of the attack, which was more of a massacre than a battle. The Pequot, who were dreaded by the English and by the region's other Indians, had earlier killed about thirty colonists in attacks on the settlements, including Wethersfield. Mason and seventy-seven men surrounded the Pequot log palisade and set fire to it. Indians who tried to escape were shot down. Between four hundred and seven hundred Pequot men, women, and children were shot or burned alive. The survivors fled west along the shore to Fairfield, where Mason defeated them in the Great Swamp Fight of July 13, 1637.

The **Denison Homestead** (Pequot-Sepos Road), built in 1717, has been restored with furnishings that belonged to eleven generations of the Denison family, ranging in date from the construction of the house to the early twentieth century. The town is dotted with Colonial homes of sea captains, all of them private.

From the early 1800s to the middle of the century, Mystic was one of the premier shipbuilding sites in the country. The town's yards built coastal sloops, fishing vessels, and the grand lords of the sea clippers. Mystic's *Andrew Jackson* set the world speed record for sailing around Cape Horn to San Francisco.

Mystic Seaport

A recreated nineteenth-century seaport with over sixty buildings on seventeen acres, Mystic Seaport is a "living" museum where craftspeople practice the traditional maritime crafts. Among the scores of exhibits are a ropewalk, rigging loft, hoop shop, printing press, drugstore, bank, cooperage, smithy, and sail loft. The most impressive exhibit is the 1841 whaling ship, the *Charles W. Morgan,* which made thirty-seven voyages from the South Seas to the Arctic, earning $1.4 million for her New Bedford owners. The 111-foot-long vessel could carry 2,700 barrels of whale oil.

LOCATION: Germanville Avenue and Route 27. HOURS: 9–4 Monday–Friday, 9–5 Saturday–Sunday. FEE: Yes. TELEPHONE: 203–572–0711.

STONINGTON

This old seafaring town, with many beautiful, Greek Revival houses, is still an active fishing village. The *Betsy* of Stonington was the first ship flying the American flag to circumnavigate the globe. The **Old Lighthouse Museum** (Water Street, 203–535–1440) is housed in a sturdy, stone lighthouse, built in 1823. The exhibits include whaling and fishing gear, swords, toys, and ship models.

The pair of cannons displayed at **Cannon Square** held five British warships, with 140 guns, at bay during the War of 1812. The British arrived off Stonington on August 9, 1814, and sent a note ashore saying that the people had one hour to get out of town or shooting would start. The town's reply was: "We will defend." In three days the British fired sixty tons of metal, including incendiary rockets, onto the town, but only one person was wounded. With their pair of cannons the defenders managed to kill twenty-one men and wound another fifty on the ships. With one ship on the verge of sinking, the British departed.

OPPOSITE: Old Lighthouse Museum, Stonington.

RHODE ISLAND

OPPOSITE: Slater Mill, Pawtucket.

Rhode Island was founded by religious dissenters from Massachusetts. In the 1630s Roger Williams settled at Providence, Anne Hutchinson at Pocasset, and William Coddington at Newport. Williams had to leave Massachusetts because he held "new and dangerous opinions," such as that the king could not grant ownership of land in New England unless the Indians were paid for it, and that civil authority could not be used to enforce religious orthodoxy. "Forced worship stinks in God's nostrils," he said. Williams was banished from Massachusetts in 1635; but before he could be shipped back to England he fled to the territory southwest of Plymouth Colony. He knew the Indians there, and was welcomed as a friend. The Indians gave him the land for his settlement at Providence ("It was not price nor money that could have purchased Rhode Island," he wrote. "Rhode Island was purchased by love."). From the very start the colony insisted upon religious freedom and the separation of church and state. King Charles recognized these principles in a charter, in which he agreed to "full libertie in religious concernements."

With its excellent harbors at Providence, Newport, Bristol, Warren, and other towns, Rhode Island was an important center of maritime commerce by the 1650s, competing successfully with Massachusetts for a portion of the trade between New England and the West Indies. Rhode Island's products, such as beef, dried fish, flour, wool, butter, lumber, and horses, as well as fine furniture, clocks, and silver made by Newport craftsmen, were shipped to the West Indies and Charleston, South Carolina. From the Caribbean came sugar, spices, molasses, and slaves. Sugar was used in distilling rum, which was then traded in the West Indies and Britain. During England's wars with France, from the 1740s to the 1760s, Rhode Island's captains sailed as privateers, preying upon French shipping. They would later put their piratical skills to use against British shipping during the Revolution.

As a maritime colony, Rhode Island was highly sensitive to the commercial policies of Great Britain, and was in the forefront of resistance to the crown when England's policies began to weigh heavily on business. The first violent acts against British rule took place in Rhode Island: In 1765 a Newport mob destroyed a boat from a British warship to protest the impressment of seamen; in 1769 a British revenue ship was destroyed at Newport; in 1772 the revenue ship *Gaspee* was burned in a daring raid. Although the British occupied Newport during the war, virtually destroying its

Detail of The Ship George Washington, *by Thomas Chambers ca. 1838.*

economy, the only major battle of the Revolution in Rhode Island was a failed attempt to dislodge the British from that town. Providence escaped harm and prospered after the war.

Once freed of British restrictions on manufacturing, Rhode Island merchants led the country into the Industrial Revolution. Backed by William Almy and Smith Brown of Providence, Samuel Slater established the country's first water-powered textile mill in Pawtucket in 1793. Throughout the nineteenth century, Rhode Island was one of the largest producers of textiles in the country. In the second half of the century, jewelry manufacturing became a leading industry in Providence.

As factories rose in Providence, Pawtucket, and the towns along the Blackstone River, each attracting large numbers of European immigrants, opulent mansions began to be built in Newport. Lured by the gentle summer climate, wealthy families from New York made Newport the warm-weather capital of society. Architects Richard Morris Hunt, Horace Trumbauer, and Stanford White built its mansions. To amuse themselves in these gargantuan "cottages," Astors, Belmonts, and Vanderbilts vied for the honor of spending the most money in the shortest span of time. They fed caviar to their dogs and stabled their horses sumptuously. Old New

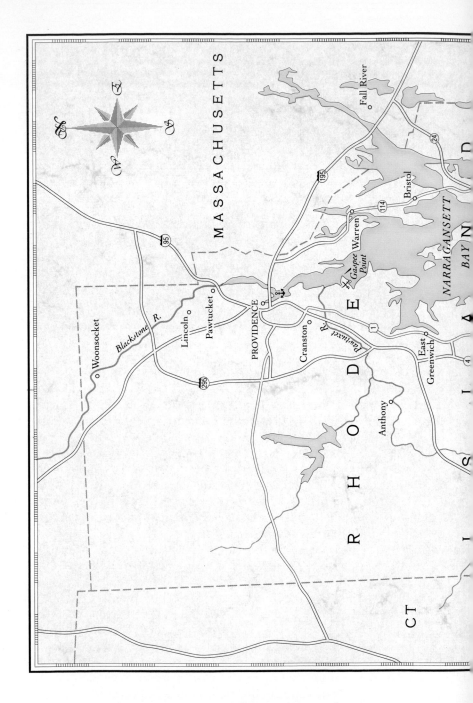

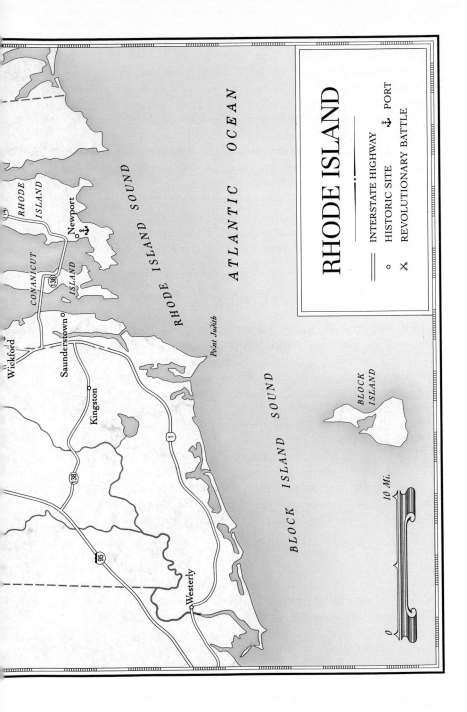

RHODE ISLAND

— INTERSTATE HIGHWAY
o HISTORIC SITE   ⚓ PORT
✕ REVOLUTIONARY BATTLE

ATLANTIC OCEAN

RHODE ISLAND SOUND

BLOCK ISLAND SOUND

BLOCK ISLAND

Point Judith

Newport

RHODE ISLAND

CONANICUT ISLAND

ISLAND

Wickford

Saunderstown

Kingston

Westerly

0   10 Mi.

England was not amused. Julia Ward Howe of Beacon Hill, who had written the stirring words of "The Battle Hymn of the Republic," said that she was ashamed to see the magnificent Belmont stables at Belcourt Castle when so many humans lived in slums.

The late-nineteenth-century mansions of Newport are the most popular of Rhode Island's historical sites, but there are well-preserved eighteenth-century districts in Providence, Bristol, East Greenwich, Wickford, and Kingston as well as in Newport itself. The cotton factory that launched the nation's Industrial Revolution still stands in Pawtucket.

This tour of Rhode Island's historic sites begins at Providence and its industrial suburb, Pawtucket. From there a traveler can proceed southeast to the port town of Bristol, or directly south along the western shore of Narragansett Bay.

PROVIDENCE

In 1636 Roger Williams, exiled from Massachusetts, established a settlement on the Providence River at the head of Narragansett Bay, twenty-seven miles upriver from the Atlantic. He called it "Providence Plantations." The site was well chosen: Not only did it have access to the sea and a fine harbor, its rivers provided easy communication and transportation to inland communities, and would later supply waterpower for industry.

The original inhabitants lived by the Providence River, along South and North Main streets (then called Towne Street). In its early decades the plantation was agricultural, but by 1700 Providence had begun to take part in the West Indian and African trade in rum, molasses, and slaves, competing with Newport. The Revolution laid Newport low and elevated the fortunes of Providence, which was saved from British attack by a series of nine forts (all since demolished) along the Providence River, and by its distance from the Atlantic.

After the Revolution, Providence, like Boston, dispatched ships to China and prospered from trade in Oriental goods. The leaders in the China trade were John Brown, whose mansion has been preserved, and his brothers. They later provided the financing for Rhode Island's first ventures in textile manufacturing, and their gifts spurred the growth of Brown University. In the nineteenth century, as maritime commerce was replaced by industry, the cove at the head of the Providence River was gradually filled in to create land for railroad tracks. The landfill was completed in the 1890s for the construction of Union Station.

Today, the Providence River partially separates the city's commercial center on the western side from the eighteenth-century historic district on the eastern bank. Brown University is on the eastern side of the river. This tour of Providence begins at the Capitol and proceeds along the eastern bank of the river, chiefly along North and South Main streets and Benefit Street. The final sites on the tour are on the river's western side.

The **State Capitol** (Smith Street, 401–277–2000) stands atop a hill overlooking the city. Built of marble from Georgia, the Capitol has an enormous dome, the second-largest marble dome without skeletal support in the world (the largest is on St. Peter's in Rome). The firm of McKim, Mead & White designed the Capitol and it was completed in 1904. A statue atop the dome symbolizes "the Independent Man." Inside, changing exhibits show portions of the state's collections. On permanent display is the 1663 charter from King Charles II, shown at the entrance to the Senate. In the elaborately appointed Governor's Reception Room is a Gilbert Stuart portrait of George Washington and the silver service given in 1905 by the Gorham Company of Providence as a gift to the USS *Rhode Island.*

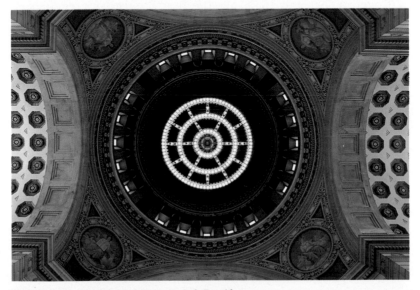

Rotunda of the Rhode Island State Capitol, Providence.

A four-and-a-half-acre park along North Main Street has been set aside as the **Roger Williams National Memorial.** The park is on the site of the spring near which Williams built his house. A **visitor center** at 282 North Main features exhibits and a slide presentation about Williams's life and the history of the Plantation. Heading east from North Main, Bowen, Wheaton, and Congdon streets lead up a hill to **Prospect Terrace,** where Roger Williams is buried. The terrace offers excellent views of the city.

The **Cathedral of Saint John** (across the street from the Williams Memorial at 271 North Main) was built in 1811 with designs by John Holden Greene.

The **Old State House** (North Main between North and South Court streets; entrance at 150 Benefit) is a plain and dignified brick building, erected in 1762, its tower having been added in the 1850s. Here the colony's assembly dissolved its bond with Great Britain on May 4, 1776, two months before the Declaration of Independence. The Old State House now houses the Rhode Island Heritage Commission and the Historical Preservation Commission.

First Baptist Church (75 North Main Street, 401–751–2266), an exceptionally beautiful Georgian church with a 185-foot steeple, was built in 1775. Joseph Brown designed it along the general lines of the London work of James Gibbs. The congregation, founded by Roger Williams in 1639, was the first Baptist congregation in America. Since Brown University's opening, the church has been the site of their commencement ceremonies.

The **Joseph Brown House** (50 South Main, private), which Brown designed himself and built in 1774, is more whimsical than the mansion he built for his brother on Benefit Street. For his own home Joseph placed the side of the house parallel to the street, in order to display an elegantly curving gable. Originally the doorway was on the second floor, reached by a double stairway. Above the door, a curved window echoed the line of the gable.

Benefit Street, which parallels North and South Main, preserves a large number of historic houses in a variety of styles and reflects the city's architectural development from the middle of the eighteenth century to the end of the nineteenth. The district of preserved houses stretches for a mile along Benefit Street, which was laid out in the late 1750s when Towne Street became clogged with traffic. A walking tour of Benefit Street could begin at Church Street and proceed roughly a mile south to Transit Street.

OPPOSITE: The dome of the Rhode Island Capitol, whose design was frequently emulated.

Number 88 Benefit (private) was the home of the poet, Sarah Helen Whitman, whom Edgar Allen Poe wooed unsuccessfully for four years. He wrote his poem "For Helen" with her in mind. At 109 Benefit is the **Sullivan Dorr House** (private), built in 1809 and designed by John Holden Greene. The front of this gracious wooden house, with a Palladian window over the doorway, is on Bowen Street. The **Brick School House** (24 Meeting Street, 401–831–7440), one of the first school buildings in the city, is the headquarters of the Providence Preservation Society.

The Gothic castle at 176 Benefit is the old state **arsenal**, designed by Russell Warren and built in 1839. The **Providence Art Club** (10–11 Thomas Street, 401–331–1114) was founded in 1880 and exhibits the work of local artists. The club's buildings were erected in 1789 and 1791. One block south, the **Carr House** (Benefit and Waterman streets, private) is a shingle-style building dating to 1885. The **Museum of Art of the Rhode Island School of Design** (224 Benefit Street, 401–331–3511) displays an excellent and wide-ranging art collection, with works from the ancient, medieval, Renaissance, and modern eras. A superb small collection of American furniture, silver, and paintings is in the **Pendleton House** adjoining the museum.

The **Handicraft Club** (Benefit and College streets, 401–831–5337) is housed in an impressive Federal mansion designed by John Holden Greene and built in 1828. The sturdy Greek temple across the street is the **Providence Athenaeum** (401–421–6970), which dates to 1838. When Poe was courting Sarah Whitman they often met in the library's stacks. Russell Warren designed the row of houses from 257 to 267 Benefit, and they were built in the 1840s. The two-story wooden house at Benefit and Hopkins streets was the home of Stephen Hopkins from 1742 to 1785. Hopkins served ten terms as Rhode Island's governor and was among the signers of the Declaration of Independence. The house has been restored and is open to the public (401–885–4222). John Holden Greene designed the **First Unitarian Church** (285 Benefit), combining Gothic and classical motifs. It was finished in 1816.

John Brown House

The most distinguished residence on Benefit Street—indeed one of the finest eighteenth-century houses in the country—is the man-

OPPOSITE: Staircase in the John Brown House.

The College Green, Brown University Campus, Providence.

sion Joseph Brown designed for his brother John. Built in 1786, the house rises a full three stories, and a balustrade surrounds the roof. The central block projects slightly and proclaims Brown's status with a pediment, a bold Palladian window on the second floor, and a handsome doorway. The decoration of the fourteen-room interior is elegant, in the refined fashion of the day. On the ground floor a handsome central hall is flanked by large formal rooms intended for Brown's entertainments. John Quincy Adams visited the house and described it as the most magnificent he had ever seen. The house, which is the headquarters of the Rhode Island Historical Society, displays fine Rhode Island furniture, silver, and china.

LOCATION: 52 Power Street. HOURS: March through December: 11–4 Tuesday–Saturday, 1–4 Sunday; January through February: By appointment. FEE: Yes. TELEPHONE: 401–331–8575.

Nearby, at 66 Power Street, is the **Thomas Poynton Ives House** (private), built in 1806 for the son-in-law of Nicholas Brown. Another fine Federal mansion, the **Edward Carrington House** (66 Williams off Benefit, private) was built in 1811. Carrington bought it the following year after returning from China, where he had been the U.S. consul. The houses at 383 and 389 Benefit, built in the 1850s, are attractive examples of the Italianate style.

Brown University

The seventh college founded in America, Brown was originally located in Warren in 1764, and named Rhode Island College. It moved here in 1770, and changed its name in 1804 in honor of Nicholas Brown, Jr. The wrought-iron **Van Wickle Gates** lead into the **College Green,** the university's original focal point. The gate, built in 1901, is named after its donor and is opened only twice each year—inward for convocation and outward for commencement. Among the Colonial and Greek Revival buildings lining the Green is the beautiful Beaux-Arts **John Carter Brown Library.** Designed in 1904 by the firm of Shepley, Rutan & Coolidge to be the "classical gem" of the university, the limestone building holds a collection of Americana that was begun in 1846. The oldest building on the campus is **University Hall,** erected in 1770. It was designed by Robert Smith, a Philadelphia architect who had also done Princeton's Old Nassau Hall. During the Revolution the hall was used as a barracks by American and French troops. The **Annmary Brown Memorial** (21 Brown Street) exhibits early printed matter and American paintings.

LOCATION: Prospect and College streets. TELEPHONE: 401–863–1000.

On the western side of the Providence River, **Market House,** on Market Square, was built in 1775 to handle maritime commerce. The three-story brick building has tall arched windows on the ground floor which originally constituted an open arcade for the city's tradesmen and merchants. During the Revolution, Market House was the site of meetings. The building is now owned by the Rhode Island School of Design.

Weybosset Street has several interesting examples of nineteenth-century commercial architecture, notably the old custom house at number 24, the cast-iron building at number 36, and the 1850s Renaissance Revival building at number 50. **Providence Arcade** (65 Weybosset Street) was the nation's first enclosed shopping mall, built in 1828 in the Greek Revival style with a grand, temple-form entrance; Russell Warren and James Bucklin were the

architects. Off Weybosset at Matthewson and Westminster Mall is **Grace Church,** a Gothic Revival church designed by Richard Upjohn. The **Beneficent Congregational Church** (300 Weybosset) is known as "Roundtop" for its striking dome. The oldest part of the building dates to 1809; it was enlarged by James Bucklin in 1836.

The Rhode Island Historical Society maintains the **Museum of Rhode Island History** at Aldrich House (110 Benevolent Street, 401–331–8575), where it presents changing exhibits on the state's history, architecture, and decorative arts. The Federal-style Aldrich House, built in 1822, was occupied from 1881 to 1911 by Nelson Aldrich, an influential U.S. senator.

Governor Sprague Mansion

The Sprague family, prominent in politics and industry, built this twenty-eight-room mansion in Cranston, a suburb west of Providence. Completed in 1790, it was enlarged in 1864 when William Sprague was serving in the U.S. Senate. On display at the house is the Carrington Collection of Oriental Art. The restored carriage house contains a collection of wagons, sleighs, and carriages.

LOCATION: 1353 Cranston Street. HOURS: By appointment. FEE: Yes. TELEPHONE: 401–944–9226.

PAWTUCKET

Pawtucket is an Indian name meaning "place by a waterfall," and the city stands on hills split by three rivers: Blackstone, Moshassuck, and Ten Mile. Waterpower, combined with a good supply of wood and iron ore, the latter discovered in 1650, made it an early industrial center, its mills and forges producing equipment for farms and ships. Pawtucket took the great leap into the Industrial Revolution with the opening of the Slater Mill in 1793.

Slater Mill Historic Site

One of the most important landmarks in the history of American industry, the Slater Mill was the first textile mill in this country to be powered by water. A complex of buildings and other structures has been preserved and restored in a park on the Blackstone River: the 1793 Slater Mill and 1810 Wilkinson Mill, the 1758 Sylvanus

OPPOSITE: *Textile machinery at the Slater Mill, Pawtucket.*

Brown House, a dam, and a restored waterpower system, including an operating waterwheel. Samuel Slater, who had worked with Richard Arkwright's waterpowered spinning system in England, was hired by William Almy and Smith Brown of Providence to install and operate machinery based on Arkwright's. The mill began the transformation of American textile making from a hand-powered home industry to one of mass production.

The restored Slater Mill houses machinery for the processing of raw cotton—carding, drawing, spinning, and weaving. There are also machines for knitting and braiding. The Sylvanus Brown House contains the hand-powered spinning and weaving equipment that the mill made obsolete, while the Wilkinson Mill demonstrates the equipment of a machine shop run by waterpower.

LOCATION: Roosevelt and Slater avenues. HOURS: March through May: 1–5 Saturday–Sunday; June through Labor Day: 10–5 Tuesday–Sunday; Labor Day through December: 1–5 Saturday–Sunday. FEE: Yes. TELEPHONE: 401–725–8638.

LINCOLN

Northwest of Pawtucket, just west of the village of Lonsdale, is a group of historical buildings along Great Road (Route 123) in Lincoln. The **Friends Meetinghouse** at Great and River roads is the oldest Quaker meetinghouse still in use in New England, built in 1704 and added to in 1744. The **Eleazer Arnold House** (449 Great Road, open by appointment through the Society for the Preservation of New England Antiquities, 617–227–3956), built in the 1680s, is an impressive "stone-ender." Its massive chimney takes up an entire wall of the two-story house. The **Israel Arnold House** (600 Great Road, private) dates to the 1740s. Across the road, **Moffatt Mill** (private) is a small, waterpowered factory built in 1812. The stone mansion called **Hearthside** (Great Road near Breakneck Hill Road, private) was built around 1814 by Stephen Smith who, it is said, won $50,000 in the Louisiana lottery. Across the road is the textile mill Smith built, called **Butterfly Mill** (private) for the pattern of its stone wall. The Blackstone Valley Historical Society has its headquarters in **North Gate** (Route 246, 401–722–1839), a toll house built in 1807.

SLATERSVILLE

One of the oldest mill towns in the country, Slatersville was founded in 1805 by Samuel Slater of Pawtucket. The factory on Mill

Street dates to 1826. Houses built for the workers can be seen along
Main and Greene streets. At the center of the village is a Congregational church established in 1838.

BRISTOL

Bristol has fine houses, products of the wealth amassed in trading
slaves, rum, and molasses, and from privateering during the Revolution and the War of 1812. Many eighteenth- and nineteenth-
century houses, most of them private, can be seen in the historic
waterfront district along Hope, High, and Thames streets. The
finest of Bristol's houses were designed by Russell Warren. Warren
designed the Federal style mansion at **56 High Street** (private),
built in 1793, for one of the richest and most brazen of Bristol's
captains, James DeWolf, who also owned sugar plantations in
Cuba. In the early 1800s some of the DeWolf brothers continued to
send shiploads of slaves to South Carolina, defying the federal law
prohibiting their importation.

Linden Place (Hope and Wardwell, private), designed by Warren for George DeWolf, was built in 1810. Like his brother James,
George DeWolf made his fortune in Cuban sugar and slaving, but
lost it all when his plantations failed in 1825. The facade of his

Colt-Barrymore House in Bristol (private).

house is a proud and forceful display of Corinthian columns and an arched doorway. It is the only survivor of the four great mansions built by the DeWolfs.

The **Haffenreffer Museum of Anthropology** (Tower Street off Route 136, 401–253–8388) displays the Brown University Collection of Indian Art and Artifacts, representing cultures worldwide, but with an emphasis on North America. The museum is located near the swamp where Metacom, known to whites as King Philip, was ambushed and killed in August 1676 by a member of the Sakonnet, a tribe that was allied with the whites. The murder brought an end to the bloody King Philip's War, which had begun the previous summer at Pokanoket Neck.

GASPEE POINT

On the afternoon of June 9, 1772, the British revenue schooner *Gaspee* ran aground on this point seven miles south of Providence as it was pursuing a packet boat, whose captain knew the local waters much better than did the British commander, a Lieutenant Dudingston. The American captain, Thomas Lindsay, raced to Providence and told John Brown that the *Gaspee* would be stuck until the next high tide, at 3 AM. Dudingston had been a local annoyance with his energetic collection of taxes, so Brown had no trouble finding, on a few hours' notice, sixty-four volunteers for a midnight visit to the stranded revenuer. Led by Captain Abraham Whipple, the raiders set out from Providence in longboats.

They captured the ship in hand-to-hand fighting and burned it, after depositing the crew in Pawtuxet. A royal commission arrested Brown, but had to release him when it was discovered that not a single person in the colony had any information about the loss of the *Gaspee*. The affair rankled the British for years. Commanding an American ship during the Revolution, Whipple received a note from a British captain from whom he had just stolen a boat: "You Abraham Whipple on the 10th of June 1772 burned his majesty's vessel the Gaspee and I will hang you at the yardarm!" "Sir," Whipple replied, "Always catch a man before you hang him." Whipple escaped.

The small town of **Anthony,** founded in the early nineteenth century, is the site of the **General Nathanael Greene Homestead** (Taft Street off Route 117, 401–821–8630), a modest farmhouse which Greene built just before the Revolution. Greene was one of the most skilled American generals in the Revolution. He won important victories in the South, and was granted land after the war by grateful citizens of South Carolina and Georgia. He settled in Georgia after the war, and it was at his plantation that Eli Whitney developed the cotton gin. His homestead in Anthony has been restored and furnished with late-eighteenth-century items.

EAST GREENWICH

Now a yachting center on a hill facing Narragansett Bay, East Greenwich was a prosperous shipping and agricultural town in the eighteenth century and a textile-producing center in the nineteenth century. A cluster of eighteenth-century houses can be found along **Division Street,** such as **Windmill Cottage** (144 Division, private), which Henry Wadsworth Longfellow purchased in 1866 as a gift for a friend. The poet later bought a windmill and attached it to the house. The town's oldest house, the **Clement Weaver House** (125 Howland Road, private) dates to 1679.

Several historic buildings line **Pierce Street.** George Washington and Lafayette were guests at the **General James Mitchell Varnum House** (57 Pierce Street, 401–884–4110) which was built in 1773 by Varnum, who was the first commander of the Kentish Guards. Varnum's unit later had its headquarters at 90 Pierce Street, the **Armory of the Kentish Guards,** a Greek Revival temple built in 1842. The **Varnum Military Museum** (Main and Division streets, 401–884–8567) displays a collection of weapons and other military items. The **New England Wireless and Steam Museum** (Frenchtown and Tillinghast roads, 401–884–1710) exhibits early radio, telegraph, and telephone apparatus, and a collection of steam engines.

WICKFORD

The picturesque village of Wickford preserves a large number of late-eighteenth- and early nineteenth-century houses, built when the village thrived as a shipbuilding and fishing port. Many can be seen along Main and West Main streets. On **Pleasant Street** there are nineteenth-century summer houses, and the 1745 Updike House (all private). The town has two notable churches, **St. Paul's** (76 Main Street), built in 1847 in the Romanesque Revival style, and **Old Narragansett Church** (60 Church Lane), which was moved to this location in 1800. (It had been built a few miles south of the town in 1707.) There is a historic cemetery across the road.

One mile north of Wickford on Route 1 is **Smith's Castle** (401–294–3521), built in 1678 on the site of a trading post burned by Indians during King Philip's War. It is thought to be the only surviving building in which the colony's founder, Roger Williams, actually preached.

Just south of Wickford, off Route 1-A, is the **Gilbert Stuart Birthplace** (Gilbert Stuart Road, 401–294–3001). The nation's great eighteenth-century portraitist was born in this gambrel-roofed, two-and-a-half-story house in 1755. Stuart's father, who came here from Scotland, built New England's first snuff mill in the first floor of this house. Farther south on Route 1-A is the **Silas Casey Farm** (Boston Neck Road, 617–227–3956), a plantation begun in the early 1700s. It is still a working farm with a farmhouse built sometime in the first half of the eighteenth century.

KINGSTON

Founded around 1700 at a crossroads on the old Pequot Indian trail, Kingston prospered on a small scale in the eighteenth century and declined in the next. Today the town preserves many of its eighteenth- and early nineteenth-century houses and public buildings, many of them along Kingstown Road. The town's notable buildings include the **library,** erected in 1775, and the **Congregational Church** (2610 Kingstown Road) built in 1820. The **Old Washington County Jail** (2636 Kingstown Road, 401–783–1328), built in 1792, features old jail cells and exhibits on local history.

The **Great Swamp Fight Monument** (off Route 2) is an obelisk that stands on the site of a battle that took place in December 1675. Militia units from Connecticut and Massachusetts attacked the winter camp of the Narragansett Indians here, killing hundreds of men, women, and children. In revenge, the surviving Narragansett members attacked villages in Rhode Island.

BLOCK ISLAND

Discovered in 1524 by Giovanni da Verrazano, who named it Luisa, Block Island received its present name in the next century, in honor of the Dutch mariner Adriaen Block. The eleven-square-mile island, nine miles south of Point Judith, was colonized in 1661. The spot on the northern shore where the first pioneers landed is marked by **Settlers Rock.** The island lacks a good natural harbor, thereby preventing settlement of any significance. However, priva-

Main Street looking east, Wickford (ca. 1920). OVERLEAF: *Block Island.*

teers often stopped at the island to take on water. The inhabitants farmed and fished on a small scale until the federal government erected a breakwater in the 1870s to make a harbor suitable for large ships. The island quickly became a favored resort, sprouting hotels that today are picturesque examples of Victorian architecture.

CONANICUT ISLAND

Situated at the mouth of Narragansett Bay, Conanicut Island is also known as Jamestown, the name of its only town. It was settled in the 1650s, mainly by Quakers who made their living farming and raising sheep. The **Jamestown Windmill** (North Road off Route 138, in the center of the island, 401–423–1798) was built in 1787 and used throughout the nineteenth century. Nearby is a **Quaker meetinghouse** built in 1786.

During the Revolution the island was occupied by the British until they were forced out by an invasion of French and American troops. **Fort Wetherill State Park,** at the southeastern tip of Conanicut, was the site of an American fort and artillery battery. The park also contains Pirate Cave, one of many where Captain Kidd is said to have hidden loot.

The southwestern section of the island is connected to the main island by a narrow neck of land. At the northern point of this appendage is **Fort Getty State Park,** where Revolutionary-era earthworks can still be seen. At the southernmost tip is **Beavertail Lighthouse,** a granite tower built in 1856. Nearby is the foundation of the country's third lighthouse; built in 1749, the British destroyed it during the Revolution and it remained lost until its foundation was exposed by the hurricane of 1938.

The **Sydney L. Wright Museum** (North Road, 401–423–0436) exhibits Indian and Colonial artifacts from the island. The **Watson Farm** is a 280-acre working farm maintained by the Society for the Preservation of New England Antiquities (North Road, visits only by appointment made through the society's office, 617–277–3956).

NEWPORT

Newport was settled in 1639 by a small band of religious refugees from Boston. In the 1600s the town was a haven for Quakers and Jews, two groups that made important contributions to Newport's economy. Shipbuilding and international trade flourished from the town's very beginnings. Newport ships carried horses, wool, fish, rum, and agricultural products to Europe and the West Indies. By the middle of the eighteenth century, it was a prosperous and cultivated town, a center of "individual opulence, learning, and liberal leisure."

During the Revolution, the British, recognizing Newport's strategic location, occupied the town from late 1776 until October 1779. In the following year four thousand French troops, under the Comte de Rochambeau, arrived in Newport with the fleet that proved crucial to the final American victory at Yorktown. The British occupation had been devastating: They destroyed some five hundred houses, and half the population fled, most never to return. The economy of the town made a painfully slow recovery in the nineteenth century, and it took one hundred years for the population to regain its pre-Revolution level of 11,000 people.

British planters in the West Indies who had business connections with Newport began coming to the town for the summer as early as the 1730s. Shortly thereafter, Southern planters, particularly from Charleston, arrived. There were so many Charleston

OPPOSITE: The 1787 Jamestown Windmill, Conanicut Island.

families summering in Newport that it became known as the "Carolina Hospital." In the late nineteenth century, Newport was rediscovered by the wealthy.

The **Easton's Point** district contains many of Newport's fine eighteenth-century houses. Bounded on the east by Farewell and Thames streets, and on the west by Washington Street which runs along the water, the point was owned by the Easton family in the early eighteenth century. Populated first by craftsmen, tradesmen, and artisans involved in nautical trades, the point later attracted well-to-do ship captains. There are many houses to be seen along Thames, Farewell, Bridge, Poplar, and Washington streets, all private, except Hunter House.

Hunter House

One of the most beautiful eighteenth-century mansions in America, Hunter House displays porcelain, silver, and paintings as well as furniture made by Townsend and Goddard, Newport's great cabinetmakers. The house is renowned for its carved panelling and other wooden decorations, notably its handsome staircase and the pineapple in the pediment over the front door. (The pineapple was a widely used symbol of hospitality in the colonies.) Hunter House, named for its last private occupant, preserves the elegant way of life of Newport's eighteenth-century merchants. It was here that French Admiral Charles de Ternay died during the Revolution.

LOCATION: 54 Washington Street. HOURS: May through October: 10–5 Daily. FEE: Yes. TELEPHONE: 401–847–1000.

Washington Square

Washington Square was the political and business hub of Newport in colonial times. Brick Market, the commercial center, stands at one end and Colony House, the political center, at the other. Many of the city's prominent merchants built their houses on or near the square. One of these is **Rivera House,** occupied by the Newport National Bank since 1803. In the eighteenth century it was the home of Abraham Rodrigues Rivera, a leader in Newport's business and Jewish communities who made his fortune in the whale oil industry. His colleagues in the United Company of Spermaceti Chandlers, all non-Jewish, declined to conduct business on Satur-

days in deference to the Jewish Sabbath. Rivera was given the
honor of laying the cornerstone of Touro Synagogue.

The square was originally known as the Parade because military drills were held here. The Parade was where the townspeople
gathered to negotiate business deals, exchange news, socialize and,
before the Revolution, to air their grievances against the Crown.
Tories were burned in effigy on the Parade in front of Colony
House. Here, also, is a **statue of Oliver Hazard Perry,** the hero of
the 1813 Battle of Lake Erie, who briefly resided on the square.

Colony House

A handsome brick building trimmed with sandstone, Colony
House was built in 1739 by Richard Munday, a carpenter-architect
and innkeeper who had previously built Trinity Church. The use
of bricks, imported from Britain, was rare in the colony—only a
half-dozen brick buildings existed in Rhode Island before the Revolution. Colony House was the seat of first the colonial, and then
the state government (the latter until 1900), as Newport alternated
with Providence as capital. In colonial times citizens gathered to
hear official announcements read from the second-floor balcony.
Two joyful proclamations heard here were the repeal of the hated
Stamp Act in 1766, and the reading of the Declaration of Independence in 1776. In a session here on May 4, 1776, the colony's
legislature renounced allegiance to the king. The British comman-
deered Colony House as a barracks during the Revolution, heavily
damaging the interior. The French used it as a hospital and, when
Admiral de Ternay died in Newport in 1780, his funeral mass was
said here—the first Catholic mass to be said in Rhode Island.

LOCATION: Washington Square. HOURS: July 4 through Labor Day:
10–4 Tuesday–Saturday, 12–4 Sunday. FEE: None. TELEPHONE:
401–846–2980 or 277–2669.

Brick Market and Long Wharf

Located at the head of Long Wharf, Brick Market was designed
and built by Peter Harrison in a British style, with storage rooms on
its upper floors and a market area below. From the early 1760s
through the colonial period, Long Wharf was the busiest of Newport's wharves, and during the Revolution it was the embarkation
point for the French fleet.

North of the square, at 26 Marlborough Street, is **White Horse Tavern,** the oldest surviving tavern in America, begun in 1673. The first proprietor was William Mayes, whose chief occupation was piracy. According to local lore, Mayes concealed his booty in the tavern. Nearby is a **Quaker meetinghouse,** built in 1699 and enlarged in 1729 and 1807. The colony's policy of religious tolerance allowed Quakers to find a refuge here from the persecution they encountered in other colonies, notably Puritan Boston. Many became wealthy merchants and prominent political figures.

Wanton-Lyman-Hazard House

Built in the 1690s, the house is among Newport's oldest surviving residences. From 1750 it was the home of Martin Howard, Jr., a Tory. During riots protesting the Stamp Act in 1765 a threatening mob of Patriots descended on the house, causing Howard to flee to the safety of a British ship, never to return to Newport. During the Revolution the Wanton family owned the house and entertained French officers here. It has been restored with period furnishings.

LOCATION: 17 Broadway. HOURS: June 15 through September 15: 10–5 Tuesday–Saturday. FEE: Yes. TELEPHONE: 401–846–0813.

Touro Synagogue

The oldest Jewish house of worship in America, Touro Synagogue was designed by Peter Harrison in 1759 and built in 1763. His design is austere on the outside, but of a restrained elegance within. Twelve Ionic columns, representing the Tribes of Israel, support a gallery where women are seated during services.

The congregation that founded the synagogue had been established in Newport in 1658 by Sephardic Jews from Spain and Portugal. More came from Portugal after the Lisbon Earthquake of 1755, and Isaac de Touro came from Amsterdam in 1758. It was his influence that led to the construction of the synagogue. Although Jews were free to practice their religion in Rhode Island, they were not allowed to vote until the Revolution. In 1790 George Washington, accompanied by Jefferson, visited Newport and ad-

OPPOSITE: Interior of Touro Synagogue, Newport, the oldest Jewish house of worship in America. It was designed in 1759 by Peter Harrison.

dressed the congregation, saying that post-Revolutionary America "gives to bigotry no sanction, to persecution no assistance."

LOCATION: 85 Touro Street. HOURS: July through Labor Day: 10–5 Sunday–Friday; Labor Day through June: 11–2 Monday–Friday, 2–4 Sunday. FEE: None. TELEPHONE: 401–849–7385.

Newport Historical Society

The society's headquarters exhibits artwork by Newport craftsmen. The "Newport Room," a reproduction of a Newport merchant's parlor, displays fine examples of furniture made by the famous Newport cabinetmakers. A **marine museum,** also at this location, has models and pictures of the merchant marine and local boating activity, as well as early navigational equipment.

LOCATION: 82 Touro Street. HOURS: 9:30–4:30 Tuesday–Friday, 9:30–Noon Saturday. FEE: None. TELEPHONE: 401–846–0813.

South of Washington Square, the **Armory of the Artillery Company of Newport** (23 Clark Street, 401–846–8488) was built in the mid-1830s and houses a large collection of weapons and other military items. The Artillery Company was founded in 1639, with eighteen men, to defend the town against Indian attacks. It was chartered in 1741, the date over the door of the armory.

Trinity Church (Spring and Church streets, 401–846–0660), one of the finest colonial churches in America, was built by Richard Munday in 1726. It was modeled on the Old North Church in Boston, which in turn was inspired by Christopher Wren's churches in London. The organ, installed in 1733, was the second in America.

The **Samuel Whitehorne House** (416 Thames Street, 401–849–7300) is a museum of Newport furniture, exhibiting the works of the well-known cabinetmakers, Townsend and Goddard.

Redwood Library

The nation's oldest library in continuous use, Redwood Library opened in 1750. Peter Harrison designed the building following the precepts of Andrea Palladio. Together with the earlier Prince William's Church near Beaufort, South Carolina, it is one of the two earliest temple-form buildings in America. The exterior wooden walls were carved and sanded to give the appearance of stone. The library was named in honor of Abraham Redwood, a wealthy merchant and owner of plantations in Antigua, who donated £500 for the acquisition of books. (Redwood, a Quaker, was later excluded from his congregation for refusing to free his Antiguan slaves.) Aside from its valuable collection of books, the library displays paintings, furniture, and historical items, such as a link from the chain laid across the Hudson River to block British warships, and a wheel from the first train in America.

LOCATION: 50 Bellevue Avenue. HOURS: September through June: 9:30–5:30 Daily; July through August: 9:30–5 Daily. FEE: None. TELEPHONE: 401–847–0292.

The picturesque building of the **Art Association** (76 Bellevue Avenue), completed in 1864, was designed by Richard Morris Hunt and reflects his fascination with medieval forms. Touro Park on Bellevue Avenue is the location of the **Old Stone Mill,** often said to have been built by Viking explorers as a bastion or a lookout tower. In fact, it was the base of a Colonial-era mill, probably erected by the great-grandfather of Benedict Arnold, who was governor of the colony and the owner of this land.

Across from Touro Park is **Channing Memorial Church,** built in 1881 and named in honor of William Ellery Channing, of whom there is a statue in the park. Channing, who was born in Newport, founded the Unitarian faith in Boston. Stained-glass windows in the church were done by John LaFarge.

The streets branching from **Old Beach Road,** behind the Redwood Library, attracted well-to-do residents during and after the Civil War. Their homes were designed in a variety of Victorian styles, some by eminent architects including Richard Morris Hunt and the firm of McKim, Mead & White. While not as imposing as the cottages along Bellevue Avenue, this cluster of houses is charming evidence of the diversity and energy of Victorian architecture.

The shingle-style **Newport Casino** (194 Bellevue Avenue), built in 1881, is one of the nation's first country clubs and one of the first buildings designed by the firm of McKim, Mead & White. The club was started by James Gordon Bennett, Jr. when he was expelled from the town's haughtiest social organization, the Newport Reading Room. The club includes a theater where Oscar Wilde once appeared. Tennis was one of the prime activities at the club, and it hosted the National Men's Singles Championships from 1881 to 1914. There is a collection of tennis memorabilia at the casino's **Tennis Museum and Hall of Fame** (401–849–3990).

The Breakers, summer cottage of Cornelius Vanderbilt, Newport.

The Mansions

The famed mansions of Newport are located mainly along Bellevue Avenue, Ocean Drive, and Harrison Avenue. There are about
sixty mansions, which the occupants airily called "cottages." The
lords of the railroads, the mines, and of Wall Street ordered architects to model their houses after those of Europe, while others
adopted the American "stick" and "shingle" styles. The mansions
cost as much as $10 million to build and furnish, and many of their
owners spent another $100,000 to $300,000 on entertaining during any given summer season, which lasted but seven weeks or so.
Six mansions are open to the public under the auspices of the
Preservation Society of Newport County. A seventh, Belcourt, is
managed independently. **Cliff Walk,** a three-mile path that winds
along the coast, offers views of the houses and Rhode Island Sound.

    Kingscote, one of the most modest of the cottages, was built in
1839, long before the Gilded Age. Richard Upjohn designed it in
the Gothic Revival style for George Noble Jones, a planter from
Savannah. It was the first summer residence to be built in this
section of Newport; previously summer visitors had resided in the
town. In 1864, the Jones family sold the house to William Henry

Rosecliff, designed by Stanford White and built in 1902.

King of Newport, who commissioned Stanford White to design additions to the house in 1881. These included a beautiful dining room of mahogany and cherry, illuminated by natural light through a wall of Tiffany glass. The house was occupied by a member of the Rives family until 1972. A notable collection of silver is displayed.

The Elms was built in 1899 with the coal money of Edward Julius Berwind of Pennsylvania, son of German immigrants. Horace Trumbauer, the architect, modeled The Elms on a French chateau, and the interior is lavishly adorned with eighteenth-century French furnishings.

Chateau-sur-Mer, built in 1852 and enlarged in 1872 by Richard Morris Hunt, was the first of the large cottages and the one to set the standard for grandeur on Bellevue Avenue. The huge granite building features a forty-five-foot-high, three-story hall and a library and dining room decorated with leather and elaborately carved walnut. The house was begun by William Shepard Wetmore, whose fortune was made in the China trade, and whose notoriety was secured when his wife ran off with the coachman.

The Breakers is the most opulent of the Newport cottages. It was designed by Richard Morris Hunt, for Cornelius Vanderbilt II, in the style of seventeenth-century palaces in Genoa. The Parisian firm of Allard et Fils decorated the public rooms with the utmost luxury, while Ogden Codman, Jr. furnished bedrooms on the second and third floors in a more intimate style. Frederick Law Olmsted's firm landscaped the grounds. The stable has a collection of coaches, carriages, and riding equipment.

Rosecliff, built in 1902, was designed by Stanford White for Mrs. Hermann Oerlichs, derived generally from the Trianon at Versailles. The entire exterior of the house is covered with glazed white terra cotta. Its impressive, heart-shaped staircase is one of White's finest works. Among the house's forty rooms are the seventy-two-foot-long ballroom and a Court of Love, designed by Augustus Saint-Gaudens and inspired by Marie Antoinette's.

Marble House was the home, briefly, of William K. Vanderbilt, who spent $2 million to build the house and $9 million to furnish it at the behest of his wife, Alva. The architect, Richard Morris Hunt, made this the most extravagant of the cottages, with its Corinthian portico, Gothic Room, and two rooms inspired by Versailles: the Gold Salon, suggested by the Hall of Mirrors, and a dining room of rose Numidian marble, based on the Salon of Hercules, resplendent with a gilded ceiling and gilt-bronze trophies on the walls. Vanderbilt was able to enjoy the house only for a few years: Alva won it in a divorce settlement. She added a charming teahouse, in the Chinese style, overlooking the water.

LOCATION: Bellevue Avenue. HOURS: April through October: 10–5 Daily. In April Kingscote and Chateau-sur-Mer are open on weekends only. From July through mid-September some mansions are open until 7. November through March: Marble House, The Elms, and Chateau-sur-Mer open weekends 10–4. FEE: Yes. TELEPHONE: 401–847–1000.

Belcourt Castle (Bellevue Avenue, 401–846–0669) was built in 1892 by Richard Morris Hunt for Oliver Hazard Perry Belmont, who married Alva Vanderbilt after her divorce. Its design, inspired by a Louis XIII hunting lodge, is a medieval fantasy: The vaulted ballroom has stained-glass windows and a fireplace surmounted by a plaster castle. The rooms were all copied from chambers in

OPPOSITE: *Entrance Hall of Marble House, built of Siena marble.* OVERLEAF: *The opulent Gold Ballroom at Marble House, with carved gilt panels by Karl Bitter.*

Newporters watching what is probably the annual New York Yacht Club race.

French castles, except the English library and the Italian banquet hall. The south wing of the house contains Belmont's elaborate stables. He provided his horses with morning clothes, afternoon clothes, and evening clothes. In the salon above the stables "there stood at either end the stuffed and lifelike figures of two of the elder Belmont's favorite horses. Seated upon them were the figures of men in armor . . . ," as Maud Howe Elliott reported in her memoir *This Was My Newport.*

Fort Adams State Park (off Harrison Avenue, 401–847–2400), a twenty-acre preserve, includes massive granite walls, tunnels, and powder magazines built between 1829 and 1857 to protect the entrance to Narragansett Bay. It never saw action.

The **Naval War College** (401–849–4473) is situated on Coasters Harbor Island, just north of Newport. It was founded in 1884 as a research and educational facility for naval officers. The college's second president was the historian Captain Alfred Thayer Mahan, author of *The Influence of Sea Power upon History.* A museum, in **Founder's Hall,** offers changing exhibits on the history of the navy and naval activities in Narragansett Bay. Founder's Hall was built in 1820 as Newport's poorhouse.

Whitehall Farm Museum

Bishop George Berkeley, whose philosophical writings laid some of the foundation for modern metaphysical thought, made his home here from 1729 to 1731. He enlarged the original farmhouse with such unusual architectural features as a cruciform hall with stairway, false double-front door, and hipped roof with lean-to construction. Berkeley donated the property to Yale to provide revenue for scholarships; and the house served as tearoom, tavern, and bunkhouse to British soldiers during the Revolution. The rooms have been restored and filled with period portraits and furniture in an attempt to re-create the atmosphere of the day.

LOCATION: Three miles north of Newport, Berkeley Avenue between Route 138 and Green End Avenue. HOURS: July and August: 10–5 Daily; June and September: by appointment. FEE: Yes. TELEPHONE: 401–846–3116 July and August; 401–846–3790 September through June.

PORTSMOUTH

Portsmouth was the second settlement in Rhode Island, after Providence. Religious dissenters from Massachusetts landed at **Founders Brook** (there is a marker off Boyd's Lane) in April 1638, and were soon followed by their spiritual leader, Anne Hutchinson, another religious exile from the Bay Colony. During the Revolution, Portsmouth was the scene of the Battle of Rhode Island, the only major military engagement in the state. A few historical markers outline the sweep of the fighting.

The battle was actually the aftermath of a failed French-American plan to oust the British from Newport in August 1778. The French fleet was supposed to land troops to support an American assault down Aquidneck from Tiverton, but they were battered first by a fierce, two-day storm and then by a British attack. The French sailed to the safety of Boston and remained there, despite the pleas of Lafayette, and the American troops surrounding Newport withdrew, pursued by British and Hessian units. While the main American force took shelter in **Butts Hill Fort** (markers off Sprague Street), a rear guard fought a brave delaying action. Among them was a unit of black slaves who had been promised their freedom if they aided the Patriot cause. The **Black Regiment Memorial** (a flagpole at the junction of routes 114 and 24) stands at the place where this unit turned back three assaults by Hessian troops, halting the British advance.

NOTES ON ARCHITECTURE

EARLY COLONIAL

In New England, Europeans first built houses using a medieval, vertical asymmetry, which in the eighteenth century evolved toward classical symmetry. Roofs were gabled and hipped, often with prominent exterior chimneys. Small casement windows became larger and more evenly spaced and were balanced on each facade. The New England salt-box house evolved from a European cottage to which a "lean-to" was added. In eastern England, houses had often been covered with tiles; in New England, these became shingles.

GEORGIAN

Beginning in Boston as early as 1686, and only much later elsewhere, the design of houses became balanced about a central axis, with only careful, stripped detail. A few large houses incorporated double-story pilasters. Sash windows with rectilinear panes replaced casements. Hipped roofs accentuated the balanced and strict proportions inherited from Italy and Holland via England and Scotland.

FEDERAL

The post-Revolutionary style sometimes called "Federal" was more flexible and delicate than the more formal Georgian. It was rooted in archaeological discoveries at Pompeii and Herculaneum in Italy in the 1750s, as well as in contemporary French interior planning principles. As it evolved toward the Regency, rooms became shaped as polygons, ovals, and circles and acquired ornamentation in the forms of urns, garlands, and swags.

GOTHIC REVIVAL

After about 1830, darker colors, asymmetry, broken skylines, verticality, and the pointed arch began to appear in New England. New machinery produced carved and pierced trim along the eaves. Roofs became steep and gabled; "porches" or "piazzas" became more spacious. Oriel and bay windows became common and there was greater use of stained glass.

SECOND EMPIRE

After 1860, Parisian fashion inspired American builders to use mansard roofs, dark colors, and varied textures, including shingles, tiles, and increasing use of ironwork, especially on balconies and skylines. With their ornamental quoins, balustrades, pavilions, pediments, columns, and pilasters, Second Empire buildings recalled many historical styles.

GREEK REVIVAL

Severe, stripped, rectilinear proportions, occasionally a set of columns or pilasters, and even in a few instances Greek-temple form, had some popularity in southern New England from 1825 to 1860. It was used in official buildings and, in northern New England, in many private houses. In America, the "Greek" Revival combined Greek and Roman forms—low, pitched pediments, simple moldings, rounded arches, and shallow domes.

RENAISSANCE REVIVAL OR BEAUX ARTS

Later in the 1880s and 1890s, American architects who had studied at the Ecole des Beaux Arts in Paris brought a new Renaissance Revival to the United States. Sometimes used in urban mansions, but generally reserved for city halls and academic buildings, it borrowed from three centuries of Renaissance detail, much of it French, and put together picturesque combinations from widely differing periods.

RICHARDSON ROMANESQUE

Richardson Romanesque made use of the massive forms and ornamental details of the Romanesque: rounded arches, towers, stone and brick facing. The solidity and gravity of masses were accentuated by deep recesses for windows and entrances, by rough stone masonry, stubby columns, strong horizontals, rounded towers with conical caps, and botanical, repetitive ornament.

I N D E X

PHOTO CREDITS

All photographs are by Paul
Rocheleau except for the following:

Art Resource: 80-81
Robert S. Arnold/Old Sturbridge
Village, Sturbridge, MA: 257
(top)
Barrett and MacKay, Prince
Edward Island: 159
Bettmann Archive: 46, 358
Ira Block/Image Bank: 359
J. David Bohl/Courtesy of The
Magazine ANTIQUES: 68,
126, 127, 211, 291, 404
(bottom right)
Bridgeport Public Library
Historical Collections,
Bridgeport, CT: 295, 310
Photograph by Richard Cheek,
Belmont, MA, for the
Preservation Society of
Newport County: 396, 397,
398, 400-401
The Connecticut Historical
Society: 110, 112-113, 287, 325
Tom Doody/The Picture Cube:
102
Steve Dunwell/Image Bank: 18,
32, 82, 88, 91, 175, 179, 309,
316, 318, 333, 348, 360-361
The Essex Institute, Salem, MA:
188-189, 229 (left)
Michael Freeman: 128, 129, 151,
152-153, 202, 204-205, 207,
239, 240-241, 246, 404 (top
left)
Mark E. Gibson/The Stock
Market: 405 (top right)
Joshua Greene, New York: 136,
137
The Florence Griswold Museum,
Lyme Historical Society: 349
Mick Hales: 208-209
John Hall: 346-347
D.W. Hamilton/Image Bank:
Cover, 386-387
Steve Hansen/Stock Boston: 57

Helga Photo Studio/Courtesy of
The Magazine ANTIQUES: 267
Hill-Stead Museum, Farmington,
CT: 283
Historic Deerfield, Inc.: 248
(right)
R.P. Kingston/The Picture Cube:
95
David Larkin: 257 (bottom)
Robert Llewelyn: 59 (top and
bottom), 73
Harvey Lloyd/The Stock Market:
173
John Lutsch/Courtesy of the
Concord Museum: 105
Patti McConville/Image Bank:
340-341
Michael Melford/Image Bank:
176
Metropolitan Museum of Art: 21,
254-255
Museum of Fine Arts, Boston:
25, 77 (Pauline Revere Thayer
Collection), 78 (M. and M.
Karolik Collection)
National Academy of Design,
New York City: 229 (right)
The Newark Museum: 279
Newport Historical Society: 402
Charles Norton: 190
Obremski/Image Bank: Half-
title page, 48, 63
Nick Pavloff/Image Bank: 62
Peabody Museum of Salem: 193
(top left)
R. Perron/Art Resource: 405
(bottom right)
Rhode Island Historical Society:
367 (John Miller Documents),
374, 385
William F. Robinson, Abandoned
New England/New York
Graphic Society, Boston: 320
Paul Rocheleau/Courtesy of The
Magazine ANTIQUES: 119,
130, 133, 140, 146, 250;
Courtesy of the Chesterwood
Museum, National Trust for
Historic Preservation: 235
Printed by permission of the
Estate of Norman Rockwell, ©

1967. All Rights Reserved.
Courtesy of the Norman
Rockwell Museum,
Stockbridge, MA: 230-231
Guido Alberto Rossi/Image
Bank: 322
Stanley Rowin/Courtesy of the
Lexington Historical Society:
116
Clive Russ/Courtesy of
Goodspeed's Book Shop,
Boston: 26-27
Mark Sexton/Peabody Museum
of Salem: 193 (top right), 193
(bottom)
Erik Leigh Simmons/Image
Bank: Title page, 39
Slater Mill Historic Site,
Pawtucket, RI: 364
John Lewis Stage/Image Bank:
114, 149
Submarine Force Library and
Museum, Groton, CT: 339
Mark Twain Memorial,
Hartford, CT: 270
Wadsworth Atheneum,
Hartford, CT: 263, 285
Yale University Art Gallery: 87,
334 (Bequest of Stephen
Carlton Clark, BA 1903), 356
(The Mabel Brady Garvan
Collection)

The editors gratefully
acknowledge the assistance of
Ann J. Campbell, Kendell
Cronstrom, Amy Hughes,
Brian D. Hotchkiss, Carol A.
McKeown, Klaske Piebenga,
and Patricia Woodruff.

Composed in Basilia Haas and
ITC New Baskerville by Graphic
Arts Composition, Inc.,
Philadelphia, Pennsylvania.
Printed and bound by Toppan
Printing Company, Ltd., Tokyo,
Japan.